DAVID WILLInd
brought up in a
graduate in Mechanical Engineering from Monash University
and was a lecturer in thermodynamics and social psychology at
Swinburn Institute of Technology until 1973. His first full-
length play, *The Coming of Stork*, had its premiere at the La
Mama Theatre, Carlton in 1970 and later became the film
Stork, directed by Tim Burstall.

The Removalists and *Don's Party*, both written in 1971, were
quickly taken up and performed around Australia, then in
London and later made into films with screenplays by the
author. In 1972 *The Removalists* won the Australian Writers'
Guild Awgie Award for the best stage play and the best script in
any medium. In 1973 David Williamson was nominated the
most promising playwright by the London *Evening Standard*
following the British production of *The Removalists*.

The next play was *Jugglers Three* (1972) commissioned by the
Melbourne Theatre Company; followed by *What If You Died
Tomorrow* (1973) for the Old Tote Theatre Company; *The
Department* (1975) and *A Handful of Friends* (1976) for the
South Australian Theatre Company. *The Club* (1977) broke all
previous box office records and in 1978 had seasons at the
Kennedy Centre, Washington, on Broadway and in Berlin. In
1980 the Nimrod Theatre production went to London. The
film, directed by Bruce Beresford, was released in 1980.
Travelling North was performed around Australia in 1979 and
in London in 1980. The film version was released in 1987. It
was followed by *Celluloid Heroes* (1980), *The Perfectionist*
(1982), *Sons of Cain* (1985) and *Emerald City* (1987) which
played in London and New York in 1988. The film version of
Emerald City was released in 1989. *Top Silk* was first produced
in Sydney and Melbourne in the same year, followed by *Siren* in
1990. *Money and Friends* was performed around Australia in
1991, in Los Angeles in 1992 and in London in 1993. *Brilliant
Lies* was first produced in Brisbane in 1993.

David Williamson has won the Australian Film Institute film
script award for *Petersen* (1974), *Don's Party* (1976), *Gallipoli*
(1981) and *Travelling North* (1987) and has won eleven
Australian Writers' Guild Awgie Awards. He lives in Sydney
with his novelist wife Kristin Williamson. Between them they
have five children.

Plays by David Williamson:

DAVID WILLIAMSON

COLLECTED PLAYS

Volume II

CURRENCY PRESS · SYDNEY

AUSTRALIAN DRAMATISTS SERIES
General Editor: Katharine Brisbane

The Department first published 1975 by Currency Methuen Drama Pty Ltd.
A Handful of Friends first published 1976 by Currency Press Pty Ltd
The Club first published 1978 by Currency Press Pty Ltd
Travelling North first published 1980 by Currency Press Pty Ltd.
This edition first published 1993 by Currency Press Pty Ltd
P.O. Box 452 Paddington, NSW 2021 Australia

Cataloguing-in-Publication data:
Williamson, David, 1942- [Plays]. Collected
plays. Volume II
   Bibliography
   ISBN 0 86819 287 2

   1. Williamson, David,1942- . Handful of
friends. II. Williamson, David, 1942- . Club.
III. Williamson, David, 1942- . Department.
IV. Williamson, David, 1942- . Travelling
north. V. Title: Handful of friends. VI. Title:
Club. VII. Title: Department. VIII Title:
Travelling north.
Australian Dramatists Series
A822.3

Typeset in Baskerville by The Master Typographer, Sydney
Printed by Griffin Paperbacks, Adelaide
Series designed by Kevin Chan

CONTENTS

Frank Wilson as Frank and Carol Raye as Frances in the Nimrod Theatre, Sydney production of Travelling North, 1979. Photo: Peter Holderness.

INTRODUCTION

KATHARINE BRISBANE

This is a vintage volume of Williamson plays. It shows a consolidation and maturing of his style of social satire and a move outward from the domestic and personal dilemmas explored in the early plays into the public arena. Just as he did overtly in *Don's Party* and *The Removalists*, here more subtly he draws parallels between private desires and public issues.

The primary themes covered in these plays are bureaucratic pettiness; artistic and professional integrity; committee-room power games; and the legacy of ideologies. The average man and woman's experience of life is present in all of them and none of the themes are new: and yet in retrospect each of them is very clearly a direct response to the progress of the 1970s — to the political and social turmoil of the Whitlam period and the financial crackdown which followed, and the gap Williamson perceived between the opportunities offered the reformers and their achievement. The vested interests uncovered, the betrayals, the accession of entrepreneurial management to what once were community affairs; the disappointments and mid-life crises of the baby-boomer generation — such are the preoccupations of this collection.

The plays are easy to read. They have a clear narrative and the first three plays still acknowledge the unities of time and space — though *A Handful of Friends* has a composite set and the time stretches over a week. *Travelling North*, which closes the book on this period of Williamson's life, is also transitional in form, owing something to his film-writing experience in its intermittent short scenes and its use of visual and musical statements to accompany the verbal. These would be his tools for the 80s.

The Department was first presented in November 1974. Its action takes place in the thermodynamics laboratory of a technical college in which already are being heard the rumblings of what a decade later became a restructuring of most such colleges into the university system. Williamson had been a lecturer in such a department and had resigned in 1972 after the royalties from his work began to show that he might make a living as a writer. He had also become a foundation member of the reconstructed Australian Council for the Arts, now called the Australia Council, and a member of a government committee appointed to select a national anthem. The frustrations of academia upon a young writer itching for his freedom, and a young artist plunged into the territorial imperatives of arts politics, went into the making of The Department, which depicts a power struggle monumental in its fatuity. At the same time he gives us, parallel to the personal agenda, an image of an Australia wracked by divisions and unable, or unwilling, to see the opportunities with which the years of struggle and change had placed within their grasp.

The setting is an image of the play's dilemma: a stage filled with the technology of education. Below are two outdated engines once central to the teaching system' above a new towing tank — a hugely expensive piece of equipment standing idle because it has been improperly installed. Suspended between on a mezzanine, amid ill-matched, temporary-looking chairs and tables, are the equally ill-matched academic staff' each with their own agenda and only Robby, the Head, with his heart in the work ahead.

Robby has a vision for his Department: to make it the biggest in the college and thereby win the prize of a glossy new building which promises to come its way. He needs his staff to pull together in this task but the methods he uses are not those of a visionary. Instead he is devious and timid, seeking expansion and yet demanding control, emotionally dependent upon his colleagues and yet constantly fearful of betrayal and the reproofs of his senior, the invisible Fletcher.

He attracts no loyalty from his colleagues, who take their tone from him, expending their intellectual energies on gaining points and frustrating plans. They believe in nothing which might bind them, neither in the college, which was founded by a crook, nor in their vocation or their students. The most extreme example is Peter, too bright for his present appointment, who takes a malicious joy in concealing his knowledge of the towing tank as a way of nursing a sense of superiority. Here is Australia in 1974 as Williamson saw it — divided and incompetent, its workers patching up old engines and old methods while the bureaucrats bicker over their vested interests and dream of the elusive world of power.

Such a divided world we see again in *The Club*, two years later, where the assault on the old loyalties is in full affray. But in between Williamson began a further exploration of the nature of friendship and the ethics of the artist who exploits them.

A Handful of Friends (1976) is an unjustly neglected Williamson play. Today it reads as eloquently as any of his work and for this edition the author has made some judicious cuts to what he calls the 'filigree' enhancing the structure. The most prominent cut in the text is to Jill's monologue in Act One scene three. Williamson advises that anyone producing this play should refer to this definitive edition.

The play deals, as the title suggests, with five friends: Russell and Wendy, an academic and his wife recently returned from the United States; Mark and Sally, a film-maker and his wife who is an actor and former journalist; and Jill, Russell's sister, a journalist. At the outset we learn that Mark has just released a movie in which Sally plays her first major role. Mutual friends who have seen it believe the principal characters to be based on Russell and Wendy, and that they are cruelly satirised. Jill, who is devoted to her brother, is especially angry, and also nurses resentment against Sally for incidents in their earlier lives. In the course of a day old memories and antagonisms surface, triggered by the film; and what at first appear as envy and malice take on a different perspective as the group explode briefly into violence and settle for an uneasy reconciliation. No one emerges honourably but they share the wisdom of hindsight.

At the time Williamson himself had been accused of betrayals similar to Mark's — for *Don's Party*, for *Juggler's Three* and for *What If You Died Tomorrow*, all of which bear a surface resemblance to the changes in Williamson's own life. In 1976

Dorothy Hewett had a writ for defamation issued against her over fictional material in two plays and a poem. The Law Reform Commission's inquiry into the law relating to the invasion of privacy was directed chiefly at the press, but it gathered into the same embrace works of biography and fiction. Betrayal of associates by holding them up to ridicule and contempt was an issue in the late 70s — and there were profits to be made from defamation action against some writers. It was, however, a passing fear which perhaps made them more judicious.

In that climate *The Club's* worry was that it might be identified as the Collingwood Football Club, then the champion of champions whose recent stocks had sunk disastrously. And the more Williamson protested that he was not privy to the debate within its, or any other club's, committee room, the more people insisted on his accuracy. Such is the nature of the creative imagination. Collingwood, as it proved, was flattered.

Williamson is quoted in *Meanjin* as being in the mood for a fight and finding his subject in the sports pages: 'Coach Sacked', 'Club in Distress'. And, as he demonstrated, human nature is common property: not only sportsmen but political party members, company directors — in fact members of any institution feeling the rise of the entrepreneur in that prelude to the 80s, recognised their own experience in the danger and the absurdity of the members of *The Club*.

The Club (1977) deals with a turning point in the history of a professional football club, once great but now on the skids. By tradition players have come through the junior league; and the coach from among the long-serving seniors. But now the club has a corporate-style manager, Gerry, who has already talked the committee into paying money for a star. He is also manipulating for the removal of the president, Ted, a pie manufacturer and faithful follower, in favour of a corporate mogul; and of Laurie the coach in favour of a more bankable name. Over one evening Gerry and Jock: Gerry, the smooth, cool-headed businessman; and Jock, old-style ex-president and former champion, gather their forces and disarm the weaker members. At the centre is Geoff, the outsider star, too intelligent and a stranger to the club culture, who is not pulling his weight on or off the field. His failings bring into question the new methods and the coach's competence: and place on the line the loyalties of those who backed them. Other pressures to the old fabric are brought by the threat of a team strike and of further buying and selling. The play ends with a rueful hope that some integrity might yet be retained; and a final come-uppance for Jock, a victim of his own obduracy. *The Club* is the last of Williamson's genuine comedies for a decade.

Travelling North (1979), which some critics believe is Williamson's best play to date, is a watershed, marking the end of certainty and dramatic simplicity; and the beginning of a series of personal explorations into the gains and losses of the post-war generation. Williamson begins by exploring in *Travelling North* firstly both time and space; and secondly his parents' generation. And he sets the play in 1969, the year of *Don's Party*, and the beginning of that period which Donald Horne has called the Time of Hope. Frank (70s) and Frances (50s) have fallen in love and decided to shake all cares and business from their age and leave wintry Melbourne for sunny Queensland. But no sooner have they established their love nest than Frank's health begins to fail.

Prior to writing *Travelling North* Williamson had made an Australian adaptation of *King Lear* as an exercise and its influence upon *Travelling North*, is significant. Frank, an old communist martinet has cruelly to realise, as he unburdened crawls toward death, that 'while I've always loved mankind in general, I have been less than generous to some of those I've been involved with in particular'. Frances, a single mother of two married and ungrateful daughters, equally learns that her too-artistic temperament and apparent neglect of her children, have left a legacy of insecurity which may have damaged them for life. Frank, who has done no better as a husband and father, has been all will and Frances all feeling. This time the realisations within the play are not a metaphor for the state of the nation; but reflect Shakespeare's warning that the pursuit of happiness cannot be taken on the ship of state but only through the inner realms of man and woman kind in particular. It is a play which questions much more than it answers and it faces Williamson, the tribal scribe, for the first time in his writing with the existentialist notion that we must each take responsibility for the direction of our own lives; and like Frances, refuse the support of those friends whom circumstance have bound together and alone take up the challenge to 'travel further north'.

The structure of *Travelling North* also differs markedly from the earlier plays. Its shape is cone-like, with Frank as its axis, building itself cumulatively in 33 scenes, each suggested by the minimum of properties. As the characters are drawn into the fabric, they moves between cold, urban Melbourne and lazy, tropical Tweed Heads. Music for the first time becomes an important key to the characters and the mood — Mozart and Vivaldi in the north, Beethoven in the south. Each scene adds to our understanding of the characters until the play reaches its apex and dissolves in a burst of Bach.

One of the reasons for Williamson's lasting popularity is the simplicity of his choice of language. His writing is extremely economical, pared down to those elements he believes essential to the audience's understanding. He aims to surprise but never to mystify and his opening scenes are crucial in setting up his audience's expectations for the tone, the pace and the theme of the play. At the start of *The Department* we are awestruck by the complexity of machinery; the opening lines tell us it doesn't work — and in the most commonplace terms. The light switch has been on the blink; the diesel engine has been a dangerous handicap for years; the newest acquisition is an embarrassment. And it is the handyman, not the engineers, who is in control: the whole laboratory is inefficient, bureaucratic and out of date. The language used is pedestrian, the pace lackadaisical; and the scenes that follow build and develop the tensions within all these elements to a level of absurdity.

At the opening of *A Handful of Friends* Wendy and Russell are unpacking his library. Fiction, and what one reads into it, is the essential substance of the play but Russell opens by saying he can't remember the contents of some of the books, though he has read them twice. In short order attention turns from the books to a set of dockets, factual data which tell their own story; and we begin to see the battle lines being drawn in preparation for the coming encounter with Mark and Sally. They move swiftly on to university politics, Russell's sexual peccadilloes and hints of some personal problem of Wendy relating to work. The pace is medium, bowling the information at steady intervals; and there is also evidence of a pattern of role-playing in Russell, a suggestion that things may not be what they seem. Acting, another form of fiction, is to emerge as strongly present in all the characters. By the time Jill arrives we are alert and prepared for manoeuvres.

The Club's battle-lines by contrast, are not domestic but male, full-frontal assault. This competitive, hard-hitting environment is established at curtain rise by the rows of champions whose photographs line the walls. The play opens briskly with short exchanges: Ted the president defensive, Gerry the manager preoccupied. Within a few lines it is established that a difficult meeting is about to occur, that Ted feels inadequate to the task. Scotch is introduced to heighten the tension and there is a brief exchange about a wife which smartly establishes the fact that women are low on the agenda.

Our expectations of a fight to come are already high by the arrival of Laurie for a conciliatory meeting; and Ted swiftly explodes it. The pace accelerates through this scene, the next with the captain Danny; and is capped by the arrival of Jock. It is language of thrust and parry, the emotions out in the open. Only Gerry, the manipulator and the sceptic, keeps his own counsel. This structure is repeated in the second act with the running gag of Geoff's family problems, one story capping the next till it dissolves in ridicule.

Lastly, *Travelling North*. Here the first impression is gracious, full of sunlight. Frances is looking out into the audience and listening. It is a play about listening. The conversation is idle and yet it quickly establishes that the harmony is not complete: Frank's observations are practical, hers romantic; he seeks for control, she for adventure; she, as a creature of feeling, already has undefined anxieties and restlessness. By the end of the scene we have learnt why they are there, from what they have escaped and we hear an ironic edge to their expectations which begs to be denied. Love, as old Lear was to discover, needs sterner stuff.

In Williamson's earlier plays a dramatic image realising the play's central dilemma became a crucial part of their force, connecting the private world of the characters with the public world of the audience: the election broadcast in *Don's Party*, the ping-pong in *Jugglers Three*, for example. These images are still there in these plays, providing an important clue to the author's intent: the engines in *The Department*, repeated references to the Third Reich in *A Handful of Friends,* the photographs in *The Club* which are torn down at the end of the play; and the light and music in *Travelling North*. In the plays which follow, in which the fluid scenic devices are further explored and developed, this aspect of Williamson's work becomes less evident. The 1980s, with its confusions of prodigality, injustice and total restructuring of government, business and Australia's place in the world; and in which Williamson himself was to face middle-age, the questions begun in *Travelling North* needed further attention, and in a form reflecting a less assured command of the issues and a more penetrating insistence upon individual responsibility.

THE DEPARTMENT

*Neil Fitzpatrick as Robby, Carole Skinner as Myra and
George Szewcow as John in the SATC production at the Parade
Theatre, Sydney 1975. Photo: Robert Walker.*

The Department was first performed by the South Australian Theatre Company at The Playhouse, Adelaide, on 15th November 1974 with the following cast:

ROBBY	Neil Fitzpatrick
JOHN	George Szewcow
PETER	Patrick Frost
MYRA	Carole Skinner
HANS	Leslie Dayman
AL	Alan Becher
BOBBY	Brian James
GORDON	Don Quin
OWEN	John Larking
SUE	Barbara Dennis

Setting designed by Michael Pearce
Directed by Rodney Fisher

Willie Fennell as Gordon, John Clayton as Robby in the Northside Theatre Company, Sydney production 1986. Photo: Branco Gaica

CHARACTERS

GORDON, 55, the departmental mechanic. Grizzled, spare, tough, sceptical.

BOBBY, 50, department member. Cheerful, puckish in appearance, darting and slightly nervous in manner.

SUE, 26, the departmental secretary. Pleasant and relaxed.

HANS, 36, department member. Thick-set and jovial.

ROBBY, 40s, head of the department. A large and rather impressive man in an unkempt sort of way. His hair sticks out in a kind of unintentional Afro fashion.

PETER, 28, department member. A tall man, rather striking in appearance, with something of the air of an anarchist larrikin.

JOHN, 24, department member. Bearded, intense, apparently humourless but displaying on occasions a subtle sense of irony.

AL, 32, department member. Slight, intense, prickly.

OWEN, late 30s, department member. A jovial, easy-going man, impressionable, good-natured and sleepy-looking.

MYRA, about 30, Humanities lecturer. Boisterous, good-natured and attractive. Her clothes are a little too brazen and she can be quite domineering when the occasion warrants it.

SETTING

The set is a naturalistic reproduction of a heat engines (thermodynamics) laboratory in a small tertiary technical college in Victoria in the year 1967. A mezzanine floor of iron gratings sits above an old Tangye steam engine on one side of the stage, and an old Rushton diesel complete with detachable ratchet starting handle, on the other. Separate desks and small tables, most with chairs drawn up to them, are scattered around the mezzanine floor. This furniture, purloined from classrooms, is used by the staff during the meeting in lieu of a single large table. Papers, magazines and tin mugs are scattered on desks, tables and chairs.

Silver piping descends through the mezzanine, piping high pressure steam to the Tangye from the boiler and carrying the exhaust steam away. A black pipe takes the exhaust fumes of the Rushton diesel out of the laboratory through a side wall. Thinner green pipes descend through the mezzanine, circulating cooling water for the diesel and the steam engine. Funnels rise out of the concrete floor to take the condensate from the Tangye and return it to the water sump under the floor. A few Pomona-type pumps stand behind the machinery to return the water from this sump to the cooling tower (unseen) on the roof of the laboratory.

The pipes in the well-lit area above the mezzanine are vertical and clean; this whole area contrasts with the tangle of pipes, machinery, pressure gauges, steam traps, safety valves, pumps, etc below the mezzanine. This latter area takes on a slightly brooding, nightmarish quality under certain lighting conditions.

There is separate access to the mezzanine level and the lower level. A fairly steep steel ladder joins the two levels.

ACT ONE

As the play opens, GORDON *is tinkering with the fuel injection on the Rushton diesel. The lighting is such that at first he can hardly be seen.* BOBBY *enters. In his interaction with* GORDON *there is no hint of any status difference between them.* BOBBY *looks around in the gloom and turns on a fluorescent light. He sees* GORDON.

BOBBY: Do you always work in the dark?
    [GORDON *looks up at the fluorescent tube. He raises his eyebrows and continues working.*]
GORDON: New tube? Didn't bother to try the switch it's been blown so long.
BOBBY: [*indicating the diesel*] What's wrong this time?
GORDON: Fuel pump, I think.
BOBBY: It's starting to give a lot of trouble, isn't it?
GORDON: Starting? It's been giving trouble for twenty-seven bloody years, as well as nearly wiping out three students. Were you round the day young Swansea got hit?
BOBBY: Neigus was hurt last week.
GORDON: Who?
BOBBY: Neigus.
GORDON: Neigus? The big fella?
BOBBY: Mmm. Broke his wrist.
GORDON: It's quite safe as long as they hang on to the bloody thing. [*Indicating the starting handle*] Did it kick back?
BOBBY: Mmmm.
GORDON: We should get rid of it. Ford've been offering us a new diesel for ten years or more.
BOBBY: Robby set up this lab and he hates to see anything go out of it.
GORDON: Yeah.
BOBBY: [*patting the diesel*] They're like old girl-friends. He can't bear to be nasty to 'em.
GORDON: Were you here the day Swansea got hit?
BOBBY: I was teaching over the other side.

7

GORDON: It's a wonder you didn't hear him. Christ, he yelped. Blood everywhere. I thought I was back in the Navy. Did he ever finish his diploma?

BOBBY: Swansea? Yes.

GORDON: He was the most useless student with machinery that ever went through this place.

BOBBY: He wasn't too hot on his theory either.

GORDON: How come he got through?

BOBBY: Special circumstances. Robby was pretty soft in those days.

GORDON: Special circumstances? Swansea? What special circumstances?

BOBBY: His father died just before the final exams. Three years in a row.

GORDON: What brings you over here today?

BOBBY: [pointing to the table] Meeting.

GORDON: Gawd. Don't you blokes do any teaching these days?

BOBBY: Robby has gone mad on meetings lately. It's all this upgrading. I wish they'd left us how we were.

GORDON: [pointing to the table] What's the panic this time?

BOBBY: I don't know, to tell you the truth.

GORDON: He'll take us into his confidence about something one day. I walked into the store-room yesterday and there was a ten foot searchlight sitting there.

BOBBY: A searchlight?

GORDON: [nodding] A bloody searchlight.

BOBBY: Why do we want a searchlight?

GORDON: That's what I asked Robby. 'Got it cheap from the Army,' he said. 'What're you going to do with it,' I said, 'dazzle the pigeons that shit on our cooling tower?'

[SUE enters. She carries a sheaf of typewritten papers, which she distributes at the table during the following conversation.]

SUE: Hello Bobby.

BOBBY: Hello Sue. What've you got there?

SUE: Agendas. I've just finished duplicating them.

GORDON: Doesn't she look lovely today? You know what, Sue? You should've been a model or an air hostess. You're too good for this place.

SUE: What do you want done?

GORDON: The pretty ones are always the most suspicious. Have you got time to do a little job for me?

SUE: What sort of job?

GORDON: Duplicating.

SUE: What?

GORDON: Gawd. I feel like I'm in the witness stand. Treasurer's report. Blackburn RSL.

BOBBY: Are you treasurer down there?

GORDON: Yep.

BOBBY: They must have rocks in their heads.

GORDON: How do you think I paid for my new car?

SUE: I'm not supposed to do outside work. Mr Robinson goes mad at me.

GORDON: Don't worry about Robby. He's an old woman.

UE: How many copies?

GORDON: I, er, need a fair few, actually. A hundred and twenty.

BOBBY: A hundred and twenty?

SUE: How many pages?

GORDON: Two. Look, a hundred will do. They've got to be posted out tomorrow. It's all typed up. Did it myself.

SUE: Two hundred sheets?

GORDON: Two hundred sheets. For the jokers who fought for your freedom in the stinking jungles of New Guinea.

BOBBY: Don't fall for that one, Sue. He spent most of his time sun-baking in the Indian Ocean.

GORDON: Sun-baking? Flat on my back in the engine room with a spanner in my hand.

SUE: [*descending the ladder*] I'll see what I can do. Have you got it there?

GORDON: It's in my locker. I'll get it for you.

[*He puts down his tools, preparing to leave.* HANS *enters.*]

HANS: [*to* BOBBY] No one here yet?

GORDON: I'm here.

HANS: You don't count. Have you welded my tow bar yet?

GORDON: No. It'll have to wait until next week.

HANS: Like hell! I'm taking the boat up to Eildon on Friday night.

GORDON: Gawd, Hans. The college does expect some work out of me.

HANS: They gave up expecting that years ago.

GORDON: They're cruel to me, aren't they, Sue?

SUE: Shocking.

GORDON: [*following* SUE *as she leaves*] I'll just grab that thing from my locker.

[*They both leave.*]

HANS: The shit's hit the fan.

BOBBY: What's happened?

HANS: Haven't you read the student rag?

BOBBY: No. What's in it?

HANS: [*taking a copy from among the books he is carrying, and reading*] Riddle: what piece of equipment cost the College fifty-seven thousand dollars three years ago and can never be used? Answer: see this man, and if he won't tell you, we will. In next week's issue.

BOBBY: Ooh hell.

HANS: [*showing* BOBBY *the paper*] Not a bad likeness, is it?

BOBBY: Oooh hell.

HANS: His hair does stick out like that.

[HANS *chuckles.*]

BOBBY: He's going to be furious.

[ROBBY *enters. It is obvious that he is the person who has been caricatured by the students. He is furious.*]

ROBBY: Where is everyone?

BOBBY: I think they're on their way.

ROBBY: Have you read it?

[BOBBY *nods gravely.*]

HANS: I don't think the cartoon did you justice.

ROBBY: It's not funny, Hans. I've had Fletcher on the phone already asking what it's all about. [*Looking at his watch*] Where is everybody? This is no joke, Hans. Fletcher's going to rip us to shreds on this one. Rip us to shreds.

BOBBY: Do you think he'll play it hard?

ROBBY: Play it hard? He'll rip our guts out. He's been waiting for something like this for years.

[ROBBY *looks up at the mezzanine door. It almost seems as if he expects the missing members of staff to have materialised. He frowns.*]

He's got the scent of blood in his nostrils and there'll be no stopping him.

[ROBBY *leaves to look for his missing staff members.*]

HANS: I think he's a little worried.

[PETER *comes in.*]

PETER: What's wrong with Robby?

HANS: [*handing him the student article*] Fletcher versus Robinson, round two hundred and fifty-seven. Fletcher's opened with a nicely placed phone call to Robby's ulcers.

PETER: [*exultant as he reads the article*] Jesus, eh? How about that!

BOBBY: Don't sound so pleased. I was responsible for it.

PETER: The towing tank? Bullshit.

BOBBY: [*glumly*] I was.

PETER: Bullshit. Robby should have checked it. [*To* HANS] Hey! How about that? I wondered why he called the meeting.

[JOHN *comes in.*]

PETER: [*to* JOHN] Have you seen this?

JOHN: Mmm.

PETER: [*noting* JOHN's *sombre expression*] I seem to be the only one extracting a sense of malicious delight. I must be a bastard.

JOHN: It'll make it harder for us to get new equipment.

BOBBY: It will too. Fletcher will use this against us for years.

JOHN: I tend to think the effect will be pretty marginal in the long run.

BOBBY: [*more hopefully*] Do you think so?

JOHN: I think so.

PETER: [*to* HANS] Are you worried about the tank, shithead?

HANS: Christ, no. I'm more worried about the holidays. What's the latest on that?

PETER: They're going to try and make us work right through. Fletcher had all the heads of department in his office last Thursday and told them they had to bring all their staff in and make them work right through.

JOHN: What was the reaction of the heads?

PETER: Robby fell into line straight away. Predictably. Fletcher only has to raise his eyebrows and Robby shits himself.

BOBBY: He wouldn't have much choice, Pete.

PETER: Why not? Joe told Fletcher to go to buggery.

HANS: Really?

PETER: Really. Evidently he told Fletcher that he was going to tell his staff that as far as he was concerned he didn't care if he didn't see them around for the full two weeks.

JOHN: [*to* BOBBY] Why's Fletcher doing it, Bobby? There isn't much for us to do when the students aren't here.

BOBBY: Apparently his reasoning is that seeing as we're getting University salaries now, we should be working University conditions.

JOHN: Four weeks annual leave?

[BOBBY *nods*.]

PETER: Four weeks annual leave? Bullshit. The only time I was ever on campus was when I was giving a lecture or a tute. The real reason's that it shits Fletcher off that he has to work through the break and we don't.

HANS: I'm not working through. I'm going skiing. I've booked in at Buller already.

PETER: That's a thought. I'll book in myself.

HANS: [*to* BOBBY] What's the staff association doing about it?

PETER: The executive's going across to get stuck into Fletcher on Thursday. [*To* BOBBY] Aren't they?

BOBBY: [*embarrassed*] I think so. I couldn't make it to the last meeting.

HANS: [*to* PETER] Going to Buller this year?

PETER: Hotham. Snow's better.

HANS: Too bloody far.

PETER: [*to* HANS] I'll tell Robby I've booked in too, but you've got to come in on this one.

HANS: I'm going to let him know how I feel.

PETER: Don't sit there like a stuffed dummy.

HANS: I'll tell him straight out. Don't worry.

BOBBY: I doubt if we'll get past discussing the tank.

PETER: I'll make sure we get past discussing the tank.

JOHN: So will I. Have any of you read that proposal I left on your desks?

PETER: Yeah. I'll support it.

BOBBY: I started it this morning but the phone rang.

HANS: What proposal?

PETER: Don't you ever read what's put on your desk?

HANS: If I read all the papers that landed on my desk, I'd be here twenty-four hours a day and my brain'd go soft.

JOHN: I've been working on Robby to set up an informal committee of staff and students to meet him for an hour each week.

HANS: What for?

JOHN: To let him know how we're thinking.

HANS: He doesn't give a stuff how we're thinking.

JOHN: Right. Which is exactly why I'm trying to get it through. Have you heard about the syllabus change?

PETER: Yeah.

HANS: No.

JOHN: If Robby gets his way there'll be something like five extra hours of teaching time per week in second, third and fourth year.

HANS: When?

JOHN: Next year.

HANS: Five hours? How are we expected to teach it?

JOHN: That's not a problem. If Council approves the extra hours they'll approve the extra staff. It's the students who are going to suffer and they're bloody furious.

ANS: How many more staff will we need?

PETER: Two.

HANS: Shit, Fletcher won't let anything through Council that's going to get us two extra staff.

PETER: He wouldn't if he could help it but Robby's got the numbers.

HANS: Really?

PETER: He's been lobbying for weeks.

JOHN: The students are ready to cut his throat. They've got a heavy enough load as it is. Can I count on your support?

HANS: I don't know what good it will do.

JOHN: He'll know that the students want to cut his throat. That's what good it will do. I'm sure he'd be a little more careful if he knew how hostile they felt.

PETER: I'll support it.

BOBBY: It puts me in a bit of an awkward position . . .

JOHN: No, look, I wasn't . . .

BOBBY: I agree with the idea in principle but . . .

JOHN: No, look, as long as these buggers support me, that's all I need.

HANS: I'll support you. I don't know what good it'll do.

PETER: [reading newspaper] Hey. How about Calwell?

JOHN: Yes. Thank God he had the grace to step down at last.

PETER: When's the next federal election?

JOHN: Late sixty-nine. We'll go close to winning it now.

PETER: I rather liked old Calwell but his face was disastrous on television.

HANS: Did you hear the one about him doing door to door campaigning in Toorak? [As they shake their heads] He wasn't doing too well. Getting very dispirited. He dragged himself up to the door of the largest mansion he'd ever seen, knocked, waited, it swung open and there was an impeccably spoken lad of fifteen or so. 'You're Arthur Calwell!' he said. 'I've got a picture of you hanging in my bedroom.' Arthur was overcome. A Labor supporter in the heart of Toorak. 'You're one of us,' he said. 'Not rahly,' said the lad. 'Mother put it there to show me what I look like when I masturbate.'

[*They laugh.* ROBBY *enters.* GORDON *follows him.*]

ROBBY: It's not funny. When Fletcher gets his teeth into this one the whole department will suffer.

PETER: We were laughing at Arthur Calwell's face.

GORDON: Don't talk to me about Calwell. He started the immigration scheme after the War. Filled the country up with Poms and Dagos.

JOHN: Enriched our cultural bloodstream, Gordon.

GORDON: Enriched? [*Pointing to* HANS] Bastards like Hans? Straight out of Hitler Youth.

JOHN: [*interested*] Were you in the Hitler Youth?

HANS: Of course. I got a medal. From the hand of Der Fuhrer.

JOHN: Really? What for?

GORDON: Baring his arse for the Nazi brass.

ROBBY: [*irritated*] Where are the others, Bobby? Al and Owen? I've been all over the place.

JOHN: Owen might be in at the hospital.

BOBBY: No. He's not going in this time.

ROBBY: Going in for what?

JOHN: Jill's in labour.

ROBBY: Again? The Church ought to give them a medal.

JOHN: They need one more.

ROBBY: What? They do give medals?

JOHN: [*straight-faced*] Mmm. I read it in the Catholic Weekly. A medal for half a dozen, and a return flight audience with the Pope for twelve.

ROBBY: [*realising it is a joke*] I can't wait all day. We'll just have to start.

[*He goes to the table and picks up an agenda.*]

Subject preferences for second semester. We've wasted enough time already. Could you please take your seats. Subject preferences. Now that we've moved to a halfyearly system I need your preferences by the end of next week at the latest. I stress again that there's no guarantee that I'll give you the subjects you ask for. I know there's been some mumbling in the ranks about this one but there are very good reasons why you can't teach exactly what you want to teach, and one is that it's damn hard to juggle the timetable to achieve this end, and secondly because I don't think it's good for you to teach the same subject year in year out. I don't want this department to lose its flexibility. I want every man to be able to teach every subject.

PETER: Why?

ROBBY: Because I don't want you to get complacent and lazy. That's why.

[*Pause.*]

JOHN: I think perhaps that's not entirely rational, Robby. There'd be quite a few benefits if we specialised a bit more.

ROBBY: I'm sorry, John, but while I'm head of the department I'm not having anyone carve themselves out little empires. With half an hour's warning I could teach any subject on our syllabus and so could all of you and that's how I want it to stay.

BOBBY: I can't teach every subject.

ROBBY: [*quickly*] You could if you had to.

JOHN: I hate to make a nuisance of myself, but I really can't understand the reasoning on this issue. The wider we spread ourselves, the more superficial our grasp of the subject matter. The idea that we should be swapped around to keep us from getting lazy seems a strange one, to say the least.

ROBBY: I didn't give that as a reason. I —

PETER: You did.

ROBBY: That is not the reason!

GORDON: How'd it be if I suddenly decided to specialise?

ROBBY: Gordon!

GORDON: Get to know diesels in depth and bugger the rest. Nice mess you'd be in then. Wouldn't you?

ROBBY: Gordon!

GORDON: I'm only trying to support you.

ROBBY: Are you going to be working there long?

GORDON: Could be a while yet, boss.

ROBBY: I want your subject preferences in next week. Don't expect to get every subject you ask for because I won't hesitate to flush out anyone I find hiding in some stagnant little pocket of knowledge. I want rounded men in this department, rounded men.

[AL *comes in.*]

AL: [*to* GORDON] Haven't you finished yet?

GORDON: Nope.

ROBBY: I've been looking for you all over the place. Where in the hell have you been?

AL: Sitting in your office.

ROBBY: In my office? What were you doing in my office?

AL: You wanted to see me at two.

ROBBY: I cancelled that when I called the meeting.

AL: What meeting?

ROBBY: This meeting.

AL: I didn't know we were having a meeting.

ROBBY: What are you here for?

AL: To see if Gordon's fixed the diesel.

GORDON: Not yet.

ROBBY: Didn't Sue tell you?

AL: What?

ROBBY: About the meeting?

AL: When?

ROBBY: Just then.

AL: What? When I was sitting in your office?

ROBBY: Yes. Didn't she see you sitting there?

AL: No. She's not at her desk.

ROBBY: Where is she?

AL: I've got no idea.

GORDON: Oh, er, I think she's doing a little job for me.
  [ROBBY *fumes*.]

ROBBY: Didn't she get in touch with you this morning?

AL: About the meeting?

ROBBY: [*losing patience*] Yes.

AL: No.

ROBBY: Well, she was told to.

AL: Well, she didn't.

ROBBY: I can't understand that. Were you in the Fluids lab?

AL: No.

ROBBY: Well, that's where I told her she'd find you.

AL: Well, that's why she didn't. I wasn't there.

ROBBY: Well, where were you?

AL: In 207 where I'm supposed to be. Prac finished three weeks ago.
  [ROBBY *fumes and sits down at the table, indicating that the meeting is about to begin.*]

ROBBY: Have you got anything else you could work on, Gordon?

GORDON: Dozens of things but this one's got priority.

AL: I need it for a prac class tomorrow morning.

ROBBY: [*irritated*] I wish you'd start scheduling your maintenance earlier than one day ahead.

GORDON: Fair go. I was only told about this one this morning.

AL: I reported it six days ago.

GORDON: [*pulling out greasy slips of paper*] I've got the memo here somewhere with today's date on it.

AL: I reported it six days ago.

GORDON: [*unable to find it*] Bloody memos. Why didn't you just come and tell me six days ago.

AL: All requests for maintenance have to be routed through Robby's office.

GORDON: Since when?

BOBBY: [*quickly*] Since —

ROBBY: [*loudly*] Since last meeting.

　　　[*A short pause.*]

GORDON: First time I've heard about it. Why not just come and tell me?

ROBBY: [*loudly*] Because we can't have you at the beck and call of anyone in the department. There has to be a list of priorities!

JOHN: There does seem to be quite a time lag though, Robby. I wonder if it might be possible to cut it down a bit?

ROBBY: [*irritated*] You might not all know it, but I'm working a twenty-four hour day for this department. I get in here at seven each morning and Bobby gets in at eight.

BOBBY: [*self-deprecating*] That's only to escape the missus.

JOHN: I'm sorry, Robby. I didn't mean that to sound like criticism. I think everyone realises how hard you're working, in fact what I was suggesting was motivated by the thought that if we could come up with some alternative scheduling system we could take some of that load off your shoulders. Perhaps we could form a sub-committee to look into it?

GORDON: Gawd. I've never heard so much crap. If you want something done, come and see me and I'll do it.

ROBBY: It isn't a very satisfactory state of affairs, Gordon, when the head of a department finds it difficult to get a rig built for his final year students because his departmental technician is too busy making [*searching for a word*] gadgets for classes in first year Applied Mechanics. There will be a list of priorities, and I will decide those priorities.

JOHN: I couldn't agree more, Robby. If there'd been a list of priorities I wouldn't've had such a hassle trying to get those [*searching for a word*] teaching aids of mine built. However, the system at present does seem to have a time lag. That's why I'm suggesting we form a sub-committee to look into it.

ROBBY: Yes, well, we'll come back to that issue later if you don't mind. We've got more pressing matters on our plate.

[*He brandishes the student paper.*]

You've all seen this, I suppose?

GORDON: Good likeness.

[*A silence.* ROBBY *glares at* GORDON.]

ROBBY: Gordon. Would you go and do something elsewhere?

[GORDON *glares and gathers his tools.*]

GORDON: I'll have to come back soon or it won't be ready for the morning.

[*He goes.*]

ROBBY: [*still holding up paper*] Who's been sounding off to the students?

[*A silence.*]

Come on. They've found out about it from someone in the department and I'd like to know who.

[*A silence.*]

PETER: They're not morons, Robby.

ROBBY: Who?

PETER: The students. When we've got a hundred foot long towing tank sitting up there on the mezzanine floor of the Fluids lab, conspicuous as crown jewels on black velvet, and when that tank, which is meant to be filled with water and used, is not filled with water and used for three bloody years, then somebody is going to start thinking.

ROBBY: Especially if someone starts them thinking.

PETER: Meaning?

ROBBY: Meaning that someone might have started them thinking.

PETER: And that someone might have been me?

ROBBY: Someone fed those students and I want to know who!

PETER: I've been trying to suggest, Robby, that it might not have been anyone. They might just have used their brains. I realise that the whole emphasis of this course is to rid them of that habit, but you just never know.

ROBBY: [*glaring at him*] All right. If nobody's got the guts to own

up, then let's just say there's a Judas in the department and
leave it at that.

JOHN: That's not quite fair, Robby. Peter may be right. The
students may have worked it out for themselves.

    [OWEN *and* MYRA *enter. They have just finished a counter lunch
    and are both showing the effects of alcohol.*]

OWEN: We're late, aren't we?

    [ROBBY *scrutinises them.*]

    [*To* MYRA] We're late. [*To* ROBBY] Ah. Ah. [*Clearing his throat*]
Myra and I have just been lunching together.

ROBBY: I can see that.

OWEN: And, er, we thought that seeing as she spends so much of
her time teaching our students, it would be a good idea if she
came to our meetings. I think that's a very good idea, don't
you?

AL: She's Humanities.

MYRA: I'm not taking no for an answer.

BOBBY: Any news from the hospital?

OWEN: No. She's taking her time again. I've brought my cigars in
anticipation.

    [OWEN *and* MYRA *climb the ladder and move towards the table.*
OWEN *puts his cigars on the table.*]

ROBBY: [*embarrassed*] Normally we'd be very glad to have you,
Myra, and it is a good idea that you do sit in on our meetings
occasionally, but we do, er, have some pretty confidential stuff
to get through today.

MYRA: [*good-natured but firm*] No. No. No. No. I'm not having
any of that one.

OWEN: The main thing we both felt was a lack of communication.

    [*He looks at* MYRA. *She nods.*]

Between ourselves and the Humanities department, and we
thought that seeing as she spends most of her time teaching
our students . . .

MYRA: Eighty per cent of my load.

OWEN: That she's the ideal person to go about bridging that gap.

ROBBY: I appreciate your point, Myra, but this is an Engineering
staff meeting and whatever and whoever you teach, you are a
member of the Humanities staff.

MYRA: Are you scared I'll tell them what you say?

HANS: [*pulling up a chair for her*] Don't be a bastard, Robby. Let
the lady stay.

ROBBY: [*sighing*] I'm sorry, Myra. You'll have to leave.

MYRA: Too bad. I'm not.

HANS: She's drunk again.

MYRA: I'm not drunk, and what do you mean again?

HANS: I've heard some bad reports about you.

ROBBY: I take it you're not going to leave?

MYRA: No.

ROBBY: I see. Well, in the circumstances we'll have to consider that last matter I raised as being closed.

MYRA: I bet it was about the towing tank.

   [ROBBY *looks at her.*]

I know about the towing tank.

ROBBY: What do you know about the towing tank?

MYRA: That you can't fill it.

ROBBY: Who told you?

MYRA: It doesn't matter who told me. What matters is that it's a bloody disgrace. Fifty thousand dollars worth of equipment you can't use and I can't get two hundred dollars for a tape recorder. I've said so too. Don't worry.

ROBBY: To who?

MYRA: To my students. It's a classic example of the relative value placed on Science as compared to Humanities.

ROBBY: You've told your students about our tank?

MYRA: Often. I use it as a basis for discussion in tutorials.

ROBBY: How long has this been going on?

MYRA: [*airily*] Months.

ROBBY: Have you seen this week's Super Stude?

MYRA: Yes. Very good likeness.

ROBBY: Myra. Fletcher is going to rip us to pieces over this tank.

MYRA: Fletcher is not going to let you have fifty thousand dollars every time you click your fingers in future, and bloody good show.

HANS: She is drunk.

ROBBY: What idiot was foolish enough to tell this woman about our towing tank?

MYRA: Don't let him bully you.

ROBBY: Who was it?

MYRA: Don't let him bully you.

ROBBY: All right. I won't pursue the matter any further, but I'd like whoever it was who opened his big mouth to note the result.

MYRA: Why didn't you work out what was going to happen before it was installed? Isn't that what engineers are supposed to be able to do?

ROBBY: It's an extremely difficult calculation, Myra, but being innumerate you wouldn't appreciate that.

MYRA: Innumerate?

ROBBY: You've called me illiterate more than once.

MYRA: It doesn't seem very difficult to me.

PETER: It is.

MYRA: Isn't the whole problem that when you put the water in it's going to be too heavy for the mezzanine floor?

ROBBY: Yes.

MYRA: Well, couldn't somebody have worked out how much the water was going to weigh before you put it up there?

PETER: Yes. That's not the problem.

ROBBY: Myra. The mezzanine is made up of two-inch strips of steel, patterned and welded together at touchpoints. The edges of this floor are welded intermittently along the front edge, continuously along the back edge, and bolted intermittently on both sides. The bottom of the tank rests on this floor. It is very difficult to predict how such an irregular floor surface will deflect under load, [louder] in fact it is a plate deflection problem of the highest order of difficulty.

MYRA: Well, why did you put it up there if you couldn't work out what was going to happen?

[There is a pause during which GORDON comes in relatively surreptitiously and starts work on the diesel again.]

ROBBY: It wasn't intended to go up on the mezzanine in the first place. [Looking at BOBBY] It got there by accident.

BOBBY: It's all my fault, actually. The architects came in one day when Robby was away at a conference and told me the plumbing'd be easier if they put the tank up on the mezzanine. I didn't argue. I thought they must've checked it themselves.

AL: It's not your fault, Bobby. It should have been checked at final blueprint stage.

ROBBY: It was checked at final blueprint stage. I simply missed the fact that the tank had suddenly leapt from the ground floor where I'd put it, to the mezzanine where no one but a donkey would put it. It went out under my signature. It is my fault.

BOBBY: I made a big note on my pad to let you know about it the minute you came back, but it slipped my mind.

MYRA: [*to* ROBBY] Weren't you here when it was being made?

ROBBY: It was constructed during the summer break when the labs weren't in use, and for the first time in twelve years I didn't come in during the summer break. I took a holiday.

MYRA: And now what? If it's filled the whole mezzanine floor will collapse?

ROBBY: I wish we knew. Some people around here seem to think that the whole building will collapse.

AL: It will.

ROBBY: Rot.

JOHN: The mezzanine will come down, but not the building. No way.

AL: Well, it won't if you treat the main stanchions as Euler beams but unfortunately that's so far from being an accurate assumption . . .

JOHN: You're wrong, Al. I haven't assumed that. In fact, just the reverse. I'm assuming a residual bending moment at each joint.

HANS: [*to* MYRA] There's three schools of thought, actually. The extremists think the building will go, the moderates think the mezzanine will go and the conservatives think the mezzanine will buckle and the tank might deform.

GORDON: And I think nothing will happen at all.

MYRA: Well, this has thoroughly disillusioned me. I'd hate to let you loose designing a bridge if you can't even work out whether your own building's going to collapse.

GORDON: Those who can, do. Those who can't, teach.

MYRA: What are you going to do about it?

ROBBY: How the hell would I know what we're going to do about it? It's there. We can't take it down. We can't fill it up. It cost fifty-seven thousand dollars. The students know. Fletcher knows. We're going to get kicked and kicked and kicked.

HANS: We're working on a plan to half fill it and breed trout.

ROBBY: Sometimes your sense of humour eludes me, Hans.

AL: [*agenda in hand*] Seeing as you've gone to all this trouble and prepared us an agenda, do you think we might get onto it?

[OWEN, *genuinely surprised, picks up an agenda.*]

OWEN: An agenda?

AL: I'd like to prepare lectures some time today.

HANS: Breakdown of adviser scheme.

OWEN: Has it broken down?

JOHN: I wasn't aware that it had.

ROBBY: Neither was I until I got Sue to check around and find out how many of your allotted students had actually been contacted.

AL: They don't come.

PETER: You can't give 'em advice if they don't want it.

ROBBY: [to AL] Have you actually gone out and looked for them?

AL: No. I haven't got time.

JOHN: I know it's time-consuming, but I think we've got to be prepared to chase them to a certain extent. Most of them tended to be a bit sceptical of that first letter we sent out.

ROBBY: You're putting me in a very awkward position over this scheme. We're the only department to try something like this and I've made quite a noise to that effect at Council, and, believe me, there'll be a lot of people around this place who'll be only too willing to fang me if they find out that the whole thing's collapsed.

AL: If they want to come and talk to me they can come and talk to me but I haven't got time to go chasing them.

PETER: Isn't the whole thing a bit artificial?

JOHN: I wouldn't think so, Peter. Not if we're really committed to the idea of making it work, and as far as its being a useful exercise I can only quote my own experience as a student. It's really quite demoralising when you only come into contact with staff in a lecture situation. It really is. Sometimes you'd like to talk to someone for no other reason than a feeling of wanting to belong to the place.

HANS: One of mine came.

JOHN: They'll come if you make them feel welcome.

HANS: I did. I offered him a fag and he told me all about his sex life.

[MYRA *is not impressed.*]

AL: All that's going to happen is that they'll come in and whinge about other members of staff.

ROBBY: They won't if you make it quite clear from the start that you're not going to listen to that sort of thing.

HANS: Come on, Robby! That's half the fun. You should've heard what my guy said about Al.

ROBBY: [*glaring at* HANS] Despite the fact that some of you seem to have been trying your best to white-ant it, the scheme

will continue, and I will check again in two weeks to ensure
that all your allotted students have been contacted. You'll just
have to get used to looking after the students a little better
than you have in the past. I've had more complaints this year
than I've ever had before.

BOBBY: [*glumly*] Mostly about me.

ROBBY: They've been about everyone. Except John.

[*Good-natured, jeering approval from* OWEN, HANS *and*
PETER.]

It's about time some more of you started putting some effort
in. We're starting to get a reputation as a department that
neglects its students and it's something we can't afford.
Enrolments this year were only up eighteen.

MYRA: Humanities were up eighty-six.

ROBBY: Yes, if I had my time over again I'd take Humanities too.
Why exercise your brain when it isn't necessary?

MYRA: Nasty, nasty.

ROBBY: Oh, and when the students take the trouble to organise a
social function, see if a few of you can take the trouble to turn
up.

OWEN: I went to the third years' wine and cheese tasting.

JOHN: And made a fine speech to boot.

OWEN: Did I? What about?

JOHN: You seemed to cover just about everything.

ROBBY: Myra and I were the only two staff representatives who
bothered to turn up to the final year party last month.

HANS: Yes, we, er, heard that you two were the only ones who
bothered to turn up.

ROBBY: Yes. And we thoroughly enjoyed ourselves.

HANS: We heard that too.

[PETER, OWEN, BOBBY *and* HANS *look at each other.* OWEN *tries to
suppress a grin.* ROBBY *looks at him narrowly.* MYRA *is furious.*]

ROBBY: I want that adviser scheme to work. Right? Now the —

AL: Where do we find all the extra time? I've got over seven
hundred prac reports to mark.

[*There is some head-nodding and murmuring from* HANS,
PETER *and* OWEN.]

ROBBY: Well, why are you all that far behind?

[*General uproar.*]

AL: [*with heat*] I had to rush a year's Applied Mechanics prac
through in four weeks because nobody had worked out that

the third years had to be in there by April.

ROBBY: There was bound to be a bit of difficulty changing over to the half-yearly system, but as I understand it you're supposed to be on last year's schedules until the new one comes out.

[*There is a general outburst of protest. The general tenor is that last year's schedule cannot be used because the second year Mechanics class has been split into two groups this year.*]

JOHN: We really do need that new schedule, Robby. Prac work's in a hell of a mess.

[*General assent.*]

ROBBY: You'll have it within a week.

GORDON: Who was the idiot who left the bypass valve open in the steam line?

PETER: Me.

GORDON: Gawd. I might have known.

JOHN: I'm sure a couple of us could get together and knock this one over in a few hours.

ROBBY: I'd rather handle this one myself, thanks John. Scheduling prac can be a lot more tricky than it appears.

JOHN: Fair enough.

MYRA: Can I say something at this point?

ROBBY: No.

MYRA: It won't take long.

ROBBY: If it's not in the agenda you'll have to raise it under general business. We've got a lot to get through.

AL: Let's get through it then.

[ROBBY *emits a weary sigh.*]

MYRA: Robby. I really want to say something.

ROBBY: I'm sorry, but we must stick to the agenda. Bring it up under general business.

GORDON: [*to* BOBBY] Billy Sproule says it won't collapse.

ROBBY: Billy Sproule? D'you mean to tell me that Billy Sproule knows about our tank? How does Billy Sproule know?

GORDON: [*shrugging*] I don't know.

ROBBY: Did you tell Billy Sproule? My God. He gossips like a fishwife. Why in the hell did you tell him?

GORDON: Because he's been a boilermaker for nearly thirty years and if anyone around the place is going to know whether the thing's going to collapse, he will.

ROBBY: Who else have you told?

GORDON: No one. No one at all.

[*He catches* MYRA's *eye.* ROBBY *sees the look and emits his most gigantic sigh to date.*]

ROBBY: Gordon. A couple of months before he died Charlie called me into his office and told me how sick he was. 'I've got to give it away, Robby,' he said. 'You're the boss here now. You'll need another teacher and it's about time we had a technician. Get Bobby across from Physics to teach, and get Gordon from the junior school to do your maintenance. He's a loudmouth and a smart alec and he won't exactly kill himself with overwork but the buggers are in such short supply at the moment I doubt if you'll do any better.' Now if you don't mind, I'd like you to find something to do elsewhere, and I'd like you not to come back until we're finished.

GORDON: [*surly, packing his tools*] I'll tell you what he said to me. He said: 'Gordon, young Robby's going to come over and ask you to work for him. Don't refuse straight off. Think about it. He'll be a lot better in ten years.' I'm sorry, Al. It doesn't look like this'll be ready for you in the morning.

AL: [*shrugging*] That's okay. Teaching's the least important of our duties around this place!

ROBBY: Al!

AL: What!

ROBBY: Shut up!

GORDON: [*as he goes*] Ten years!

MYRA: Can I say something?

HANS: [*quickly*] Yes.

MYRA: [*quickly*] Is there any truth in the rumour that my subject is being cut by an hour a week next year?

ROBBY: Nothing's been finalised on the matter of next year's courses. Nothing at all.

MYRA: Firstly, I'd hope the rumour wasn't true and secondly, if there was any truth in it I hope I'd be consulted on the matter before any decision was taken.

JOHN: I don't quite see how this fits in with yours, Myra, but I think I should mention that there's a very strong rumour doing the rounds amongst the students to the effect that course hours are going up by five hours a week next year.

[*Pause.*]

ROBBY: There's one thing that this college isn't short on and that's rumours. Nothing's been finalised.

MYRA: [*to* JOHN] Going up five hours?

JOHN: That's what the students seem to think.

ROBBY: [*tersely*] Nothing has been finalised!

MYRA: I'll tell you what, Robby. That's going to really make me angry. It's one thing to be cut back if hours as a whole are being cut back but if hours are going up then that amounts to a calculated slap in the face. I know you think that what I'm teaching them isn't worth much

ROBBY: You're jumping to conclusions. Nothing's been finalised!

MYRA: Engineers should be getting more Humanities. Not less.

ROBBY: Myra. Nothing has been finalised.

JOHN: What is the current position then, Robby?

ROBBY: Current position on what?

JOHN: When you say nothing's been finalised, I take it that there are moves afoot to change the course structure.

ROBBY: Nothing's been finalised!

JOHN: But there is a proposal to change the course structure in the process of being formulated?

ROBBY: There is a draft proposal before Council. Council has not made a decision.

JOHN: Could you possibly tell us something about the contents of the proposal?

ROBBY: No, I could not. The proposal is before Council and is therefore to be treated as confidential.

PETER: [*bored, half asleep*] Shit.

ROBBY: It's rather stupid of the students to get upset about a proposal when they don't even know what that proposal contains.

JOHN: They're worried about the five extra hours. Final year's got twenty-four contact hours already.

ROBBY: It won't be anything like five hours. Three and a half to four at the most.

JOHN: That's still pretty substantial.

ROBBY: If the students had half a bloody brain in their head they'd realise it's in their own bloody interests. Knowledge is growing at an exponential rate and if we don't keep them abreast of it their qualifications'll be useless.

OWEN: What's getting the big push? Systems and Control?

ROBBY: I can't say.

HANS: Give us a clue.

ROBBY: I can't say.

HANS: Blink your left eye if I'm warm. Numerical Methods?

ROBBY: You'd have to be an idiot if you didn't think Numerical Methods had to go in.

AL: I wondered how long it would be before we jumped on the computer bandwagon.

ROBBY: Computers are a fact, Al. They're scarcely a bandwagon.

MYRA: I see. We're allowed to guess. Could I guess that a subject called H might be reduced from two hours a week to one.

ROBBY: Myra. Certain subjects are definitely going in. Certain subjects may be reduced or cut, but the fine details haven't as yet been worked out.

MYRA: Well, before they are worked out, could you do me the courtesy of consulting me if my subject is to be cut out.

ROBBY: Yes!

MYRA: Thank you.

JOHN: I take it Graphical Solutions will go?

ROBBY: [*sharply*] Why?

JOHN: If we're looking for subjects to chop then I would've thought that would be the first to go.

> [*General assent except from* BOBBY, *who looks embarrassed and fidgets.*]

ROBBY: [*tersely*] Graphical Solutions still has a place.

HANS: In the museum.

ROBBY: Peter! Would you mind waking up!

> [PETER *jerks to attention from a semi-doze.*]

Fletcher's had a complaint that you hung up on someone who was making a phone enquiry.

PETER: Eh? When?

JOHN: When is something likely to be finalised, Robby?

ROBBY: When Council considers the recommendations.

MYRA: And those recommendations, although they contain definite ideas about what subjects are to go into the course, don't as yet specify which subjects, if any, are to be deleted?

ROBBY: [*exasperated*] That's right, Myra. I've told you that already.

MYRA: I'm just trying to make sure I know precisely what the position is.

ROBBY: Could we leave this whole issue and come back to it later?

AL: Do all these extra hours mean that our teaching loads are going up?

ROBBY: Will you please all stop talking as if the extra hours were already a fact. The proposal has not been considered by Council.

AL: If we do get extra hours does it mean our teaching load will be going up?

ROBBY: If Council approves of the principle of an expanded syllabus they'll automatically approve of new staff to teach it. That goes without saying.

AL: How many more staff? One?

ROBBY: Quite possibly two.

HANS: Will that make us bigger than Physics?

ROBBY: Possibly. Why do you ask?

HANS: Just interested.

MYRA: Who's the biggest department in the College at present?

HANS: Physics.

ROBBY: I think we can stop that line of inference right now if you don't mind.

AL: Where will they fit? I'm not sharing an office.

ROBBY: We'll deal with questions like that if and when they arise. Now can we drop the whole subject and get on with the agenda.

PETER: When did it happen?

ROBBY: What?

PETER: This phone call I'm supposed to have hung up on.

ROBBY: Last Friday.

PETER: Friday?

ROBBY: Yes. Friday. You hung up in some woman's ear. I've got to report back to Fletcher on it.

PETER: Oh, that one. I didn't hang up on her.

ROBBY: What did you do? I've got to report back to Fletcher.

PETER: I told her to hang up, think about what it was she wanted to ask me, write it down, then ring me up again.

ROBBY: Do you think that's the proper way to handle a telephone enquiry?

PETER: It is when the caller's a fuckwit.

ROBBY: When someone calls this department and asks for information they will be treated with civility and respect. Now if you don't mind we'll proceed with the agenda. The design competition. It's getting a bit out of hand.

[*A silence. Most people glance at* OWEN.]

OWEN: What do you mean, Robby?

ROBBY: I mean it's tending to get out of hand.

MYRA: I thought it was marvellous.

ROBBY: It's got to the point where the whole department practically comes to a standstill for upwards of a week.

AL: Upwards of a bloody month.

OWEN: I know there's a bit of disruption on the day itself.

ROBBY: There's bloody bedlam on the day itself.

MYRA: It has been getting the department some wonderful publicity, Robby.

JOHN: Right. We've had cover on three of the four television channels this year, haven't we, Owen?

OWEN: So they tell me.

AL: Wonderful.

JOHN: I thought it was good.

AL: Fantastic. Our students neglect the entire course while they're busy making toy paddleboats. Fantastic.

JOHN: Oh come on, Alan. I thought it was an excellent project. They had to use an enormous amount of basic theory.

HANS: It was bloody good television, too. Eleven batterydriven paddleboats butting the Christ out of each other in the College moat.

MYRA: Whose boat won?

OWEN: Neigus'.

ROBBY: It's got right out of hand. We're here to teach, not to get our heads on television.

OWEN: Look, I'm sorry, Robby. I thought it was a good showcase.

[SUE *enters.*]

ROBBY: What is it, Sue?

SUE: Excuse me interrupting, Mr Robinson. Phone for you.

ROBBY: Did you say I was in the middle of a meeting?

SUE: Yes.

ROBBY: Made no difference, I suppose?

SUE: He said he was terribly sorry and it wouldn't take a minute.

[ROBBY *snorts, rises and leaves the room with* SUE.]

OWEN: What brought all that on, Bobby?

BOBBY: Some TV bloke asked him to shift out of his office so he could interview you.

JOHN: But didn't Robby make a boat himself?

HANS: Yeah. He's been making it down in the workshop before anyone gets in. Gordon told me.

PETER: Yes, he's been at it for weeks. [*To* BOBBY] Did he ever get it finished?

BOBBY: Yes. He took me down one morning to test it in the moat. I haven't seen him so happy in years.

JOHN: Why didn't he enter it in the competition? Wasn't it fast enough?

PETER: It should have been. He put in a huge iron flywheel to cut impact losses. Bloody clever idea.

JOHN: What was the problem?

BOBBY: It sank.

[*A pause.* AL *shifts uncomfortably.*]

OWEN: I'm sorry, Al. I didn't realise my design competition was interfering with your classes.

AL: [*embarrassed, defensive*] It used to be enough teaching them. Now you've got to entertain them as well.

[*Awkward pause.*]

[*Getting up to leave*] Will you tell Robby I'll be back shortly?

BOBBY: How long will you be gone?

AL: A few minutes.

[*He goes.*]

PETER: Whingeing little prick.

BOBBY: He's got problems.

HANS: [*to* MYRA] Enjoying the meeting?

MYRA: I'm very glad I came.

HANS: Robby's a pretty good operator, isn't he? Enrolments stagnant and he still manages to get himself two extra staff.

MYRA: He won't get it through Council.

HANS: Pete says he will.

PETER: He will. The word is that he's got the numbers.

MYRA: I can't believe it. If we can see through it what do you think Council's going to do?

PETER: He's got the numbers. He's been wheeling and dealing for weeks.

MYRA: All for the sake of becoming bigger than Physics? Ridiculous.

PETER: Kings used to measure their importance by the size of their army. Jesus, Al makes me sick.

[*A silence.*]

HANS: He's getting worse. I just couldn't stop this student talking about him the other day.

JOHN: I know. Mine are the same.

HANS: The kid showed me an assignment he'd set them and it

was impossible. He sets them impossible assignments and then screams at 'em.

JOHN: I know.

BOBBY: Robby's pretty concerned about him, actually.

OWEN: He seems to spend a lot of time in his office now.

BOBBY: He'll be in there now. I go in there and try to talk to him sometimes, but you can't get through to him. We end up talking about Thermodynamics.

OWEN: We invited him over for a meal, but it didn't go very well. Jill invited her sister and I'm sure he thought it was all a plot.

HANS: It sounds like it was.

OWEN: [*in all innocence*] Oh no. Rosemary doesn't want to get married again. She made that quite clear several times but he still got jumpy.

MYRA: Has he got any outside interests or hobbies or anything?

BOBBY: He used to belong to a choral society but he had a big blue with them.

PETER: He was the only one in tune.

BOBBY: They weren't practising hard enough. He showed me the letter he wrote them when he resigned. Hell, what a ripper.

HANS: What'd it say?

BOBBY: I can't remember it all but it ended up accusing them of wasting seven years of his spare time and telling them they were nothing but a social club who were more interested in small talk and alcohol than in music.

[ROBBY *re-enters, furious.*]

ROBBY: Well. We don't have to wait for next week's edition. Fletcher's found out about the tank and wants a full report.

BOBBY: Oooh hell.

ROBBY: To take to Council.

BOBBY: Ooooh hell.

ROBBY: I don't know what you're ooh helling about. It's my fault. I signed the drawings. [*Sighing*] Well. We can say goodbye to our wind tunnel. We'll never get it through Council now.

HANS: Ah well. With our expertise we'd probably put the fan in back to front and blast the roof off.

[ROBBY *is not amused. He picks up the agenda.*]

ROBBY: Founder's Day ceremony. The Council has — where's Al?

BOBBY: He'll be back in a minute.

ROBBY: The Council has decided that despite last year's fiasco the ceremony will proceed as usual, and I hope that this year I am spared the acute embarrassment of having to watch my own students behave like hooligans. It is not the acme of civilised behaviour when a ninety year old lady is drowned out by moronic interjections, and when the college chairman is narrowly missed by a flour bomb.

HANS: You won't sit next to him this year, will you?

ROBBY: Hans, for the last time will you spare us your humour? I'm serious about this matter. Deadly serious.

OWEN: Is Miss Milton coming again this year?

ROBBY: No. She died.

PETER: When?

ROBBY: Two months ago.

PETER: Wasn't she the last relative?

ROBBY: Yes.

PETER: I thought Council was going to stop this Founder's Day thing after the last relative died?

ROBBY: Well, they can't now, can they?

PETER: Why not?

ROBBY: It would look like straight out capitulation.

PETER: Shit.

ROBBY: And I can see their point! I'm damned if I'd give in to mob rule either.

[*Pause.*]

It might help, Myra, if you didn't get them working on a provocative project just before the ceremony this year.

MYRA: Provocative project?

ROBBY: I don't think it was entirely a coincidence that last year's blow-up occurred straight after you'd given them that project.

MYRA: It might not have been but I don't think you can blame the project. It was a simple, straightforward research exercise. I can hardly be blamed if they weren't very impressed with what they found.

ROBBY: I don't care whether they were impressed or not. They've got no right to act like animals and taunt a ninety year old lady. If your subject can do nothing more constructive than turn our students into hooligans then it's really no wonder if I do occasionally have second thoughts about its value.

[MYRA *is upset and speechless.*]

JOHN: Robby. That's a bit much.

ROBBY: They were like a pack of bloody animals!

MYRA: I'm not condoning the way they behaved.

ROBBY: Frederick Milton may not have been a model of virtue, but he founded this College with his own money, and this College means something to me. As a student and a teacher I've spent most of my life here and it means something to me.

MYRA: Robby. I'm not condoning the way they behaved.

ROBBY: Why set them on that particular project just before Founder's Day?

MYRA: Because it was topical. And relevant.

JOHN: That's fair enough, Robby. If we're going to make a big thing about Founder's Day then it's fair enough to ask your students to find out something about the Founder. It's scarcely Myra's fault that Milton was a crook.

ROBBY: He was not a crook.

PETER: He was a crook.

ROBBY: He was not a crook.

PETER: He sold government contracts to his own businesses.

ROBBY: He started this College.

PETER: Yeah. Because his factories were short of mechanics.

ROBBY: All right. Everyone's rotten. Everyone's corrupt. Dig up muck. But the point is that even if it was all true, and it's not, nothing excuses that animal behaviour we saw at last year's ceremony. Nothing!

JOHN: I don't think we're disputing that, Robby. The point at issue was the implication that Myra was in some way acting unethically by setting her students the task of finding out something about the College Founder.

ROBBY: I would just like to know one thing. Could Myra honestly sit there and tell me that she had no idea, when she set them the project, that they'd unearth something ambiguous?

JOHN: I don't think —

MYRA: No, I can't. I knew they'd find out he was a rat and I'm glad they bloody well did.

[*Pause.* ROBBY *is pleased.*]

JOHN: Which still doesn't mean that Myra was in any way unethical.

MYRA: Shut up.

JOHN: [*hurt*] I'm sorry Myr —

MYRA: I can speak for myself.

ROBBY: The classroom is for instruction. Not for propaganda.

I think that's something you might well bear in mind yourself,
John.

JOHN: Sorry. I'm not with you.

ROBBY: The classroom is for instruction. Not propaganda.

JOHN: Of course.

ROBBY: It's something you might well bear in mind yourself.

JOHN: I'm sorry. I'm afraid I don't know what you're referring to.

ROBBY: Perhaps you'd just better think about it for a while.
   [*Looking at the agenda*] Now the −

JOHN: I'm sorry, Robby. What exactly were you referring to?

ROBBY: Did you take your students on a tour of Ford Australia
   recently?

JOHN: Yes.

ROBBY: Did you follow up that tour with a lecture to the students
   on the evils of the car industry?

JOHN: No, I didn't. Who told you that?

ROBBY: I respect your point of view, John, but you're not
   employed here to ram it down students' throats.

JOHN: I'm afraid I take very strong objection to that statement,
   Robby. I don't know who was the source of your information
   but if they'd reported me accurately they certainly
   wouldn't've described my talk in the way you've described it. I
   merely stated the fairly obvious truth that engineering criteria
   play very little part in car design, being almost totally
   outweighed by pressures towards ostentation, model
   proliferation, excessive engine power and poor passenger
   protection. If that's forcing politics down my students' throats
   I offer you my resignation right here and now!

ROBBY: Don't be ridiculous.

JOHN: I mean it.

ROBBY: It's all very clear-cut to you, but we place dozens of our
   students with Ford for vacation experience, and they take on
   two or three of our graduates every year.

JOHN: My offer still stands.

ROBBY: They also, I might add, equipped half of our Engines lab
   for nix. I'm sorry. I shouldn't've brought it up, but it's been
   raised at Council level and I'm getting the kicks.

PETER: Tell Council to go and get stuffed! And Ford Australia!

ROBBY: [*looking at* PETER] That's interesting.

PETER: What?

ROBBY: Coming from you.

PETER: Why?

ROBBY: Don't you do most of your consulting work for big business?

PETER: I solve problems for a fee. I don't initiate their policies.

ROBBY: Fletcher wants to see you.

PETER: What about?

ROBBY: About your consulting work.

PETER: It's none of his business.

ROBBY: He thinks it is.

PETER: Why?

ROBBY: Because he wonders how you find the time to be doing so much of it. So do I.

PETER: Have you had any complaints about my teaching?

ROBBY: The administration is still waiting for last year's roll checks.

PETER: Well, they're going to have to wait a long while. I don't call rolls any more.

BOBBY: I see. You've taken the law into your own hands?

PETER: Yes.

ROBBY: Perhaps you'd better see Fletcher about that one too.

JOHN: I'm sorry to come back to it, Robby, but I'm very upset about that complaint. I intend to take it further.

BOBBY: Don't make an issue out of it, Johnny. Milton is littered with the corpses of men of principle. Look at me.

[AL *re-enters and starts to climb the ladder.*]

HANS: What principle did you ever stand for?

BOBBY: Incompetence as a way of life. I think the urn should be boiling if anyone's interested in a cuppa.

ROBBY: We'll break and start again in fifteen minutes.

[HANS, OWEN *and* BOBBY *rise like schoolboys released at recess.*
JOHN, *still angry, hangs around to speak to* ROBBY. *So does* MYRA. PETER *leaves in a leisurely manner. The following dialogue occurs as the first three climb down the ladder and make for the door.*]

HANS: My mug's been missing for two days. Did you whip it off again, Owen?

OWEN: No.

HANS: If I find it in your office this time I'll hide your bloody chalk-box.

[AL *begins to climb down the ladder again.*]

AL: Why don't you put a label on your mug like I do?

HANS: That's got its dangers, Al. I spit in yours every morning. [AL *leaves.* OWEN *and* HANS *laugh as they leave.* PETER *leaves.* JOHN *sees that* MYRA *is determined to stay and leaves too.* MYRA *stands there looking at* ROBBY. *He looks evasive and shifty.*]

ROBBY: I knew you knew they'd dredge up some muck.

MYRA: So what!

ROBBY: You just wanted to stir up trouble.

MYRA: I couldn't stand the thought of them sitting through that charade again without knowing the truth.

ROBBY: Do you really think it'd have been a terrible crime if Miss Milton had've gone to her grave with her illusions intact?

MYRA: Oh migod!

ROBBY: Well I'm sick of it. And thanks very much for letting the whole world know about the tank.

MYRA: It had to come out sooner or later.

ROBBY: Fletcher's going to hold that over me for God knows how long.

MYRA: You've been bottling that Founder's Day stuff up for a year, haven't you?

ROBBY: It's pretty destroying to watch your own students behaving like louts. When there was just Bobby and I we knew our students as well as our best friends. They were our best friends, and they respected us as well.

MYRA: I hope my subject isn't being cut. Especially if it's because of Founder's Day.

ROBBY: It's purely a matter of finding time. I'll see if I can chop an hour out somewhere else.

MYRA: How's your wife?

ROBBY: The specialists still haven't found anything.

MYRA: How many have you taken her to?

ROBBY: Three.

MYRA: What are you going to do?

ROBBY: Take her to another.

MYRA: Do you think that's wise?

ROBBY: Probably not.

MYRA: There's obviously nothing organically wrong with her.

ROBBY: I know.

MYRA: Do you think it's worth her talking to . . . someone?

ROBBY: A psychiatrist?

MYRA: I'm not suggesting she's —

ROBBY: I don't need a psychiatrist to tell me what's wrong with her. She hates my guts. That's what's wrong with her. Charlie's wife paid him out by hanging herself in his toolshed, so I suppose I can count myself lucky.

MYRA: There must be a reason for it.

ROBBY: Of course there's a reason for it. I've neglected her all my life. When we were setting up this lab about fifteen years ago I slept on a couch in my office for over a week. See that Tangye? That was built in 1872. I found it in an old riverboat and hand-machined the replacement parts myself.

MYRA: Have you heard from your daughter?

ROBBY: Yes. I got a postcard from Tess. Work always came first. Now it shits me but it's too late to do anything about the other. Am I boring you?

MYRA: No.

ROBBY: I am. I'm sorry about the party.

MYRA: What are you sorry about?

ROBBY: I made a fool of myself.

MYRA: So did I.

ROBBY: I was going to ring you.

MYRA: Why?

ROBBY: To apologise.

MYRA: There was no need to.

ROBBY: [a sudden inspiration] Why don't you get interested in Peter?

[MYRA stares at him incredulously.]

No. Seriously. He needs a steadying influence. He's provoking the administration into a major conflict over that consulting work. He's not going out with anyone regularly as far as I know. He knocks around with those brainless tarts he meets skiing and they're not going to do him any good.

[MYRA stares at him.]

What's wrong?

MYRA: Do you realise what you've been saying?

ROBBY: I was just —

MYRA: I understand perfectly why your wife's neurotic.

ROBBY: You're misinterpreting what I —

MYRA: It might interest you to know that I don't relish being thought of as the type of girl who is a steadying influence, and it might also interest you to learn that I don't particularly want to channel my affections in the way best suited to serve the interests of your department!

ROBBY: Myra, you're misinterpreting —

MYRA: You're incredible!

ROBBY: What do you want out of life? To end up a bitter old spinster like Maggie Symons?

> [MYRA, *incredulous, stops her progress towards the door and stares at him. She starts on her way again.*]

[*Brusquely*] Do you know anything about this committee that John wants me to form?

MYRA: No.

ROBBY: He hasn't spoken to you about it?

MYRA: No.

ROBBY: You'd approve, I'm sure. They want me to set aside an hour each week to sit and listen to their whinges. They must think I'm stupid. If they think I'm going to end up like your boss then they've got another think coming.

MYRA: There's nothing wrong with Joe.

ROBBY: Except that he's a bloody rabbit. He's too scared to poke his head outside his door for fear of offending one of his staff.

MYRA: Rot. He just can't get away with blue murder like you can.

ROBBY: Get Robby is the favourite game around here these days. I wouldn't mind so much if they were paragons of virtue themselves. I had a deputation of thirty students in my office last week complaining about Al.

MYRA: I'm not interested.

ROBBY: They're perfectly entitled to set up a committee to let me know what they think of me, but I'm not allowed to breathe a word of complaint about them. Al failed over half his students in Thermo last year. Set an impossible paper and failed over half of them.

MYRA: Isn't he upset at the moment?

ROBBY: All right. His wife's left him, but that's no excuse for him to single-handedly create a nation-wide shortage of engineers. He's going to do exactly the same again this year. I've had thirty students in my office already and I have to sit there and defend him.

MYRA: Have you talked to him?

ROBBY: About what?

MYRA: Have you told him you think his standards are unreasonable?

ROBBY: Al? Are you joking? You couldn't tell Al anything like that.

MYRA: So what are you going to do? Sack him?

ROBBY: Sack him? Here? A person has to be certified dead by three independent medical practitioners before you can claim they're unfit for duty around here.

MYRA: What are you going to do then?

ROBBY: What can I do, short of setting and marking his papers myself?

MYRA: You could talk to him.

ROBBY: That's the solution to everything, isn't it? Talk, talk, talk. Talk solves everything. That's what Chamberlain thought at Munich.

MYRA: I'm going to get a cup of coffee.

ROBBY: I'm sorry. I didn't mean what I said about Maggie Symons.

[*Before she can reach the door,* PETER *enters carrying a cup of coffee in one hand, a sheaf of papers under his arm, and a slide rule in the other hand. She looks at him, nods and leaves.* ROBBY, *descending the stairs on his way out, looks at him.*]

[*Sarcastically*] Catching up on some work?

PETER: [*smiling politely*] That's right.

[ROBBY *glares at him and leaves.* PETER *moves up the ladder to the table. He spreads his papers, sits down and starts calculating. He uses the slide rule frequently, scribbling the results rapidly. Sometimes he does a long stretch of algebraic analysis without using the slide rule. Sometimes he sits and thinks. He takes rapid sips of coffee in such a way that they scarcely interrupt him. Early in this process of calculation the house lights come up indicating interval.* PETER *remains calculating throughout this interval.*]

END OF ACT ONE

ACT TWO

GORDON *enters.* PETER *looks up from his calculation.*

GORDON: [*a little worried*] Hey, you seen Bobby?
PETER: Who?
GORDON: Bobby.
PETER: No.
GORDON: I've done something stupid.
PETER: What?
GORDON: Locked the door of the Fluids lab and started the pumps.
PETER: The pumps?
GORDON: I'm filling the tank. It's quarter full already.
[PETER *raises his eyebrows and recommences his work with apparent unconcern.*]
I got fed up.
[PETER *nods, still looking at his work.*]
It got beyond a joke.
[PETER *looks up and nods.*]
Someone had to do something.
PETER: [*with a trace of a grin*] Don't look so worried.
GORDON: It's all right for you. I'll probably get the sack.
PETER: Don't look so worried.
GORDON: [*irritated*] You'd be bloody worried. You'd be shitting yourself and don't bloody tell me you wouldn't. I'd better go and turn them off.
PETER: Leave 'em on. It won't collapse.
GORDON: That's what I think, but what if it does?
PETER: It won't. I've checked it.
GORDON: Checked it?
PETER: It'll deflect about three sixteenths at the middle. It's quite safe. I did a complete computer simulation of the whole system.
GORDON: When?
PETER: Over a year ago.
GORDON: It'll deflect three sixteenths?

41

PETER: Plus or minus ten per cent.

GORDON: And that's safe?

PETER: Perfectly safe. It won't collapse.

GORDON: You're sure?

PETER: I'm sure.

GORDON: You didn't make a mistake when you were working it out?

PETER: No.

GORDON: It's safe to leave the pumps on?

PETER: Yes.

GORDON: Do you think I should?

PETER: Christ, yes. Just make sure I'm there when Robby sees it full.

GORDON: I hope you haven't made a mistake. If Robby asks you where I am, tell him I've gone to Pritchards to chase an impeller that didn't turn up.

PETER: You're one of the best, Gordo.

GORDON: [*glumly*] Probably get the boot and do my long service leave.

[*He goes.* PETER *gives a silent whoop of satisfaction.* OWEN *comes in, tea in hand.*]

PETER: Any news?

OWEN: No. I rang a little while back and she's still hard at it.

PETER: How are you managing?

OWEN: At home?

PETER: With the boys.

OWEN: Jill's Mum's over looking after things.

PETER: That'd keep her busy.

OWEN: Have you got an odd letter recently?

PETER: What kind of letter?

OWEN: Young Greg's got himself this book of joke letters and he's been annoying the hell out —

PETER: Is that who sent the bloody thing!

OWEN: Which one did you get?

PETER: I got the Reverend Oliver Pott, a touring temperance lecturer.

OWEN: Inviting you to attend a meeting?

PETER: No. Apparently a lot of the success of his lectures was due to a drink-sodden creature he used to exhibit as a warning, but the guy had just died and someone had suggested me as a replacement.

OWEN: [*laughing*] He went out on his first hike last weekend with two of his mates and they came on a tiger snake sunning itself in the middle of the track.

PETER: What happened?

OWEN: [*laughing*] You know what a young smartarse he is.

[PETER *nods enthusiastically.*]

'Don't worry,' he told his mates. 'Tiger snakes are basically timid and will move off if approached.'

PETER: What happened?

OWEN: [*laughing*] Chased them three miles. He's just written a letter to the guy who wrote his snake book.

PETER: What else has been happening?

OWEN: Two of the male white mice are pregnant, Tim's foal kicked a chook and broke its leg, Brian's ferret bit his finger and the dog killed the kitten.

PETER: The dog killed the kitten? They were the best of mates last time I was up there.

OWEN: The stupid little thing wandered across his feed bowl while he was eating.

[OWEN *snaps his jaws, imitating a big dog crushing a small kitten and tossing it aside.*]

The funny thing was that as soon as he'd done it he got all full of remorse and went across and tried to lick it back to life.

PETER: Do you remember the day we tried to train it not to take baits?

[HANS *walks in carrying a mug of coffee.*]

Did I tell you about the time we tried to train Owen's dog?

HANS: Dog? That's no dog. That's a cross between a wolf and a water buffalo. I'm not coming anywhere near that menagerie of yours ever again, Bourke. Not unless you chain the bastard. [*To* PETER] I was just giving young Greg a well-deserved boot up the arse for calling me a fat Kraut when it bailed me up against the wall with its paws on my chest. I'm a decorated war hero but I was not unafraid. That dog is a menace.

PETER: You don't have to convince me.

OWEN: It's usually as docile as a lamb.

HANS: You've got a weakness for gross ferocious creatures, haven't you, Bourke? Look at Jill.

PETER: What about Ingrid?

HANS: Ingrid is fat but jolly. That's the difference.

PETER: [*to* OWEN] Go and ring the hospital again.

OWEN: I might in a minute.

HANS: What were you saying about training the dog?

PETER: Oh, we, er, put mustard and chilli in some steak to teach it not to take baits but it dragged the meat over to its water dish and cooled its mouth between bites.

HANS: It ought to be shot.

[MYRA *comes in.*]

Back for the second half?

MYRA: Yes. Damn it. I'm going to stick it out to the end. [*Looking at her watch*] I thought he said quarter of an hour. [*To* OWEN] Any news yet?

OWEN: I think I might go and ring.

[*He goes.* PETER *looks at his watch.*]

PETER: He's probably into his drinks cabinet to fortify himself for the second half.

[*Pause.*]

HANS: If he can do it, so can we.

MYRA: [*looking at her watch*] We'd better not go to the pub, had we?

HANS: [*shaking his head and nodding towards the door*] No need. I've got a flagon of red in my filing cabinet.

PETER: I'll be in that.

[JOHN *comes in.*]

Want to join us for a quick red?

JOHN: [*looking at his watch*] Where's Robby?

HANS: Into the barley juices, I'd say. Coming?

JOHN: Thanks. I think I'll leave it this time.

HANS: Have you ever seen inside it?

PETER: The drinks cabinet? No.

HANS: You name it, it's there. I got a Scotch myself a couple of weeks ago.

PETER: [*opening the door*] You're joking. That cabinet's only opened for heads of State.

MYRA: [*going out door*] Don't be cruel.

HANS: [*as he goes*] He wanted me to take two classes so he could go to a conference in Adelaide.

[JOHN *paces up and down, alone in the laboratory. He is still upset over* ROBBY's *earlier accusations. He looks at a typewritten and duplicated foolscap sheet he is carrying. He begins to practise the speech he intends to make in a low voice.*]

JOHN: I'm sorry, Robby, but it's very difficult to continue in a job when fairly basic accusations are made relating to one's integrity. I can't agree with you that I in any way overstepped the area of my professional competence, or used my position to propagate political views, nor do I relish being in the position where my future prospects at the College may be influenced by complaints lodged by unknown persons and of which I never hear. I'm afraid that my earlier offer of resignation has firmed to a definite decision. [*Holding out the typed forms*] I've enjoyed working here.

> [*He nods and re-reads his resignation letter.* ROBBY *enters. He looks around and frowns, initially not seeing* JOHN *on the mezzanine floor. He turns to leave.*]

Could I see you for a moment, Robby?

ROBBY: [*jumping guiltily*] I didn't see you there. Where is everyone?

JOHN: I'm not sure.

ROBBY: [*looking at his watch*] I said quarter of an hour.

> [*He turns to go out, ostensibly to chase his staff, actually to avoid the confrontation.*]

JOHN: Could I speak to you for a moment, Robby?

> [ROBBY *sighs, turns, and reluctantly climbs the stairs.*]

ROBBY: I'm sorry I brought up that Ford business, John. You get pressed from all sides in my job. Pressed from all sides.

JOHN: I'm sorry, Robby, but I can't — Well I, er I've written a letter.

> [*He hands his resignation letter to* ROBBY, *who takes it, sits down at the table and sighs, without looking at it.*]

ROBBY: Resignation letter?

> [JOHN *nods.* ROBBY *looks at the letter without opening it. He screws it up.* JOHN *looks at him in surprise.*]

I'm afraid I can't accept it. You're too good a man to lose.

JOHN: I'm sorry, but I've decided.

ROBBY: I apologise for what I said. I'll apologise in front of the rest of the boys if you like.

JOHN: I'm sorry, but I've decided.

ROBBY: I feel exactly the same way about the car industry as you do. I'm an old Labor Party man myself, you know. Carried a card for years, but what can you do? They give jobs to your students and build your labs.

JOHN: Yes. I can understand the pressures to compromise quite clearly. I'll type the letter out again.

ROBBY: Now listen. You're resigning because of what I've said. I've apologised for what I've said so there's no need to resign. Right?

JOHN: I'm resigning, not so much because of what you said, but what you revealed in saying it. My whole career here could obviously be influenced by complaints I never hear about.

ROBBY: [*wearily*] The things that affect your career are always the things you never hear about. That's how institutions work. Anyway, you've got nothing to worry about career-wise. You stand out like a pearl amongst the swine around here.

JOHN: I'm very flattered by the compliment but I've made up my mind.

ROBBY: What will you do?

JOHN: I haven't decided.

ROBBY: You won't get a job at another college.

JOHN: Why not?

ROBBY: All the CAEs have an agreement.

JOHN: What agreement?

ROBBY: A gentleman's agreement. Not to pinch each other's staff.

JOHN: I hope you're joking.

ROBBY: I'm not joking. If staff could flit from college to college just to advance themselves it would throw the whole system into chaos. There's nothing official, but you try and get a job and see.

JOHN: That's very interesting.

ROBBY: You won't get into a Uni without a PhD. Look, I'm not trying to be a bastard. I'm just giving you the facts.

JOHN: Thanks.

ROBBY: You could get a job in industry but you don't want a job in industry, do you? Look. Bugger you! I don't want you to leave. Right? What've I got to do? Apologise fifty times? Get down on my knees? What've I got to do? Beg? I don't want you to leave! I want you to withdraw your resignation. I am sorry for what I said!

JOHN: I'm not worried about what you said! I'm worried about the general situation. If there are complaints made about me I'd like to hear about them.

ROBBY: Fair enough.

JOHN: Who made this complaint?

ROBBY: One of your students' fathers runs a place that supplies

Ford with piston rings. He rang Fletcher. Young Teddy Roberts.

JOHN: Teddy Roberts?

ROBBY: You probably thought he was lapping your lecture up, eh? And all the time he was waiting to get home and tell his old man what a bastard you were. [*Chuckling*] It takes you years to work out which of those smiling faces you pass in the corridor is knifing you behind your back. [*Changing mood*] Have you talked to the others about your committee idea yet?

JOHN: Yes. I've spoken to most of them.

ROBBY: Are they pretty enthusiastic?

JOHN: I'd say so.

ROBBY: That's good. That's good.

    [*Pause.*]

Some hurt you more than others.

JOHN: Sorry?

ROBBY: The knife jobs. Some hurt you more than others. Do you know much about Peter?

JOHN: How do you mean?

ROBBY: How he came to the department?

JOHN: Mmmm.

ROBBY: As soon as I heard about the run-in he had with Cheeseman I took the next plane up there and offered him a job. Have you heard this?

JOHN: I heard that you were pretty quick off the mark.

ROBBY: It was a mistake, but when what you think is a never to be repeated opportunity crops up, you don't stop to think out the long-term implications. You can't put a thoroughbred into a paddock full of pack-horses. Not meaning to be insulting, John, but Sydney Uni still gets something like twenty requests a year for copies of his PhD from all over the world.

JOHN: Why did he come?

ROBBY: Well for a start, I practically begged him to come. He's not averse to a bit of begging, I can tell you.

JOHN: He wasn't too popular at the time either, was he?

ROBBY: Well, no. That's true. You don't endear yourself to all and sundry by destroying your Prof's academic reputation at an international seminar. Especially someone as popular as Cheeseman. He waited for over a year to spring it, you know. Cheeseman gave him his paper for comment. In good faith. That bastard found a couple of flaws and didn't tell him. Made a fool of him at an international seminar. Waited for over a year to spring it. Should have warned me. Yes. He had to get out and find himself a quiet little backwater. That was part of it. Should've warned me, shouldn't it? I'm speaking out of school now and I know I shouldn't, but I treated him like a crown prince when he first came here, and all the time, unbeknown to me, he's knifing me left, right and centre. Poking fun at me to his students, spraying confidential information to other departments. I'm sorry. I shouldn't be saying these sort of things. This committee won't become a whinge session, I hope?

JOHN: Whinge session? How do you mean?

ROBBY: When you get people together to discuss things it can get very negative.

JOHN: I think it should prove quite positive. An informal little forum to exchange ideas.

ROBBY: That's good. That's good. There are a few things that worry me.

JOHN: What sort of things?

ROBBY: I'm all for discussion but sometimes it's just not possible to be as open about some things as you'd like to be.

JOHN: For instance?

ROBBY: This committee idea has got a bit to do with my proposals for course changes, hasn't it?

JOHN: No, although course changes would be a fruitful area of discussion once the committee gets under way.

ROBBY: Mmm. Now, for example. You mentioned Graphical Solutions before. In the meeting. Graphical Solutions is redundant. Right. I agree. Scrap Graphical Solutions? No. Do you know why? It is the only subject Bobby believes he can still teach. He borrows Al's notes to make sure he's still on the right track with the others. Of course, this computer thing scares hell out of him. Now it's illogical and stupid of me to put all our students through the agonies of Graphical Solutions to maintain one man's pride. I couldn't justify it for a moment in an open meeting and I wouldn't try. But I am going to retain Graphical Solutions until I have got Bobby a job as head of the junior school. Now I shouldn't have said that and if you make it public I'll deny it, but I put it to you as an example of a situation in which it is impossible for me to be completely open.

JOHN: There are other subjects you could cut out or prune.

ROBBY: So what are you saying?

JOHN: I'm saying that there's no reason in the world why you can't put your new subjects into the course without increasing course time by three and a half to five hours a week, Graphical Solutions or no Graphical Solutions.

ROBBY: So what are my motives?

JOHN: Quite frankly, I don't like to say.

ROBBY: You must think they're pretty reprehensible.

JOHN: If course hours are going up in order to get two extra staff members, in order that we will then be the biggest department in the College, then they are pretty reprehensible.

ROBBY: What possible advantage is it for me to be head of the largest department in the College?

JOHN: I suppose there are certain psychological benefits?

ROBBY: It makes me feel a little bit more important?

JOHN: Possibly.

ROBBY: I'm going to tell you something in the strictest confidence, and if you break that confidence I'll break your neck. State government is about to approve a fairly massive reallocation of tertiary finance for the next triennium. The Colleges of Advanced Education are going to get a comparatively larger slice of the cake, the Universities comparatively less. It's entirely pragmatic. It's cheaper to pump money into us than to build more Universities. Milton is going to get sufficient funds to erect one new building straight off. This new building will be air-conditioned, have University standard offices and lecture theatres and superbly equipped laboratories. The building is up for grabs and it's either Physics or us and it's going to be us. Nobody else in the College knows what you've been told. Not even Fletcher. We either get that building now or wait eight to ten years for a second chance and I haven't got that sort of patience. That's all I'm going to say. I'm quite in the wrong morally. I know. I'm loading up my students to win a political point. I've done worse than that. I've offered Mal Edgar of Physics an extra hour of teaching in our first year if he'll vote with me on my proposals next Friday. He's never going to speak to me again when he eventually finds out that I conned him into voting himself out of a new building. I've spent three months planting the idea around Council that the knowledge explosion is far more serious in Engineering than elsewhere. I've done every dirty little trick it's possible to do to get this course change through next Friday. It might be wrong but I'm going to have that building and I'm not about to tell any committee what I just told you, and if all of that disgusts you then I suppose you'd better resign.

[*Pause.*]

What does this country need? Physicists or engineers?

JOHN: Engineers.

ROBBY: There are four jobs offering for every graduate. Physicists are lucky if they can find one. All right. The carpeted, air-conditioned offices, the sound proof tutorial rooms, the acoustically perfect lecture theatres with all their electronic gadgetry, the escalators, the lot. They're all very tempting but it's our students that are ultimately going to benefit. Right? I'm sorry that our present students are going to get loaded up a little more than they should, but it's for the ultimate benefit of those students who are coming after them, and I'm sorry that it has to be done this way, but in a mad bureaucracy that gives a new building to a department simply because it's the biggest without even considering which department really needs it, then I've got to play these crazy games. Right?

JOHN: I don't know.

ROBBY: Think about it. I was an idealist myself once and —

[AL *comes in and looks around.*]

You were supposed to be back here half an hour ago.

AL: I don't notice anyone else here.

ROBBY: I don't care whether anyone else is here or not. You were supposed to be here twenty minutes ago.

[OWEN *comes in.*]

OWEN: Sorry I'm late. I've been on the phone.

JOHN: Any news?

OWEN: It's well advanced according to the doctor.

[BOBBY *comes bustling in looking embarrassed.*]

BOBBY: Sorry I'm late, boss. Old Norm caught me in the corridor.

OWEN: What's his worry now?

BOBBY: The snails ate his lettuce and his wife broke her leg in the bath.

AL: If nothing's going on here I'll go. I've got plenty of work to do.

ROBBY: [*moving to go down the ladder*] Just stay here, will you? [ROBBY *moves towards the door. Just as he approaches it, however,* HANS, PETER *and* MYRA *burst in. They are showing just the slightest trace of their two or three glasses of claret.*]

ROBBY: Where have you lot been?

HANS: Sorry, boss. We got here early and no one was around.

ROBBY: [*climbing the ladder*] Yes, well multiply eight by thirty minutes, and you'll find out how many man hours you've just lost us.

[HANS *attempts the calculation as he climbs the ladder.*]

All right. Seeing as we've wasted all this time, let's get down to it, shall we? Department representative on the staff association executive. Bobby's indicated to me that he's willing to do it again, and personally I think we should count ourselves lucky that he has. I don't think we could get a better man.

BOBBY: Don't lay it on too thick.

ROBBY: I mean it. [*Looking at the agenda*] Now the next matter —

JOHN: Sorry to be obstructionist, but isn't the staff representative meant to be elected by the staff?

[*A silence.* ROBBY *looks at* JOHN, *frowning slightly.*]

BOBBY: I'd be only too happy to stand down.

ROBBY: I'm sorry. I'd assumed there were no other nominations.

JOHN: This is certainly not meant to be a reflection on Bobby or on the job he's been doing for us, but I think it would be more proper to call for nominations.

ROBBY: [*to everyone*] Would you like me to call for nominations?

HANS: Do we have to make a big issue out of it?

ROBBY: I wouldn't've thought so.

JOHN: It's not so much a matter of making it a big issue as a matter of correct procedure. The staff association constitution calls for an election.

MYRA: Nominations should be called as a matter of course.

ROBBY: I'm sorry. I'd assumed there were no other nominations. Are there?

PETER: I'll nominate John.

JOHN: Well, er, that puts me in a rather embarrassing position. I didn't really press this point in order to get a nomination.

ROBBY: Are you accepting it or aren't you?

JOHN: Well, er, having made a point of it I suppose I'm morally obliged to.

ROBBY: Do we have any other nominations?

[*A silence.*]

What do we do now? Get Gordon to make us a ballot box?

AL: You don't need it. There was only one nomination.

[ROBBY *glares at him.*]

ROBBY: Would somebody care to nominate Bobby?

BOBBY: I'd be just as happy to see some new blood on the executive. Really.

HANS: I'll nominate Bobby.

ROBBY: Well. What do we do now?

BOBBY: We both leave the room and you vote, I suppose.

AL: It should be a secret ballot.

ROBBY: We don't need to go to those lengths, surely?

JOHN: I'm not fussy.

AL: It should be a secret ballot.

ROBBY: What in hell are you scared of, Al? It's a simple little election and nobody's going to worry one jot which way you vote.

JOHN: Look I don't mind us both leaving the room. It seems the simplest way to go about it.

AL: It should be a secret ballot.

ROBBY: This is absurd. Absolutely absurd. I suppose we have to hold an election to see how we run the other election.

HANS: Make a decision.

ROBBY: Will you both step outside for a minute and we'll have a show of hands. No. Go out this way.

[BOBBY *and* JOHN *get up and begin to leave.*]

BOBBY: The last time I did this I was voted in as form captain of 3C.

HANS: You're just angling for the sympathy vote.

BOBBY: I need it.

[*They leave.*]

ROBBY: All those in favour of John?

[PETER *puts up his hand.*]

Bobby?

[HANS *puts up his hand.*]

[*To* OWEN *and* AL] What's wrong with you two?

AL: I'm not voting unless there's a secret ballot.

ROBBY: Sometimes you stretch my patience to the limit, Al.

AL: I know that principles don't mean much around here, but they still mean something to me.

[ROBBY *sighs and fixes his gaze on* OWEN, *who appears nervous.*]

ROBBY: [*almost barking*] What about you?

OWEN: I'd prefer not to vote. They're both good men.

MYRA: I can't vote. I'm Humanities.

ROBBY: Democracy at work. The constituency is tied at one vote all. Owen? Do you possibly feel you could make a decision?

OWEN: No. They're both good men.

ROBBY: You couldn't possibly bring yourself to regard one as just a tiny bit gooder than the other?

OWEN: I'd rather not.

ROBBY: I suppose this means I've got to exercise my casting vote?

PETER: You haven't got one.

ROBBY: What?

PETER: The staff association constitution debars heads of department from voting for departmental rep.

ROBBY: I'm a paid up member of the bloody staff association!

PETER: You can vote for general rep but not for department rep.

MYRA: Peter's right, Robby. I think the clause was put in to safeguard the head of department feeling any embarrassment.

ROBBY: Embarrassment?

MYRA: At having to indicate preference for one member of his staff over another.

ROBBY: You know what the trouble with the staff association is? The staff association doesn't know where its real support lies. Who do they think fight the battles against the administration? We're the ones who stick our necks out for the staff and we're barely tolerated as members!

[BOBBY *puts his head in at the door.*]

BOBBY: Can we come in yet?

ROBBY: Yes. You may as well.

[BOBBY *beckons* JOHN. *They come in.*]

JOHN: Well. Tell us the worst.

HANS: Toss a coin.

BOBBY: Dead heat?

ROBBY: Dead heat.

HANS: Dead heat.

JOHN: Look, er, in that case I'll withdraw and let Bobby take it.

BOBBY: Thanks very much, John, but I can't accept.

ROBBY: You can accept and will accept. Say thank you to John for his kind and generous offer, sit down and let's get on with the meeting.

MYRA: Guided democracy.

ROBBY: Yes, well, someone's got to guide things around here or we'd get nothing bloody well done. [*Reading from agenda*] Engineering staff and students consultative committee. John has come up with the suggestion that we should have an hour set aside each week in which those staff members who are interested, and a number of elected students, can meet with me and discuss things of a general nature that they're happy about or unhappy about in an atmosphere of frankness. Would you care to comment, John?

JOHN: Yes, well there's not much I can add. I see this predominantly as a chance for a little bit of informal cross-fertilisation of ideas between students, staff and Robby on, er, general educational issues.

AL: What sort of general educational issues?

JOHN: Well, for instance, I found out the other day, purely by accident, that Owen's going to dispense with an end of year exam in Design.

[OWEN *starts to look alarmed, but* JOHN *fails to notice.*]

And replace it with a series of tests. Now as soon as I heard that it opened up all sorts of possibilities in my mind, but the point is that if we had a committee operating I'd probably've heard about it months ago.

ROBBY: [*grimly*] So would've I. [*To* OWEN] Might I ask on whose authority you've abolished end of the year examinations?

OWEN: It was just an idea I had. It seems to keep up their interest more.

ROBBY: Well, would you kindly revert to the standard procedure until such time as there is a general policy decision to change it. That goes for all of you.

JOHN: Sorry. I appear to have put my foot in it, but all the same a committee of the type I've proposed could possibly discuss this very issue and come to the conclusion that a series of tests had advantages over one final exam.

MYRA: We've been running tests in some of our subjects for over two years.

ROBBY: I'm afraid that it's my prerogative to decide what type of examination system I have in this department and I'd take a pretty dim view of any committee trying to dictate to me on this issue.

JOHN: I don't think there's any question of dictating, Robby —

ROBBY: The thing that worries me about this committee is where exactly do you draw the line between discussion and straightout pressure?

JOHN: I don't think anyone's questioning your authority, Robby. You'd always have the final say.

ROBBY: That's all very well, but what if you're all in there screaming for tests instead of final exams? Don't you think that constitutes pressure on me?

JOHN: Well —

PETER: If everybody's in there screaming for tests rather than final exams then maybe they're right and maybe you should feel under pressure.

ROBBY: I see.

JOHN: I think what Peter's trying to say is that you might come across some good new ideas yourself in the course of discussion.

ROBBY: I don't really think that was what Peter was trying to say at all, and in fact if he meant what I think he meant then I'm very worried about the whole concept of a committee. Very worried indeed. I won't tolerate a situation in which I'm expected to justify my every action and opinion. I'm making some pretty important decisions on what I see as the longterm interests of the department, and I don't intend to be hamstrung by committees. Do you understand my point of view, John? There has to be a clear understanding that this committee will not give rise to conflict.

JOHN: I'm sure if there were matters you'd prefer not to discuss the committee would respect that feeling.

PETER: It should give rise to some sparkling debate. I can hardly wait.

ROBBY: [*ignoring* PETER, *addressing* JOHN] All right. If I can have that assurance then I can't see why we shouldn't go ahead with your plan. I think we'll wait till next year and set it up if you don't mind. The new course'll be under way by then and that should give the committee a solid basis on which to begin discussion.

[PETER *looks astounded at this barefaced postponement obviously intended to avoid any embarrassing questions about the new syllabus, and is about to say something when* JOHN *either catches his eye or kicks him under the table or in some rather positive way indicates that he should shut up.*]

JOHN: That seems reasonable.

ROBBY: Fine. I'll leave that to you to organise. [*Looking at the agenda*] Oh yes. Misuse of staff amenities. Al's brought to my attention a rather annoying practice that we'll have to do something about. I haven't experienced it myself yet but I'd like to know just how widespread it's become. How many of you have come across students in staff toilets?

[PETER, HANS *and* MYRA *look at each other with bemused, rather incredulous glances.*]

OWEN: I was going to mention that myself.

ROBBY: It's happened to you?

OWEN: A couple of times in the last few weeks. It's very embarrassing too. You get annoyed but you'd feel stupid if you ordered them out.

BOBBY: I've noticed it a couple of times.

PETER: Does it really matter?

AL: They've got their own toilets.

BOBBY: And they're much bigger than ours.

JOHN: Ours is more tasteful.

ROBBY: I think we should treat this seriously, John.

MYRA: I can't believe it.

PETER: No, Myra. You don't understand. When men stand up at a urinal an element of competitiveness creeps into it. If a fellow staff member has the drop on you that's bad enough, but if a student beats you that's humiliating.

HANS: It's worse now that Neigus has broken his wrist. You've got to unzip his fly for him.

BOBBY: Neigus came in while I was there and I dried right up. Sorry, Myra.

OWEN: Neigus is one of the main offenders. The first one I saw was Gary Minter, but the next two times it was Neigus.

ROBBY: [*to* AL] Was Neigus the one you saw?

AL: No. It was Terry Brescini.

ROBBY: It seems a small matter to some of you but if it's the start of a conscious policy of defiance then it could lead to other things.

HANS: Another six months and they'll be shitting in our offices.

ROBBY: It seems a small matter to some of you, but I'd like it to stop.

JOHN: How exactly do we tackle the problem, Robby?

ROBBY: Well, er, I, er, suggest that in the first instance those who feel strongly about it speak up about it when they encounter an offender and, er, if that doesn't work I'll, er, speak to Fletcher. Now, er, the next matter. [*Reading from agenda*] Uniform standards.

PETER: What does that mean?

ROBBY: Well I'm, er, not quite sure how we're going to go about tackling this one, but I've, er, noticed a bit of a tendency for there to be consistently high fail rates in some subjects and not in others. Now it may, er, be that some subjects are, er, intrinsically harder than others and so this differential may in fact be justified. I'm not quite sure what to do about this matter so I'll throw it open for general discussion.

AL: Which subjects in particular were you worried about, Robby?

ROBBY: Your, er, Thermodynamics does seem to be one of the problem areas, Al.

AL: I pass every student who reaches the required standard and fail those who don't. Is there some other way I should behave?

ROBBY: Of course not. It just might be that some of us are expecting a little too much of our students and some not enough and we may need to find some kind of acceptable average. Now I don't know how we're going to achieve —

JOHN: Just a thought, Robby. What if we exchanged exam papers amongst each other so we could make general comments about standards. I could give my Applied Mechanics paper to Peter and he could give his paper to me — Nothing formal. Just for comment and suggestion.

OWEN: What if someone commented and suggested and you didn't want to change the paper you'd set?

JOHN: I suppose if the pair of you became deadlocked then you could go to Robby to arbitrate.

ROBBY: [*seizing on it*] That's not a bad idea, John.

AL: The way I set my papers is my own business and I don't think I should have to tolerate interference.

ROBBY: It's not exactly interference, Al.

AL: It sounds like it to me. Under that sort of set-up you could have the final say about the paper I set.

ROBBY: Only in exceptional circumstances.

AL: I wouldn't tolerate it in any circumstances.

BOBBY: I don't think John was suggesting a —

ROBBY: Let's be blunt, Al. Some of your papers have been pretty stiff and quite frankly last year's was beyond what I consider reasonable.

PETER: I don't want to offer a comment on standards but I will note in passing that two of the questions were badly worded and ambiguous and the last question was just plain bloody-minded.

ROBBY: [*placating*] Well I wouldn't . . .

AL: [*furious, wounded, upset*] There was nothing on that paper that a student who knew his subject couldn't handle. [*Erupting fully*] If anybody tries to tell me there's some kind of commitment to academic excellence in this College I'll laugh in their face. It's a farce. The whole bloody place is a farce! The College is a farce! The department is a farce! And this bloody meeting is the greatest farce of all! and I 'm damned if I'm staying. I've got more important things to do!

[*He storms out, tripping on the bottom step of the ladder. There is an awkward silence.*]

ROBBY: [*to* JOHN] That's not a bad idea of yours, John. I think we'll get that one going.

JOHN: [*indicating door*] What about . . .?

BOBBY: Leave him cool down for a week or two and I might be able to talk him around.

ROBBY: You needn't've been quite so tough on him, Peter.

PETER: I'm sick and tired of that little prick.

[*An awkward silence.* MYRA *looks at* PETER *thoughtfully and frowns.*]

ROBBY: [*reading from agenda*] New duties.

HANS: What in the hell's that?

ROBBY: [*sighing*] It's a nasty one to have to bring up, but I'm afraid the administration are after their pound of flesh. Now that we're getting University salaries the administration is wielding the big stick over holidays. I know that we've been taking the term break as a holiday for years but under the new terms and conditions of appointment we're only entitled to twenty days a year and it looks very much like the administration are going to hold us to it.

[ROBBY *sighs. An ominous pause.*]

HANS: That's ridiculous.

[*General chorus of assent.*]

ROBBY: I know. I know, but there's not much I can do about it. They've got us over a barrel.

JOHN: What are we supposed to do?

ROBBY: There's plenty of work. The phones run hot with enquiries and from what you said earlier there's plenty of prac work to mark, but all the same I realise that's not the point. You've been getting this holiday for years —

BOBBY: For twenty-seven years.

ROBBY: Right, and it is pretty rough to suddenly —

HANS: I'm booked in at Buller. Thirty dollars deposit.

ROBBY: I know. We should have heard about this earlier.

PETER: I'm booked at Hotham.

ROBBY: I'm sorry, but they've got us over a barrel. There's nothing I can do.

PETER: How come Joe's told his staff that they can have the holiday?

[ROBBY *looks at* MYRA.]

ROBBY: Is that right? Has Joe told you that?

[MYRA *nods.*]

Well, if Joe told you that, he's going to get rolled. Fletcher is going to Council on this one and he's determined to get it through at all costs.

PETER: Why don't you tell him to stuff off for once in your life?

ROBBY: Let's get one thing straight. You're not entitled to that holiday. You're entitled to four calendar weeks. I'd take on Fletcher any time but it's like going into the ring with two hands tied behind my back to fight him on something you're not entitled to.

PETER: Joe is. Wally is. Arthur is.

ROBBY: [*wildly*] Well, they're all going to get rolled. Every one of them. They're all going to get rolled because he's absolutely adamant on this one. Adamant! It's something you're not entitled to and I can't fight him on something like that! He's absolutely adamant, and I'll tell you what, if Joe's been stupid enough to tell you all that, then he's going to get the biggest rolling he's ever got. They're all going to get rolled! Wally, Joe and Arthur. Rolled into one. Rolled!

[*An awkward pause.*]

HANS: What am I supposed to do about my booking at Buller?

ROBBY: You'll just have to cancel it, I'm afraid. [*Another outburst*] Why shouldn't you all come back during the break? I've been coming back during the break for over twenty years. I don't often agree with Fletcher, but I think he's right on this one. I really think he's right. You'll have to cancel that booking I'm afraid, Hans.

[HANS *screws up his face but is obviously going to obey.*]

PETER: I'm not cancelling mine.

ROBBY: [*enraged*] You'd better cancel it. You'll come back here and work during the break or you won't come back at all!

PETER: I'm not cancelling it.

ROBBY: I run this department, Peter! You'll work during the break or you'll get out!

[*An awkward silence.* PETER *says nothing.* ROBBY *nervously gathers his papers together and gets up.*]

That's all I want to cover today. Will you come and see me in my office for a few moments, Bobby?

[BOBBY *nods. A silence as* ROBBY *descends the ladder. He turns at the door.*]

You'll work in the break or you'll get out!

[*He goes.* BOBBY *scurries after him. Pause.*]

OWEN: I, er, best get on the phone again.

[*He goes.*]

PETER: [*to* HANS] What did you back down for?

HANS: No sense pushing it too far.

JOHN: I'd be a bit careful if I were you, Pete.

PETER: Who wants to work in this rat-heap anyway?

HANS: [*to* MYRA] Is Joe going to stick to his guns?

MYRA: I'd say so.

HANS: Who's going to win? Him or Fletcher?

MYRA: I can't see Joe backing down.

HANS: [*to* PETER] If we're going to get a holiday in any case it's stupid to go sticking your neck out.

PETER: Bugger him. Let him sack me.

JOHN: He's not going to sack you but there's no sense making things even more unpleasant around here than they are already. Tell him you'll cancel the booking and let him win the battle. If Joe holds out he'll lose the war so what does it matter?

PETER: Bugger him.

HANS: And when you do tell him you've cancelled you'd better book pretty quickly because Buller's full already.

PETER: No. Bugger it. I'm not backing down on this one. [*To* JOHN] Why didn't you speak up when he torpedoed your committee?

JOHN: He didn't torpedo it.

PETER: What? You're allowed to start it up next year when the whole course-change controversy's over.

JOHN: It was either that or not get it started at all.

PETER: It may as well have been not at all.

JOHN: That's your opinion. [*As he goes*] See you, Myra. Will you be coming again?

MYRA: I don't think so.

JOHN: [*to* MYRA] See if you can talk some sense into our resident hot-head. He has a bit of trouble relating to authority figures.

PETER: You have trouble standing up to them.

JOHN: I try and steer a middle course.

[*He goes.*]

HANS: [*preparing to go*] It's not a good issue to push, Pete.

PETER: It's a splendid issue to push. He's going to look pretty stupid moving against me if we're going to get the holiday in any case.

HANS: [*to* MYRA] He just likes a fight. See you.

MYRA: Goodbye, Hans.

[HANS *goes.*]

PETER: If we had a man like your Joe we wouldn't have any of this sort of trouble.

MYRA: You'd have other sorts. I've been waiting three years for my two hundred dollar tape recorder.

PETER: Is eight thirty all right for tomorrow night? I'm sorry about the short notice. These bloody things creep up on you. It should be quite a fun type night. A lot of the guys I go skiing with are going. It'll be bloody good, actually.

MYRA: Would it inconvenience you much if I couldn't come?

PETER: Couldn't come?

MYRA: I'm sorry. I tried to ring you this morning.

PETER: What's wrong? Are you sick?

MYRA: [*shaking her head*] I've changed my mind. I'm sorry. I tried to ring this morning.

PETER: It's pretty short notice.

MYRA: I tried to ring this morning.

PETER: Come on. Don't be so stupid.

MYRA: I'm sorry. I've changed my mind.

PETER: Why? You sounded pretty enthusiastic yesterday.

MYRA: I don't think it's a good idea to get involved with the people you work with.

PETER: Except Robby?

MYRA: Why do you say that?

PETER: You'll go out with Robby but you won't go out with me.

MYRA: I've never gone out with Robby!

PETER: That's not what I've heard.

MYRA: I don't care what you've heard. It's wrong.

PETER: What about that party?

MYRA: I was drunk and he was drunk and that's it.

PETER: A pretty demonstrative 'it' from what I've heard.

MYRA: I don't think it's any of your business.

PETER: Well, why in the hell carry on with Robby? Christ. Robby?

MYRA: [angrily] What gives you a proprietary interest over who I associate with and who I don't associate with? Since you've been here you've hardly as much as spoken to me except for the obligatory little bit of condescending flirtation over end of year drinks.

PETER: Suit yourself. I'm not hard up. You're only one on a list of dozens.

[MYRA looks at him, turns and walks down the ladder.]

[Angrily] What did you think he was? Some kind of prize catch or something? He's a weak turd and you made a bloody fool of yourself.

MYRA: Yes. I'm not making the same mistake twice.

[GORDON enters looking pleased with himself.]

GORDON: My God, Myra. You get more beautiful every time I see you. You should've been a model or an air hostess. Are you coming to our next meeting?

MYRA: [strongly] No!

[She slams the door as she goes. GORDON is surprised. He turns to PETER.]

GORDON: No worries.

PETER: [still upset] What?

GORDON: No worries.

PETER: It's full?

GORDON: Two inches under the rim.

PETER: How much did it deflect?

GORDON: About an eighth. Maybe less. Couldn't really tell with the tape measure.

PETER: Have you told Robby?

GORDON: No. Not yet.

[*Pause.*]

How do you reckon we should handle it?

PETER: That's a point.

GORDON: I suppose he's sure to find out sooner or later.

[ROBBY *storms in, absolutely livid.*]

PETER: Sooner.

ROBBY: [*to* GORDON] Did you turn those pumps on?

[GORDON *nods glumly.*]

What if the whole building had've collapsed?

GORDON: The building wouldn't've —

ROBBY: What if the whole building had've collapsed and killed some students? Fletcher would've made a nice mess of us then, wouldn't he? [*To* PETER] Did you tell Gordon to turn those pumps on?

PETER: We did it in consultation. It was quite safe. I did a computer simulation.

ROBBY: When?

PETER: Eighteen months ago.

ROBBY: Eighteen months ago? Why didn't you tell me?

PETER: You didn't ask.

ROBBY: [*to* GORDON] What if the mezzanine had collapsed! If you ever do anything like that again I'll have you sacked and you'll lose your super and be damned to your bloody union.

GORDON: I'm sorry, boss. I've been getting a bit irritable lately and doing things without thinking. Me knee's playing up again.

ROBBY: For someone who's been in the Navy you seem to remember precious little of what you were taught. How do you think your Captain would've reacted if you had've decided to flood the ballast to see if the bloody ship would still float?

PETER: There was no danger. I worked it out.

ROBBY: What would have happened if you had've been wrong for once in your life? Bloody smart-arse. I should have left you to fend for yourself when nobody wanted to know you.

PETER: I could've got a job in any Uni in the country!

ROBBY: I want a written statement from you that you're prepared to work during the break.

PETER: You know what you can do.

ROBBY: I know what I can do all right.

PETER: What?

ROBBY: Try the thought of teaching sixteen hours a week of Graphical Solutions.

PETER: I'll go to the staff association.

ROBBY: And I'll make it look quite accidental, I can assure you. I might cut it down to fourteen as a concession, but I'll be unable to do anything else to help. Pure chance. Terribly unfortunate. I'll sympathise with you. I might even cry. [*Angrily*] Now get out of here and cancel that booking and leave a note on my desk to that effect by tomorrow morning.

PETER: It's all bluff.

ROBBY: You try me.

PETER: [*as he goes*] I'll fuck you up one day.

ROBBY: Get out. I've been threatened by real men.

[PETER *glares at him and goes.*]

You wouldn't think a grown man could be so childish.

GORDON: Aw, the more brains they've got the stupider they are. That's what I always reckon.

ROBBY: Yes, well, you haven't been very bright yourself over this, have you?

GORDON: It's me bloody knee, boss. Every time it plays up I get irritable. I'll go and open the valves and let the water out of the tank.

ROBBY: No. Wait a minute. Seeing as you've done it we may as well make capital out of it. Who knows it's full?

GORDON: Peter and me. That's all.

ROBBY: I think we might call Mr Fletcher over.

GORDON: [*over-enthusiastic*] Why not. Christ, that'll spike his guns. His jaw'll hit the floor.

ROBBY: No. Wait a minute. Go and open those valves.

GORDON: Open them?

ROBBY: Politics, Gordon. Politics. Let's wait until Fletcher thinks he's really got us on toast over this one, then we'll fill it up.

GORDON: No flies on you, are there?

ROBBY: How long will it take to empty? About twenty minutes?

GORDON: Bit longer than that.

ROBBY: Lock the doors while you're doing it.

GORDON: [*as he goes*] Right.

[*Before he gets to the door,* OWEN *comes in.*]
Any news?

OWEN: [*excitedly*] Yeah. It's a girl. Hey. Stay here. I just came in to get my cigars. Grab one.

[*He runs up the ladder and grabs his cigars.*]

[*To* ROBBY] It's a girl.

ROBBY: Did you want a girl?

OWEN: [*handing him a cigar*] Did I what! I've got four bloody boys already.

[*He starts to descend the ladder.*]

ROBBY: I had girls and wanted boys.

[OWEN *hands* GORDON *a cigar.*]

GORDON: I had both and none of 'em turned out much good.

OWEN: [*as he leaves*] Boys are okay when they're little, but by the time they're about six they're testing themselves out against you all the time. I haven't got the energy to cope with another.

[*He goes.*]

GORDON: Want a match?

ROBBY: Yes. Yes, I will.

[GORDON *lights* ROBBY's *cigar, then his own.*]

GORDON: I'll go and open the valves.

ROBBY: Right.

[GORDON *goes.* ROBBY *stands on the mezzanine proudly surveying his kingdom. He sniffs the oily air with satisfaction, exulting in the successful defence of his territory. He switches off the mezzanine lights, puffs the cigar, and descends the ladder. He lingers by the Tangye steam engine, looks at it, pats it, moves to the door still looking at it and switches off the final neon light. Blackness as he exits.*]

THE END

A HANDFUL OF FRIENDS

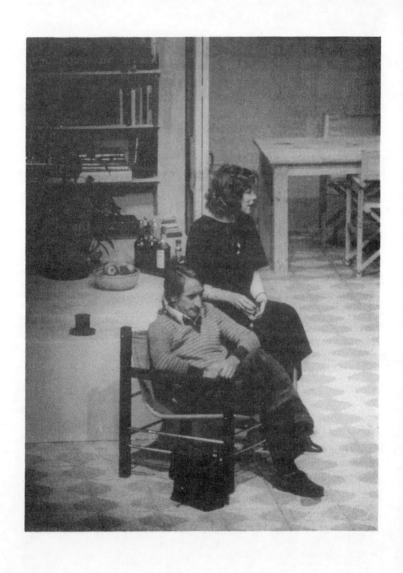

*John Gaden as Russell and Julie Hamilton as Wendy in the
SATC production at the Playhouse, Adelaide 1976.
Photo: Grant Matthews.*

A Handful of Friends was first performed by the South Australian Theatre Company at The Playhouse in the Adelaide Festival Centre on 20th May 1976 with the following cast:

RUSSELL McALISTER	John Gaden
WENDY McALISTER	Julie Hamilton
JILL McALISTER	Lyndell Rowe
MARK MARSHALL	Neil Fitzpatrick
SALLY MARSHALL	Sandra MacGregor

Setting designed by Shaun Gurton
Directed by Rodney Fisher

CHARACTERS

RUSSELL McALISTER, 40, a medium-sizzed man, slight of build and engaging in a leprechaunish sort of way.

JILL McALISTER, 35, his sister, warm, attractive, pleasant.

WENDY McALISTER, 38, Russell's wife, tall and very beautiful, soft-faced and rather detached.

MARK MARSHALL, 41, strikingly handsome, intense, nervously energetic.

SALLY MARSHALL, 30, vivacious and exceptionally attractive.

SETTING

The first and possibly largest area is a spacious, Victorian-style living room and, partly visible beyond it, a kitchen-dining room; the door at the side of the living room leads to bedrooms and bathroom. It is the house of WENDY *and* RUSSELL McALISTER. *The second area is* JILL McALISTER's *flat: there is a small living room cum kitchen area. A side door leads to the flat's one bedroom. It is a modern, tastefully decorated flat. A third area representing a room in a large inner-city hotel is needed for Act Two Scene Two.*

ACT ONE

SCENE ONE

A late afternoon in autumn. RUSSELL *and* WENDY*'s house and* JILL*'s flat are both lit by the late afternoon sun.* RUSSELL *stands in the living area, unpacking books. The room is in some disarray as* WENDY *and* RUSSELL *have only recently arrived back from overseas. One of the books he is unpacking catches* RUSSELL*'s eye as he is about to put it up in a shelf. He stands reading it.* WENDY *comes into the living room carrying a pile of letters, bills and papers.* RUSSELL *sees her, shuts the book and puts it on the shelf.*

RUSSELL: It really worries me. I've read some of these books twice and yet when I start re-reading them I can hardly remember a line.

WENDY: Yes, it's disheartening, isn't it? I have the same problem.

RUSSELL: [*in mock prayer*] Oh Lord. Give me back the countless hours I've spent consuming things I've thought good for the mind, but which have only piled confusion on confusion and dribbled out again anyway. What are those?

WENDY: Dockets and bills and letters. They were in one of the small cases.

RUSSELL: Oh. Could you sort them, love? Throw out anything we can't claim as a tax deduction.

[WENDY *nods and sits down.* RUSSELL *stops to read again. She looks at him, smiles gently and begins sorting through the pile of papers.*]

WENDY: What are you reading?

RUSSELL: 'Time that is moved by little fidget wheels Is not my time . . .' Appropriate?

WENDY: Do you still like it?

RUSSELL: Mmm. It's still a good poem. You know, it's really good of Mark and Sally to make a special point of coming down from Sydney to see us. One thing about Mark, come fame and fortune, he never forgets his old friends.

WENDY: No. He puts them in his films.

RUSSELL: Creative people do it all the time. I put Mark in the novel I tried to write, didn't I? He was the central character. I'm rather flattered to think he found us interesting enough to want to include us.

WENDY: [*dubiously*] Mmm.

RUSSELL: I'm going to have problems at Barton.

WENDY: Problems? Why?

RUSSELL: There are quite a few people in the department who think I shouldn't've got the job.

WENDY: Are you serious?

RUSSELL: Yes, I am.

WENDY: Has anyone said anything? Openly?

RUSSELL: No, but I can sense it.

WENDY: Are you sure?

RUSSELL: Yes. There's a guy there they think should have got it before me.

WENDY: Why? Is he exceptionally well qualified?

RUSSELL: Yes. Better than I am, but I don't think it's that. I gather that the Professorial Board rock the boat. That's the sort of implicit message I'm receiving from everybody.

WENDY: Have you met him? The radical?

RUSSELL: Oh yes. He's being very friendly and polite. In fact he's so polite that I'm terrified. He must have the numbers. Luckily the Dean looks pretty tough and I'm sure he'll back me if there's a showdown.

WENDY: You're talking as if the battle lines are drawn already.

RUSSELL: It's the last thing I want, but it looks as if I might have no choice.

WENDY: If people assume there's going to be a fight it invariably happens.

RUSSELL: I don't want it to happen, I can assure you. I'm an academic, not a politician.

WENDY: I know. See if you can avoid a confrontation.

RUSSELL: Look. If they're convinced that I shouldn't've got the appointment they'll manufacture issues to fight me on no matter what stand I take. Ninety-nine percent of institutional in-fighting is about power and personalities rather than issues. I had my first meeting today and found myself wishing I was back in LA working under Mitchell Ayres. I must write him a letter and let him know how things are going.

[WENDY *stops and frowns as she reads one of the dockets she is sorting. She looks at* RUSSELL.]

What's that?

WENDY: A motel receipt.

RUSSELL: Oh. Really?

WENDY: The El Rancho Torro Motel, Colorado. Mr and Mrs R. McAlister. Really, Russell. If you're going to persist in this habit I wish you'd at least be efficient enough to destroy the receipts.

RUSSELL: We've been to Colorado, haven't we?

WENDY: No, we haven't, and if we had've I wouldn't have stayed at the El Rancho Torro Motel. Mr and Mrs?

RUSSELL: Yes.

WENDY: I'm surprised.

RUSSELL: That's a little unfair.

WENDY: The last two have been men.

RUSSELL: That's hardly an issue, is it? I know it sounds corny but it really is more the need to talk to somebody.

WENDY: Apparently just about anybody will do. Wouldn't it be a lot simpler if you went to the next conference with a couple of good books, or watched television?

RUSSELL: All right. Shoot me. Right here between the eyes.

WENDY: The El Rancho Torro.

RUSSELL: Its one virtue was that it was clearly visible. It had neon-lit bull's horns twelve feet high.

WENDY: Russell, I'm not amused. Really. Who was she?

RUSSELL: I really don't want to go into it.

WENDY: I'd like to know.

RUSSELL: A research student. Please, it was all a fiasco.

WENDY: Tell me, Russell. If you can't even destroy your evidence then I've got a right to know.

RUSSELL: An appealing little mop-haired girl with a passion for the Mexican revolution and a desire to become bisexual. She was a lesbian.

WENDY: Why was she trying to become bisexual?

RUSSELL: She had some theoretical reason. There's a section of the women's movement that supports it on ideological grounds. It was a fiasco.

WENDY: Why?

RUSSELL: Nothing much worked and she cried and rang her girl friend in New York. It cost me thirty-seven dollars long distance to listen to her apologising for sleeping with me.

WENDY: She was obviously very upset.

RUSSELL: [*soberly*] Yes. She was.

WENDY: Sometimes, Russell, I think our relationship has just about run its course.

RUSSELL: Don't say that. Please. I'm sorry about these incidents. They're really not important.

WENDY: They are to me.

RUSSELL: They're not. Really.

WENDY: They are to me.

RUSSELL: I'm not doing any more of it. I mean it.

WENDY: I've heard that before.

RUSSELL: I won't be able to in any case. This is Australia, not California. They drowned a gay Law lecturer in Adelaide while we were away. We're back in the land of swift frontier justice.

WENDY: Why is our relationship important to you, Russell?

RUSSELL: I love you. That's why. If you want to know the truth, the physical side of our relationship is much better than anything I've achieved casually.

WENDY: Then why do you keep repeating the pattern?

RUSSELL: Because I like sex. I'm not very good at it but I like it. It's one of life's splendid ironies. I'm not very good at it am I?

WENDY: It's not a very important question.

RUSSELL: I'm not, am I? I get so excited that I either slow down and become terribly boring or my cup runneth over. So much of human behaviour is attributed to metaphysics and the indefinable but I've got a sneaking suspicion that a lot of it has to do with such mundane matters as the density of nerve ends around the glans penis.

WENDY: Living with you is often quite depressing.

RUSSELL: I expect it is. I really do love you. You do still love me, don't you?

WENDY: Yes.

RUSSELL: I'd be totally destroyed if you left me. The prospect frightens me more than anything I can think of and I'm being serious.

WENDY: [*screwing up the docket in anger*] Why can't you be competent enough to at least destroy your evidence?

RUSSELL: I'll go and get another load of books.

[*He leaves for the kitchen-dining room. The front door bell rings and* WENDY *goes to get it.* JILL *enters carrying a casserole dish.*]

WENDY: Hello Jill. Oh, you haven't . . . ?

JILL: Oh. Look, it's only another casserole.

WENDY: Jill. You shouldn't have. You've practically fed us every day since we've been back.

JILL: Just as long as I'm not in the way. I feel as if I've been on your doorstep ever since you arrived.

WENDY: Jill, don't be silly.

JILL: Well I have.

WENDY: You could never be an intruder. If I'm a bit distracted from time to time please don't mistake it for indifference. Thanks for the casserole. You're very thoughtful.

JILL: [*looking at the books*] Has he read all of them?

WENDY: I think he has. Oh. Mark and Sally Marshall are coming down from Sydney to see us.

JILL: Oh.

WENDY: They're coming to dinner on Saturday night. Would you like to come?

JILL: No. I don't think I will.

WENDY: Mark said that Sally would like to see you.

JILL: I'm sorry, but I'm afraid I wouldn't like to see her.

WENDY: Oh. I didn't realise you felt that strongly about it.

JILL: And I certainly don't want anything to do with Mark after seeing his film yesterday.

WENDY: Is it really that bad?

JILL: Yes, it is. And he's made an utter fool of Russell in it. I know Russell's got his faults but it's not very pleasant watching your brother being ridiculed in a public cinema.

WENDY: Are you sure the character's based on him?

JILL: He's a History lecturer with a drink problem who writes novels in his spare time and his wife was once a nurse who he met in a hospital after a car crash, so I don't think I'm exactly jumping to conclusions. There's one thing about Mark that hasn't changed. His lack of creative imagination. I'm amazed that he's even got the gall to want to visit you.

WENDY: It's because of the film that he's coming.

[JILL *looks at her.*]

He's asked us not to see it before he's had a chance to talk to us about it.

JILL: I bet! He obviously didn't expect you to arrive back the week it opened.

WENDY: But it isn't terribly successful, is it?

JILL: It's a disaster. Every critic in the country has called it self-indulgent bilge and nobody's going to see it. That's one consolation.

WENDY: Mark didn't seem worried on the phone.

JILL: He'll go on making films. He'll revert to adaptations. He does them quite well.

WENDY: And the character of the wife's based on me?

JILL: Yes. Sally plays the part. She's terrible.

WENDY: Oh.

JILL: The part itself's all right. Mark obviously feels a lot more positively about you than he does about Russell. [*Hearing* RUSSELL *approaching through the kitchen*] Try and stop him seeing it. It'll only make him depressed. It'll be off in a week or so.

[RUSSELL *enters, carrying a pile of books.*]

RUSSELL: How are you, love? Like a book?

JILL: I might as well. From what I hear, you don't even read them.

RUSSELL: There's a guy in New York who makes a living out of stocking bookshelves. You tell him what image you want to project and he gets you all the right titles. How are you?

JILL: Fine.

[RUSSELL *gives her a warm kiss.*]

RUSSELL: You've brought another casserole.

JILL: Yes. It's not exactly haute cuisine, I'm afraid.

RUSSELL: Don't apologise. Everyone still apologises back here. Your casseroles are of International standard. That's what Mark keeps saying in his letters: 'My film is of International standard.' Has he really modelled two of the characters in his latest epic on Wendy and me?

JILL: There's some resemblance.

RUSSELL: He's always been a bastard, God bless him. They're rather unkind portraits, I take it?

JILL: There's really not all that much resemblance.

RUSSELL: I must see it.

JILL: I wouldn't bother.

RUSSELL: Hey! [*Becoming enthusiastic and beckoning* JILL *to follow him*] Did you know that there's a wine cellar under the sun room?

JILL: [*moving after him*] Really?

RUSSELL: [*as he leaves*] There's a trapdoor behind the first set of shelves. No bottles, worse luck, but it's better than a kick in the teeth.

JILL: [*off*] Well, there are not many houses that can boast a wine cellar.

[WENDY *stands, temporarily forgotten by both of them as they make their way eagerly to the back of the house. She picks up the pile of bills and letters, looks at them, sheds the beginning of a tear, wipes it away, and deposits the whole lot of the papers in a rubbish bin with an angry flourish.*]

SCENE TWO

JILL'*s flat.* JILL *is unpacking her Saturday morning shopping from two large brown paper supermarket bags. She takes out cans, wrapped meat, fruit, celery sticks, vegetables, bread, packets of flour, biscuits and detergent, etc.* SALLY *and* MARK *may be seen approaching the front door as she unloads the shopping.* SALLY *rings the bell.* MARK *stands waiting.* JILL *opens the door and is surprised and confused when she recognises them.*

JILL: Sally, Mark. What a surprise. Come in.
[*She beckons them in. With a broad grin,* SALLY *hugs her passionately.*]

SALLY: Jill. You're looking absolutely marvellous. I know it's a cliche but you haven't changed a bit.

JILL: Oh. Neither have you.

SALLY: I should have rung, but we were just passing and I couldn't resist dropping in.
[SALLY *wanders around the flat, studying it.*]

JILL: Mark, take a seat. I'll make coffee.

MARK: Thanks.
[*He gives* JILL *a kiss.*]
You are looking well. It's been a long time, hasn't it?

SALLY: [*to* JILL] You've changed the curtains. They're much better.

JILL: Do you think so? Do sit down, Mark. I'll make coffee. You've caught me on the hop. I haven't even unpacked my shopping. Saturday mornings are always a bit frantic.

[SALLY *picks up a piece of pottery and inspects it.*]
You gave me that.
[SALLY *nods.*]

SALLY: [*looking around the flat*] This really brings back memories.

MARK: I've heard all about the flat from Sally and I must say it's every bit as good as she said it was.

SALLY: I'm sorry it's been so long since I've been in touch. I've been meaning to ring you for ages.

JILL: It's as much my fault as yours. I've started to write to you over a dozen times.

SALLY: It all gets so difficult when you live in different cities.

JILL: Are you down here for long?

MARK: For a little while. The main reason is to visit Wendy and Russell. Have you been seeing much of them?

JILL: Yes, of course.

MARK: How are they both?

JILL: Oh. Fine.

SALLY: You'll be there tonight, won't you?

JILL: Oh, er, yes.

MARK: Are they both glad to be back?

JILL: Wendy seems a little disoriented, but then again, that's Wendy.

MARK: She finished a degree over there, didn't she?

JILL: A degree and a teacher training qualification and after all that she went teaching and only lasted a week.

MARK: She doesn't seem the type for teaching.

JILL: Of course not, but she was determined to do it. You've never met Russell or Wendy, have you, Sally?

SALLY: No, they'd left for the States before I moved in here.

MARK: Why did she only last a week?

JILL: The classroom environment was too much for her. Russell tried to tell her that teaching wasn't her thing but she was determined. Sometimes I wonder if there isn't a little bit of self destruction lurking there somewhere.

MARK: Is Russell glad to be back?

JILL: I think so. Yes.

MARK: So he should be. It's a pretty triumphant return.

JILL: Yes, I think he's really glad to be back.

SALLY: How's the magazine?

JILL: Just the same.

SALLY: Is Iris Burke still there?

JILL: Iris Burke will always be still there.

SALLY: It seems to still be flourishing.

JILL: Yes. The issues are getting lighter and lighter. It's all style, trend shifts and the female orgasm now.

SALLY: Really? That's a pity.

JILL: D'you know, they've calculated that if you total up the column inches devoted to it in all the glossies around the world, the female orgasm is responsible for the destruction of thirty-two million hectares of pine forest per annum?

SALLY: [*in all innocence*] Really?

MARK: [*chuckling*] Sally.

SALLY: Well, it sounded feasible.

MARK: She believes anything she's told.

JILL: [*smiling*] Yes, she does. Milk?

SALLY: Mmm.

MARK: Yes.

SALLY: Oh, here, let me give you a hand. We whipped up a few quick meals in here.

JILL: Yes.

SALLY: [*taking coffee to* MARK] Here you are, love.

MARK: Thanks. Yes, well we're having to tighten our belts a little at the moment. This latest film of mine isn't doing nearly as well as it should. The critics have really crucified it.

SALLY: Very unfairly.

MARK: Ah well. There's no such thing as objective criticism in this country.

[*Pause.*]

JILL: I've, er, been meaning to see it.

MARK: Oh. You haven't been? Oh. I was going to ask you what you thought of it. Have Wendy and Russell seen it?

JILL: I don't know. Will it be running here long?

MARK: I, er, think they're going to rest it for a while and bring it back when the public taste catches up with it. It's a bit ahead of its time. Have, er, any of your friends seen it?

JILL: Oh, er, yes. One or two.

MARK: Sally collected some very good crits. That's one consolation.

SALLY: And some bad ones.

MARK: They were just from people who'd already prejudged you. Director casts wife. I bet she's terrible. You shouldn't worry in any case. Compared with what they said about the film in general, you came out smelling of roses.

SALLY: I did get some good crits.

[*Pause.*]

JILL: Does this, er, box office problem mean that there'll be difficulties in getting another film afloat?

MARK: No. Not at all. I've got a tremendously exciting project coming up and the money's almost there already. Which reminds me. Can I use your phone? I've got to get through to a few people rather urgently.

JILL: Yes, of course. You can unplug it. There's a connection in the bedroom. Take it with you.

MARK: Which bedroom?

JILL: There's only one. That door's a cupboard.

MARK: Oh.

[SALLY *looks at* JILL. MARK *looks at them both and goes into the bedroom.*]

SALLY: That made him stop and think. Is there still just a double bed in there?

JILL: [*embarrassed*] Yes.

[SALLY *gives* JILL *a kiss on the cheek.*]

SALLY: I really am ashamed I haven't rung you.

JILL: I should have rung you.

SALLY: I can't tell you how grateful I was when you took me in.

JILL: I was glad to help.

SALLY: God, that was a terrible week. Iris Burke called me into the office and sacked me on Monday and Ian threw me out on Wednesday. I didn't have anyone else to turn to.

JILL: I was only too glad to help.

SALLY: Jim was only fourteen months old. It was a nightmare.

JILL: How is Jim now?

SALLY: Oh, he's beautiful. Noisy but beautiful. Where's Morgan?

JILL: He died.

SALLY: Really? What a shame. He was terribly naughty though. Remember the day we heard Jim gurgling with delight and came out and found Morgan rolling him towards the front steps with his nose. I loved that dog.

JILL: [*laughing*] Morgan didn't really approve of young Jim. I'd love to see him again.

SALLY: You must come up and stay. Who's still at the office apart from Iris Burke?

JILL: Hardly anyone. Don't let's talk about it. It's too dreary.

SALLY: No, really. I want to, I want to. I really enjoyed those days — something was always happening. A party, drinks, a first night. Remember? Jefferson Airplane, the Doors, Ravi Shankar. Remember?

JILL: Mmm. I do.

SALLY: Heavy male journos putting the hard word on us. My God. Barry McKenzie had nothing on some of those guys. Are they still the same?

JILL: [smiling] Mmm.

SALLY: And didn't we have energy? Really. We did, didn't we? Every time some celebrity would land at the airport we'd be out there after interviews. Remember?

JILL: Yes. And you'd win out more often than not. By fair means or foul.

SALLY: Foul?

JILL: Yes, foul.

SALLY: What do you mean?

JILL: You know damn well what I mean.

SALLY: Oh. That.

JILL: Yes that. Amongst others.

SALLY: I just think he wanted to be interviewed by one person at a time.

JILL: [admonishing her good humouredly] Sally! He said: 'There are two of you in this suite and only one of you is going to get the interview and I'm randy.' I walked to the door in disgust, fully expecting you to have the decency to follow me, only to hear it shut behind me with you still on the other side.

SALLY: [laughing] Jill! He didn't say he was randy.

JILL: He did.

SALLY: [laughing] Jill. He didn't. He said: 'I'm only going to give one interview at a time.' I was surprised you weren't there when I left the suite.

JILL: You left the suite at three o'clock the next afternoon.

SALLY: [laughing] Jill. That's not true.

JILL: And to add insult to injury you had the nerve to ring me up and ask me to phone your husband with some unlikely story that you'd just had to fly interstate.

SALLY: [laughing] I'm sure I didn't. I do remember you picking up young Jimmy for me once.

JILL: Yes. I had to pick him up from the lady who minded him,

deliver him home to your husband and tell him that you were
spending the night in a patrol car doing research for an in-
depth article on prostitution.

[SALLY *laughs so hard that she practically falls off the couch.*]

SALLY: [*wiping her eyes*] Oh dear. Prostitution.

[*She kisses* JILL *affectionately on the cheek.*]

I shouldn't laugh. It was only a few weeks after that that I was
fired.

JILL: You were getting erratic. Deadlines didn't seem to mean a
thing to you.

SALLY: Yes. I did get erratic.

JILL: What's next for you now?

SALLY: I thought you'd never ask. Mark's cast me in the lead for
his new movie. I'm really excited about it.

JILL: Really?

SALLY: [*nodding excitedly*] Mmm.

JILL: What's the film? Can you say?

SALLY: I'm not supposed to but I can't stop myself. It's *The
Fortunes of Richard Mahony.*

JILL: Really? That's going to be a bit difficult to compress, isn't
it?

SALLY: Yes, it is. It's going to have to be a big, big film. Three
hours and a big budget. I'm playing Polly.

JILL: Lucky you.

SALLY: Mark thinks it's one of the best women's roles in our
literature.

JILL: It probably is.

SALLY: I'm just so excited.

JILL: Would you mind if I did an article on you for the magazine?
If I don't somebody else will.

SALLY: Not at all.

JILL: I'd like to get in first about the *Mahony* film. Can I mention
it yet?

[MARK *comes out of the bedroom looking pretty pleased with
himself.*]

MARK: Well, there's someone who's definitely interested.

SALLY: Who?

MARK: Martin Rees. He wants to see me first thing on Monday.

SALLY: That's great.

MARK: He wouldn't touch my last one, but he knows this one has
got it all.

SALLY: Terrific.

MARK: He's no fool, the old Martin.

SALLY: Mark, Jill wants to do an article on me.

MARK: An article? Why?

SALLY: Some people apparently find me interesting.

JILL: I'd like to be the first one to break the news about Richard *Mahony*. And Sally's role in it.

MARK: [*looking sharply at* SALLY] Well, I don't really know whether it's wise at this stage. We haven't gathered together all the finance yet.

JILL: I could hold the article until you gave me the all clear. [MARK *purses his lips and looks doubtful.*]

SALLY: Mark. Don't be so conservative. You know you're going to get the money. If you don't take up Jill's offer you'll be wasting good pre-publicity.

MARK: I just don't like committing myself to paper yet. I'm superstitious.

SALLY: Oh Mark.

MARK: All right, but I would appreciate it if you did hold it till everything's definite, Jill.

JILL: Sure.

SALLY: When would you like to do it?

JILL: When are you going back?

SALLY: We're here for a week or so but it looks as if we'll be doing a lot of running around.

JILL: Would it be too much trouble to tape a few comments now while I've got you here?

SALLY: Not at all. You're not in a hurry are you, love?

MARK: No. Not particularly.

[JILL *goes to a shelf and takes down a tape recorder of the portable cassette variety. She flicks the playback switch.*]

JILL: [*hearing nothing coming through speaker*] This one seems clear.

MARK: Did you want to ask me any questions as well?

JILL: Oh. You mean interview you both?

MARK: [*shrugging*] Only if you want to.

JILL: Well, I'd rather just interview Sally.

SALLY: Come on, love. This is my interview. You get your own.

MARK: I just thought Jill might be interested in the sort of approach that's going to be taken to the material. That sort of thing.

JILL: Perhaps I could get that in a separate interview.

MARK: Just as you wish. How long do you think you'll both be?

JILL: Not more than half an hour.

MARK: [*showing irritation*] I'd like to see Wally James some time this afternoon.

SALLY: We'll only be half an hour. What are you going to do?

MARK: I don't know. Go for a walk, I suppose. I had the impression that the flat was a little bigger than this.

JILL: It is quite tiny.

MARK: [*to* SALLY] Is this the way it was set up when you lived here?

SALLY: Mm. I slept out on the couch, and Jim slept in a cot.

MARK: Oh. Yes. There is only one bedroom, isn't there?

[*He walks out the front door and closes it behind him.* SALLY *and* JILL *look at each other.* SALLY *grins.*]

SALLY: He really is sweet. I love him very much.

JILL: We'd better get started. He seems in a bit of a hurry. Testing. One, two, three, four . . .

[*During this last speech of* JILL*'s the lights fade to black.*]

SCENE THREE

It is early evening on the same day. JILL *is alone in her flat. Sunset hues colour the light streaming through her windows. She sits on a long-legged stool at the bench dividing her living area from her kitchen. On this bench sit her cassette recorder and a plate on which there is an uneaten sandwich. Further away from her on the bench are a pad and biro pen. She pulls them towards her, picking up the pen. She thinks for a second then turns on the tape recorder.*

JILL: [*on tape*] But when was it that you first knew you wanted to act?

SALLY: [*on tape*] Oh. When I was four.

JILL: [*on tape*] Yes, but that's a fantasy most of us have at four. When did you first decide in a real and positive way that you were determined to become an actress?

SALLY: [*on tape*] Oh. [*Laughing*] I suppose I really became interested in it as a real possibility after I married Mark.

I started to see the rushes of the films he was making and I found myself looking at the actresses and saying: 'I could do as well as that.' I really believe that anyone can do anything if they really want to.

[JILL *switches off the tape, stands up, and with the pencil and pad still in her hands, paces around the flat. She stops by the couch, sits down and scribbles something. She looks at it, rips the sheet from the pad and screws it up impatiently. It joins quite a few other screwed up pieces of paper on the floor. She goes back to the tape recorder, switches the rewind button for a moment or two, then presses the playback button. We hear* SALLY*'s voice.*]

I really believe that anyone can do anything if they really want to.

[JILL *switches off the tape. She hesitates for a second, then throws the pencil and pad away, reaches for a fresh cassette cartridge, loads it and begins to dictate excitedly. The tract which she does dictate has the inevitable stop-starts of an extemporised piece, together with the inevitable mistakes and backtracks, which the actor can extemporise for herself. The delivery should not be too halting and hesitant, however, as the feeling to be conveyed is one of inspirational fluidity.*]

JILL: [*speaking into the microphone*] Ident. Anyone can do anything if they really want to, especially if they're Mrs Mark Marshall. This is Jill McAlister recording for first draft transcription. I've just met an old friend of mine. Sally Blackwood, or, if you prefer, Mrs Mark Marshall. If you haven't heard of her already then you soon will. She's about to become prominent, if prominence is what you call landing the plum role in a small budget, by international standards, feature film made by the most prominent, if not the most talented, director in this country's rather moribund film industry. The director? Yes, folks, you've guessed it. Husband Mark. Sally deserves her imminent success. The speed with which she dropped her old friends in Melbourne when she first heard there was a film talent on the Sydney scene and the rapidity with which she homed in on her target was remarkable. One had to admire her spunky self-confidence, but for some of us, thrust so rapidly into her immediately forgotten past, it hurt.

But let's not be too bitchy. Her ambitions mightn't have

included getting herself onto celluloid then. Perhaps she loved the man. Perhaps it was just the temptation of sharing the same bed with the man who made the casting decisions that started thoughts buzzing in her pretty little head. Who knows? Perhaps she genuinely thought she had talent. Unfortunately, however, thinking is one thing, having it is another. For my money the message, to that vast majority of the population who haven't seen the latest Marshall family epic, is: 'Don't waste yours.' Money that is. I'm no film critic, but to me the sheer boring self-indulgence of it all was breathtaking, and while one can only admire the audacity of Marshall in casting wife Sally as a sensitive, tactful and loyal academic's wife, this is one time when casting against type has come unstuck. And how.

I must admit that when she dropped in unannounced on me after all these years I did feel pleased. It's nice to be remembered by newly important old friends, and I can't deny that in the days when she shared a flat with me we did seem to have something going between us. I was bewitched, for want of a better word, by her energy, flair and grace. Attraction to other people is often more a matter of style than content — witness thirty million Germans and their protracted love affair with Adolf H — and what Sally lacked in content she surely made up for in style.

Back in the old days the magazine she used to work for didn't have quite the prestige of ours, so she left it and came to join us. It wasn't my happiest day. She was welcomed by our editor with open arms and the message was plain. She'd been getting the interviews and I hadn't, so it was clearly a case of, 'Move over, Jill, here comes the new star' — and did she live up to it. In fact she eventually became so arrogant that she started sleeping in till two o'clock in the afternoon and missing deadlines, which gave me my chance to do what any normal red-blooded, ambitious, envious girl would do. I stabbed her in the back. To be more precise, I organised the seven key staff members, without whom the magazine would have collapsed, to go to our very astute boss and say: 'It's her or us.' And our boss, not wanting to call our bluff, made it her.

Unfortunately, at about the time when we'd had enough of Sally, her husband had had enough too and threw her, and baby Jim, out onto the cold, hard streets with nowhere to go

and ah — such is the ambivalence of human emotions — I took
her in, with baby Jim; assisted her economically through her
lean times, grew to love her desperately and taught her
humility, compassion and responsibility and was foolish
enough to think she was listening, until one day she read a crit
of a new film made by my big brother's old friend Mark and
said: 'Let's go to Sydney.'

'How is it that you had the confidence to decide to become
an actress?' I asked her earlier today.

'Anyone can do anything if they really want to,' she said. 'I
really believe that.'

I really believe it too. Especially if your name is Mrs Mark
Marshall.

[JILL *switches off the tape and sits looking at it with
satisfaction. She switches it on again.*]

End of first draft for transcription. Kate, I'm marking this
tape urgent as I want to tidy it up first thing Monday morning.
Oh, when you type it up, don't let Iris see it. It's not her style.
I'm going to freelance it to a more appropriate journal.

[JILL *switches off the tape and sits back, looking very satisfied.
She has the intense calm of someone who has just finished a
burst of creativity that they believe has been very productive.
She moves over and stretches out on the couch. The lights snap
to black.*]

SCENE FOUR

In the partly visible kitchen-dining room a dinner is in progress.
MARK, SALLY, RUSSELL *and* WENDY *are present. The stereo unit,
which is in the living area, is playing, rather loudly, ethnic
Balinese music.*

WENDY *moves to the door of the living room and enters. She
stands for a few seconds inside the door and appears relieved to be
away from the others for a few moments. She looks across at the
stereo, moves across and turns the music down. She stands there,
savouring the solitude and relative quiet.*

*The lights come up in Jill's flat. The electric lights are not
switched on and* JILL *is sitting up at the bench on a long-legged*

*stool. She sits there tapping her pen on the bench, then suddenly
gets up, goes to the bedroom, emerges with the phone, plugs it in to
the connection by the bench and begins to dial. After only three
digits she stops and replaces the phone. She picks it up again and
this time completes the full six digits. Immediately the phone next
to* WENDY *begins to ring.* WENDY, *deep in her own thoughts, is
startled. She does not particularly want to pick the phone up.*
RUSSELL *appears at the doorway with an enquiring look on his
face. She indicates the phone. He goes across and picks it up.*

RUSSELL: 81 7601.

JILL: [*teasing him*] Is it now? Are you sure?

RUSSELL: Oh, it's you. How are you feeling now?

JILL: Much better. I thought I might come over.

RUSSELL: We've just finished eating.

JILL: I don't want anything to eat. Just coffee.

RUSSELL: Fine. Come over. Mark and Sally will be going soon,
though. They're both pretty tired.

JILL: I'll be there in ten minutes.

RUSSELL: All right. We'll see you then. [*Putting the phone down*]
Jill's coming over.

> [WENDY *sighs and nods wearily. It is not that she dislikes* JILL.
> *She indicates by a weary look in the direction of the dining
> room, that it will prolong the night.* RUSSELL *gives her a 'buck
> up' sort of look. She smiles faintly.*]

What's happened to my music?

WENDY: Too loud. Could you tell Mark and Sally that they can
bring their coffee in here if they like?

RUSSELL: [*going to the door*] Bring your coffee out here. It's more
comfortable. [*To* WENDY] Would you like me to change the
record?

> [WENDY *nods.* JILL *meanwhile has gathered her things together.
> She grabs her car keys, pats the cassette recorder affectionately,
> and leaves the flat, turning the lights out as she goes.* RUSSELL
> *changes the record to a gentle Ravel piano solo with the volume
> very low.* MARK *and* SALLY *come through the door into the living
> room carrying coffee cups.*]

Jill's feeling much better. She's coming over for coffee.

SALLY: Oh fine. [*Looking at* MARK, *a little tersely*] Mark wants to
speak to her.

MARK: [*tersely*] Well, it is a little premature to publish anything about the film yet. We haven't even got the finance.

RUSSELL: Trust Jill to get you down on tape. She never misses an opportunity.

MARK: It's too early to publish.

RUSSELL: [*to* SALLY] What's Mark cast you as again? I can't remember the book all that well.

SALLY: [*icily*] You mean what has Mark tentatively cast me as. Polly. It's the lead.

RUSSELL: Oh. Sorry. I didn't realise. Terrific. We'll drink to your success.

SALLY: I think we'd better save the toasts until such time as my husband makes up his mind. I had thought his decision was final, but apparently it's not.

MARK: Sally. The film isn't even final. I just won't have you presuming to give interviews before any final decisions have been made.

[WENDY *slips out of the living room door towards the kitchen area.*]

SALLY: I'm so sorry. I overstepped my authority.

MARK: I'd rather we stopped discussing this issue right now. We haven't seen Russell and Wendy for years. Where's Wendy?

RUSSELL: Packing up the dishes. It's a compulsion of hers.

MARK: Perhaps you could help her, love. I'd like to have a talk with Russell.

SALLY: Oh. Yes. Of course, dear. Any time.

MARK: Sorry. I didn't mean it that way. I'm not myself today.

SALLY: [*as she goes*] I see. Well, whoever you are now, the change hasn't been for the better!

[*She exits.*]

MARK: She's got plenty of spirit, hasn't she?

RUSSELL: Mmm.

MARK: I like a woman who stands up for herself. She's alive, Russell. Really alive. You've no idea what a difference she's made to me. I like a woman who stands up for herself and gives me something to bounce off. Her only problem is that she's ambitious. She wants to be someone. 'Why?' I keep asking her. Look at me. I'm someone and look at me. So screwed up it isn't funny. A competitive society has a built-in and fundamental contradiction. It encourages you to fight your way to prominence and as soon as you succeed it sends out the hatchet men to carve you up again, piece by piece.

Jesus, they've crucified me over this latest picture of mine, Russell. I keep a brave face in public, but there's a lot of weeping in private. God, they've made a mess of me. There's no need for me to tell you how glad I am that you're back.

RUSSELL: Thanks. I'm glad to be back.

MARK: I mean it. You don't exactly make friends hand over fist in my game and it leaves a big hole in your defences when your best friend goes overseas for seven years.

RUSSELL: I'm sorry we haven't had time to see the film yet, but . . .

MARK: It's a good movie. Utterly competent. God, Russell, they're like wolves. Every time a young director makes a film that isn't literally falling apart at the seams they hail the bastard as my successor. Forty-one and I'm a has-been. There's a hunger for novelty out there that's absolutely insatiable. God knows how any man can cope with it. I can't. I'm shot through with arthritis, can't sleep at night — all that kind of scene. Creators are the sacrificial objects of a bored society. I'll be dead in five years.

RUSSELL: Now come on.

MARK: It's true. I'm done for. If I had any sense I'd get out and buy a house on a cliff overlooking the ocean and watch the waves pounding Christ out of the rocks, but I can't. The adrenalin keeps pounding in my arteries and every time I get kicked in the face I get up for more. I'm going to make one good film before I die. It's the only motive I've got left. One good film before I die and it's going to be so good that none of those bitter little typewriter assassins will dare knock it. It's going to be this one, Russell. I haven't said it to anyone else yet, so mark these words, they're historic, it's going to be this one!

RUSSELL: I'm sure it is.

MARK: I'll tell you what, though. It's not going to be all that easy getting the money together. My last film's not doing all that well financially.

RUSSELL: You'll get it. I can't remember anything that you've ever set yourself to do that you haven't gone on and done.

MARK: This one's going to be the hardest.

RUSSELL: You'll get there, especially when it's something you feel so strongly about. I can remember you talking about *The Fortunes of Richard Mahony* before I went away.

MARK: Right. It's my film, Russell. It's my destiny and I'm ready for it. I am ready for it. Hey, I wish you knew how glad I am that you're back. I haven't been able to talk to anyone like this for . . .

RUSSELL: Seven years.

MARK: Right. Are you well?

RUSSELL: I think so.

MARK: I'm not. My body's packing up. My organs are all collapsing around me like balloons with slow leaks. The death signals are starting. What's life all about?

RUSSELL: Damned if I know.

MARK: I'm sorry I'm talking about myself all the time, I'm a bit wound up at the moment. How's your new job?

RUSSELL: I'm having my problems but I think it'll be all right.

MARK: Problems? How can you have problems? You're a professor.

RUSSELL: It doesn't matter what I'm called, I've still got to earn their respect.

MARK: Respect be damned. If they give you any trouble kick their heads in. You've got the whip hand so use it.

RUSSELL: I might too. There are a couple of young Turks who are really giving me the shits.

MARK: Kick their bloody heads in. Life's too short to go around worrying whether every young smart-arse is being given due respect. That's your one trouble, Russell. You're not tough enough. Let them know who's boss right from the start or they'll run all over you. Slap 'em down.

RUSSELL: I think you're right, actually. I might have to start getting tough.

MARK: Give it to 'em right between the eyes. Mark my words. The young Turks who are screaming loudest for democracy are tomorrow's despots — and I can quote you instance after instance to back me up. It's one of the recurring themes of history.

RUSSELL: That is a fact, isn't it?

MARK: Of course it's a fact! Give it to them right between the eyes. How's Wendy?

[RUSSELL *frowns and makes a touch and go motion with his hands.*]

RUSSELL: She doesn't seem to be coping all that well any more. She's drawing back into herself. We were in the car together

for over an hour yesterday and we didn't speak. Nothing I
thought of seemed appropriate. I was quite scared.

MARK: It took her a long while to get over . . .

RUSSELL: It took me a long while to get over it too.

MARK: Sorry. I didn't mean it like that.

RUSSELL: I know.

MARK: I'm sorry I wasn't more help at the time. In situations like
that I literally don't know what to do.

RUSSELL: There was an awful irony in the whole exercise. We
wanted that child so much.

MARK: I'm sorry. I didn't know what to say or do.

RUSSELL: [*shrugging*] You came to the funeral and cried. That was
enough.

[*There is an awkward silence.* RUSSELL *moves across and takes
the record off.*]

Do you know why it was so difficult for Wendy to conceive?

[MARK *shakes his head.*]

My sperm count was very low. I finally had it tested. Virile but
not potent. The story of my life. If I'd swallowed my pride and
adopted ten years ago things might be different now. Wendy's
been in contact with the young minister who helped her
through the crisis.

MARK: Oh . . .

RUSSELL: She's doing some voluntary work with him. It could be
the very thing she needs.

MARK: Voluntary social work. Didn't you mention in one of your
letters that she'd done a degree in the States?

RUSSELL: [*nodding*] A degree and teacher training. She tried
teaching but it didn't work out. She cracked up after a week.

MARK: You still love her, I hope?

RUSSELL: Of course I do.

MARK: I'd hate anything to happen to your relationship. You
were the two most transparently 'in love' people I ever knew.
You're not . . . ? [*He points to a nearby whisky bottle.*]

RUSSELL: No. That's all under control.

MARK: Make sure it is. You're going to need as many intact brain
cells as you can muster to squash those young Turks of yours.
Did you publish a lot in the States?

RUSSELL: Nothing much at all.

MARK: Did you finish your PhD?

RUSSELL: No.

MARK: Then how in the hell did you get your professorship?

RUSSELL: I gave a good interview.

[MARK *looks at him suspiciously.*]

I did. It's my one big talent. I always give great interviews. They soon find out I can't follow it up but by then it's too late. How long have you been with Sally?

MARK: Nearly six years. Jill brought her up to Sydney and introduced us.

RUSSELL: I know.

MARK: We were living together within a week. My God, it was passionate. Looking back I can't imagine that I ever had that sort of energy.

RUSSELL: I can.

MARK: [*looking at him sharply*] I don't know why we spent so much of our youth making such a big issue about sex. It really is such a bloody unimportant part of life. Especially when you're shot through with arthritis and can hardly climb two flights of stairs. When you see this picture of mine I want you to be absolutely honest. And about Sally's performance too. There've been some nasty cracks about nepotism from the critics, but as far as I'm concerned she is top class.

RUSSELL: You said in your letter that this film's a bit of a departure. It deals with contemporary life?

MARK: Yes. The, er, problems that people in our sort of age group face in this day and age. I don't think I'll try anything personal again. It's a bit hard to be objective when you've written the thing yourself.

RUSSELL: It's, er, pretty close to life, I take it?

MARK: Not really. A few things drawn from our common past which I hope you won't take objection to. It really is just a work of fiction.

[SALLY *returns.*]

SALLY: Finished.

MARK: Yes. Thanks, love.

SALLY: It's a pleasure. Any other time my presence proves embarrassing, please let me know.

MARK: Darling. Russell and I are very old friends. I just wanted a chance to talk to him.

[WENDY *returns and sits down.*]

That was a wonderful meal, Wendy. I'd forgotten how well you cook. I'm sorry I didn't eat all that much but I've got a bit of a stomach upset.

WENDY: Oh. I didn't realise. Could I get you some Alka Seltzer?

MARK: No thanks. I'm starting to feel a little better now.

SALLY: He's the greatest hypochondriac I've ever known. He's scared he'll die before the world recognises his genius.

RUSSELL: I've got exactly the same fear. No. Really. I get a recurring nightmare that I die alone and penniless and a week later my name appears as a footnote in the *International Journal of Historical Studies*.

MARK: [*testily*] I couldn't give a damn about posterity, and I've got no pretensions to genius. I just want to make a good film that makes a lot of people eat their words.

SALLY: [*to* RUSSELL] I can't really see you as a History professor.

RUSSELL: Oh. Why?

SALLY: You don't seem pedantic enough.

RUSSELL: Professors aren't necessarily pedantic.

SALLY: Historians are.

RUSSELL: Pedantic. The drama of the ages is our canvas. I assumed we were seen as the swingers of the campus. Pedantic? [*To* WENDY] Is that right?

WENDY: Quite possibly.

RUSSELL: I'm shattered. Is that why Teddy Kennedy avoided me at that faculty party? You told him I was an historian.

SALLY: What did he say to you, Wendy? You didn't get around to telling us.

WENDY: I can't remember much. I was so nervous that the only thing I can remember was thinking that I'd laughed too loudly at one of his jokes. He probably thought I was stupid.

RUSSELL: Nonsense. He was entranced. Thirty seconds with everyone else and half an hour with you.

SALLY: [*not entirely without envy*] My God. You must have made an impression.

RUSSELL: She certainly did. [*To* WENDY] Tell them.

WENDY: [*blushing*] It was just out of politeness.

RUSSELL: He offered to drive her home.

SALLY: [*sharply*] Really?

WENDY: He didn't.

RUSSELL: He said that she was the most refreshing person he'd spoken to in weeks.

SALLY: I thought you were serious. About the driving home.

RUSSELL: He hasn't got a good safety record. [*To* WENDY] Did you tell him I was an historian?

WENDY: Yes, I think I did.

RUSSELL: And what was his reaction?

WENDY: I can't remember.

RUSSELL: Well he obviously didn't say: 'Holy Jesus, take me to meet him immediately.'

WENDY: No, I think he just said: 'Oh.'

RUSSELL: 'Oh.' Well, it sounds as though Sally's right. The very word 'historian' sets discerning mouths yawning all over the world. I'm shattered. It does explain a few things though. Like that mugger who said: 'Give us your money and don't say a word.' He probably thought he was going to have to listen to a dissertation while I was counting out the banknotes. I'm going to have to do something about this. A television show to popularise the profession like that Physics professor. This is Professor Russell McAlister bringing you this week's episode of History. Where were we up to, Sally?

SALLY: The middle ages, but they weren't rating very well.

RUSSELL: Yes, I've been very disappointed with the middle ages. They've got violence and action but somehow they don't seem to add up to a significant whole. Let's move on to the Spanish Inquisition.

SALLY: I'm sorry, Professor, but our sponsors feel there's very little to be gained from dwelling on this era.

RUSSELL: Really? I'm surprised. It's exciting stuff. The clergy of Rome burning heretics at the stake. Who are our sponsors?

SALLY: Barry's Barbeques.

RUSSELL: Ah. Let's move on to one of my own personal favourites, The Rise of the Third Reich.

[RUSSELL *and* SALLY *are by this time giving a spirited performance.* RUSSELL *begins to shift the furniture with manic zest.* SALLY *helps him.*]

Mark, off that couch.

MARK: Do I have to?

RUSSELL: [*to* SALLY] Mark and I used to stage epic battles in our back yard when we were kids.

SALLY: Really?

RUSSELL: Oh, yes. Mark was always the general and I was the infantry. He was a very stirring orator. Mum's pumpkins were the advancing Japs. He got me so worked up one day that I hacked them to pieces.

[RUSSELL *has used the couch, its cushions, and various other odds and ends to create the impression of a small spare room. He walks into this room, opening either an imaginary door, or a door made of cushions, assumes the grave air of a narrator and faces the audience of* MARK *and* WENDY.]

It was in this very room, in this very inn, in this very town on the border of Austria and Bavaria, where at half past six, on a cold night on the evening of 20th April 1889, Fritz Holder, a lonely Austrian bank clerk, toasted rye bread in front of this very fire, while twenty miles away, in a very similar inn in a very similar room, which unfortunately we could not photograph because of copyright difficulties, Adolf Hitler was born. From the very beginning his mother Klara noticed a truculent and aggressive streak in her young son.

[RUSSELL *suddenly transforms into the young Adolf, and plays with an imaginary toy car, crashing it repeatedly and noisily into a wall. He indicates to* SALLY *that she should play Klara Hitler.*]

SALLY: Adolf, little vun. Your poor mutter's nerves are not so gude. Could you be please a little more quiet?

[RUSSELL, *as the young Adolf, eyes her truculently, pauses and deliberately smashes his toy car against the wall even more loudly than before.* RUSSELL *transforms into the narrator again.*]

RUSSELL: At school —

[*The door bell rings.* RUSSELL *breaks his performance, races to the door, lets* JILL *in and motions her to join the audience and not interrupt the performance.*]

At school he was described as wilful, arrogant and lazy, reacting with extreme hostility to advice or reproof of any form. Already he was spending an estimated ninety-nine percent of his conscious hours daydreaming of his future greatness as an artist.

[RUSSELL *transforms himself into the young Hitler, sitting at a school desk dreaming grandiose dreams.* SALLY, *as his schoolteacher, comes up behind him and looks over his shoulder at his schoolwork.*]

SALLY: Ah. Adolf. I am so glad to see that you have started your sums and are hardtrying at last. Chust one little thing. Two and two are almost five, but not quite.

[RUSSELL *simmers, turns his head slowly and glares at* SALLY, *who becomes nervous.*]

Shall we try again? Two plus two equals . . . ?

[*She smiles sweetly, if nervously, and waits.*]

RUSSELL: [*bellowing*] Five!

[RUSSELL *resumes his role as narrator.*]

Be sure to be with us again next week as we watch this unlikely and unlovely little chap rise to supreme power by pandering to the infantile power fantasies of the German lower middle class.

[*The act has been very polished for an improvised routine, and draws genuine applause, especially from* WENDY *and* MARK.]

JILL: [*to* RUSSELL] You make an excellent Hitler.

RUSSELL: Thanks.

JILL: The same compulsion to perform. [*To* MARK] You should go to one of his lectures. It's like a miniature Nuremberg rally.

MARK: I heard they were more akin to a night club act.

RUSSELL: I do tend to throw in a few jokes.

SALLY: Hello, Jill. Glad you could come.

JILL: Yes, I feel a lot better now. Hello Mark, Wendy. Sorry I messed things up.

WENDY: Not at all. I'll get you a drink.

JILL: Thanks.

RUSSELL: [*to* SALLY] I thought we did that very well.

SALLY: So did I.

WENDY: [*to* JILL] Did you go to Russell's lectures often?

JILL: Once or twice. When I had nothing else to do. I used to be impressed by cheap histrionics in those days.

RUSSELL: I'm so glad you came.

JILL: [*to* WENDY] Did you ever go to see them?

WENDY: Yes, I did. Often. I used to enjoy them immensely.

SALLY: [*to* RUSSELL] I keep forgetting that you and Mark grew up together.

RUSSELL: Yes. In the same country town. Mark's father was the local baker and our Dad was the clerk in the Dairy Farmers' Cooperative. We're from good solid bread and butter stock.

WENDY: I had a nightmare the other night. I was sitting watching him lecture and everyone around me was laughing and clapping and I turned to the people around me and said, 'He's my husband,' but nobody heard, so I said it still louder and nobody heard, and suddenly I found myself sitting up in bed in the middle of the night shouting: 'He's my husband.' That's not terribly hard to interpret, is it?

[*Pause.* WENDY *appears to be a little nervous, embarrassed and distracted. She gets to her feet.*]

I'll put on some more coffee.

MARK: We must go.

WENDY: Please don't. You've all got a lot to talk about.

[WENDY *moves towards the kitchen area.*]

SALLY: She seems a little tense.

RUSSELL: Yes, she is a little tense at the moment.

SALLY: Jill says she started teaching in the States?

RUSSELL: Yes, she did.

SALLY: Is she going to work at something now you're back?

RUSSELL: Not teaching.

SALLY: Why's that?

RUSSELL: It doesn't seem to suit her temperament. She's going to do a little bit of voluntary social work.

SALLY: Voluntary social work?

RUSSELL: Helping old age pensioners and things like that. I'll get you another coffee.

[*He picks up their coffee cups and begins to make his way to the kitchen.*]

MARK: We really must go.

RUSSELL: Have another coffee.

[*He exits.*]

SALLY: Helping old age pensioners? Teaching would be more interesting than that.

MARK: She's not suited to it.

SALLY: What do you mean she's not suited to it?

MARK: It doesn't suit her temperament.

SALLY: I'm sure she'd be a lot happier if she was doing something challenging and involving.

MARK: [*a little irritably*] She's going to do something.

SALLY: Helping old age pensioners?

MARK: What's wrong with that?

SALLY: It's all very high minded but it will bore her stupid. She'd be much better teaching. I didn't particularly like journalism but I had to stick to it. It was better than nothing. When I got the sack I nearly went out of my mind until I got another job.

MARK: [*getting exasperated*] She can't teach. She had some kind of a breakdown after a week.

SALLY: Maybe it was a tough school. Why doesn't she try a small private school or something?

MARK: [*irritably*] She can't teach.

SALLY: What a stupid thing to say. Of course she can teach. Anyone can do anything if they really want to. If you encourage someone to be some kind of fragile goddess figure then she'll never try anything. All right, Teddy Kennedy thought she was wonderful but she can't fall back on that for the rest of her life.

[JILL *exits to the kitchen.*]

MARK: Really, Sally. Sometimes you don't have much feeling for other people.

SALLY: Of course I haven't. I'm just tough and ambitious. Aren't I?

MARK: I think we'd better go.

SALLY: That's what you told me this afternoon. That's what you told Russell too when you sent me out of the room. Isn't it? [*Getting heated*] That I'm an ambitious bitch who'll stop at nothing to get what she wants and that I was awful in the film and that there's no way you're going to cast me in *Mahony*? Isn't that what you said? That you wished you were damned well rid of me?

MARK: Calm down, Sally. I said nothing of the sort.

SALLY: Well it's what you said to me this afternoon.

MARK: I told Russell you were excellent in the film, as a matter of fact.

SALLY: Yes, I bet you did. That's why you shunted me out of the room. To tell him I was excellent.

MARK: [*calling*] Russell!

SALLY: Don't bring Russell into it.

MARK: Russell!

[RUSSELL *appears at the doorway without the coffee cups.*]

What did I tell you about Sally's performance?

RUSSELL: Er . . .

MARK: Before. When I was talking to you.

RUSSELL: You said she was good. Very good.

SALLY: [*to* MARK] Then why won't you cast me in *Mahony*?

MARK: Because it's not even certain that I'll be doing it.

SALLY: That's absolute nonsense, Mark. Of course you're doing it. You know you're doing it. If you want me for the role, tell me. If you don't, tell me. All I want you to do is to make up your mind. I can't stand people who say one thing one minute and another thing another. Mark. Are you going to cast me as Polly or aren't you? Mark! For God's sake have the guts to look at me! If you're not going to use me, please say so. I couldn't stand finding out about it from someone else.

MARK: Sally, will you listen to me? How can I definitely cast anyone when I don't even know whether the damn film will be shot!

SALLY: You did think my performance was terrible, didn't you?

MARK: Russell. What did I tell you about Sally's performance?

RUSSELL: You said it was very very good.

SALLY: Then why won't you cast me?

MARK: [*getting exasperated*] I've told you .

SALLY: There's no doubt that the film will be shot. No doubt at all.

MARK: I haven't even bought the rights to the book.

SALLY: You have. I phoned the agent last week.

MARK: You what?

[RUSSELL *slips out unobserved.*]

SALLY: I phoned the agent last week. You've signed the option and paid the money.

MARK: Sally. This is intolerable.

SALLY: It's intolerable of you to lie, too! Now am I right for that part or aren't I?

MARK: Yes. You are!

SALLY: Then why won't you cast me?

MARK: Because I've got reservations about whether it's wise.

[*There is a pause.* SALLY *looks at him narrowly.*]

SALLY: Wise?

MARK: I've decided that it isn't always a good idea to cast someone you're intimately involved with.

[*Pause.*]

No matter how good your performance is people are going to say that you got the part because you're my wife, and because I happen to love you I want to spare you that sort of bitchery.

SALLY: Let me worry about the bitchery. I just want you to trust your own judgement.

MARK: Well, that's the other problem.

SALLY: [*narrowly*] What is?

MARK: When you're intimately involved with someone you can't be sure that you can trust your own judgement.

SALLY: What do you mean?

MARK: I really do think you're a fine actress but I might be unconsciously biased.

SALLY: Mark! I will be good in that part. I will be very good. Do you hear me? I will be very very good. Now for heaven's sake trust your own judgement!

MARK: If you're so good why don't you go and get yourself a part in some other film?

SALLY: I see.

MARK: No one could be bitchy then. You'd have proved yourself.

SALLY: I see. That's the manoeuvre, is it? Who have you got in mind for the part, Mark?

MARK: No one. Absolutely no one.

SALLY: I pleaded with you to get the rights on the book, Mark. I pleaded with you but you weren't interested, and now, because of me, you've got the most valuable film property in the country.

MARK: I've been going to do *Richard Mahony* for years. Russell!

SALLY: Don't call Russell into it again. What is he? Your yes man?

MARK: Russell!

[RUSSELL *appears, a little hesitantly, at the doorway*]
Russell. Haven't I been going to do *The Fortunes of Richard Mahony* for years?

RUSSELL: Mmm. You did talk about it.

SALLY: You might have talked about it but you would've never got around to doing anything if I hadn't prodded you. Do you know that it's the most valuable film property in the country now?

[RUSSELL *disappears again.*]

MARK: It's not . . .

SALLY: It is! The agent said that if you hadn't have signed the option when you did he could have sold it two days later for twice the price.

MARK: Rot.

SALLY: Ron Carroll came to him two days later offering straight cash. The agent's kicking himself. I've steered you into the best film buy you've ever had and now you want to toss me aside, and don't think I don't know the reason. Sheer pragmatism. Now you're onto a big budget you're going to get yourself some overseas star.

MARK: Don't be ridiculous. She's got to be Australian.

SALLY: You're just going to keep your options open until the last minute, aren't you? If I was ninety-nine percent right for the part and little miss ninety-nine point two came along you'd ditch me without a minute's hesitation.

MARK: There's a certain amount of truth in that. The film comes first.

SALLY: I see. For the sake of point two percent you'd ditch me?

MARK: The film comes first. [*Flaring*] Look. I refuse to be pressured like this. I don't care if you did help me decide on the property, it's my film and I'm the director and I'm responsible for the final product and I will make all the administrative and aesthetic decisions about it. Do you understand that? It's on my skills and judgement that this film stands or falls and those skills have taken me a hell of a long time to accumulate and they are considerable skills, Sally. Considerable. This is my film and nobody makes decisions but me.

SALLY: I see. It's all right if I exercise my skills and judgement to get you the option but now I've done my bit I can go to hell. You've got the power now and you're going to use it.

MARK: That's right. I have got the power, and I've got it because I've earned it and I've earned it because I've spent a long time learning the skills of my trade.

SALLY: So now it's lick my boots or else. Yes, yes, yes. I can see where I went wrong. I should have been born a man and have had a father who was a baker or a grocer or whatever in the hell he was, and he would have told me to be hard working and diligent and to have direction in my life, and I wouldn't have wasted so much time tramping through Europe and Africa and Asia seeing what the world was all about, loafing about in the little cafes . . .

MARK: . . . in the foothills of Firenze, or lived through the Monsoons of Burma or drifted through the blue blue blue Aegean seas tra la tra la tra la . . .

SALLY: Seeing what the world was all about! No! I would've stayed at home and become qualified and become the sales manager of the fastest growing ladies underwear manufacturer in the country, and even though I found this vocation quite spiritually enriching, my basic driving ambition might have led me on from there to apply for a sales manager job in a television company which I would have taken up after a tearful farewell from my old ladies underwear chums who might have been so moved as to present me with a beautiful leather briefcase filled with silk panties, for they would surely not be without wit and humour. Then by a combination of diligence, industry, bullying and backstabbing I might have wormed my way into production and got to direct and produce my very own soap opera, the first of many such gifts of mine to the culture of the nation.

MARK: Shut up. I'm warning you, just shut up!

SALLY: After producing and directing this epic for three years I might have even got up enough courage to launch out and make a movie. Perhaps I would have even be lucky enough to meet a woman who urged me to keep making them and who was intelligent enough to talk to me about scripts and casting and which scenes to drop and which scenes to retain ...

MARK: What have you ever told me about scripts and casting that's ever been of any use? Nothing. Absolute nothing! All you've ever done is waste my bloody time ...

SALLY: However I'm not a male and my father wasn't a grocer and I'm not hard working, diligent, sly, opportunistic, persistent and deceitful and I'm rather glad because that self-righteous, small town, grocer's-son-made-good, self-congratulatory, paranoiac manner of yours makes me sick.

[MARK *glares at* SALLY *with barely contained fury.*]

Go on. I'm an arrogant bitch. Why don't you say it?

[SALLY *picks up a knife lying next to a platter of cheeses and hands it to* MARK.]

Go on. Carve me up. That's what you'd like to do, isn't't? I'm arrogant. Carve me up. Here. Right across the throat.

[JILL *walks in and beats a hasty retreat.*]

MARK: Put it down. You're being ridiculous.

SALLY: You might as well. I'm no use to anyone. I was taught the wrong set of values for this country. This is the original grocer's son land.

MARK: He was a baker!

SALLY: There's no place here for someone who's courageous and self-sufficient and holds nobody in awe.

MARK: No one in awe and everyone in contempt.

[MARK *snatches the knife from her and puts it back on the cheese tray.*]

SALLY: Go on. Carve me up. I'm no use to anyone. I'm not humble enough. Uriah Heep has got nothing on you grocer's son lot.

MARK: Shut up, Sally. I'm warning you.

SALLY: Our family might have lost its money but you can't stamp out an attitude towards life. An appreciation of beauty and grace and art and music and a fundamental belief in oneself. Our grandfather told us on his deathbed never to bow down before anyone and anything. That's the sort of family I come from.

MARK: Your grandfather was an arrogant shit who knew nothing about farming or management or any other bloody thing except affecting a regal air and thinking everyone would be terribly impressed by the fact that his father was a phony German count.

SALLY: He wasn't phony. He was genuine.

MARK: Genuine my arse. Every peasant that ever left Europe for Australia became a count as soon as he got through the Suez Canal.

SALLY: He was genuine.

MARK: What in the hell does it matter?

SALLY: It must be wonderful to be so smug and untouchable. You've got your little bag of tricks, haven't you? You know where to point your camera and how to get performances. Nobody can take that away from you, can they? What have I got to look forward to. Nothing. Nothing at all. No future. Nothing.

[JILL *makes a tentative entrance.*]

JILL: Russell says there's some coffee ready if you'd care for it.

MARK: Thank you. I would.

[JILL *looks at* SALLY. SALLY *nods grimly.*]

JILL: Black?

[SALLY *and* MARK *nod.* JILL *exits hastily.*]

SALLY: Have I?

MARK: What?

SALLY: I've got no future, have I?

MARK: Shut up. You give me the shits.

[SALLY *glowers and snatches the keys of the car from the pocket of* MARK's *coat which lies over the couch.*]

SALLY: Oh I do, do I? Fine. Well, I'm going. You stay here and talk to your friends.

> [*She storms off towards the front door, slamming it behind her. There is a pause. A car starts up and screams off into the distance.* RUSSELL *reappears with two cups of coffee.*]

RUSSELL: Has Sally gone?

MARK: Yes.

RUSSELL: I'll, er, drive you to your motel if you like.

MARK: I'll get a taxi.

RUSSELL: Are you sure? [*As* MARK *nods*] Would you like to hear some music?

MARK: Music?

RUSSELL: Something soothing?

MARK: [*shrugging*] All right.

> [RUSSELL *puts a record on. Eerie melodic bleeps are heard.*] What's that?

RUSSELL: Whales.

MARK: Whales? Real whales? [*As* RUSSELL *nods*] Whales that swim around with spouts?

RUSSELL: Mmm. There's a guy who swims around underwater and records them.

MARK: I'd like a job like that.

RUSSELL: Whales practically talk. They sound friendly to each other, don't they?

MARK: Why shouldn't they be? They haven't got a film industry.

END OF ACT ONE

ACT TWO

SCENE ONE

Half an hour later. RUSSELL *has left the living room, presumably to see what* WENDY *is doing, the whale sounds have stopped and* MARK *is discovered phoning for his taxi.* JILL *moves into the living room from the kitchen-dining room.*

JILL: I take it Sally's worried that she mightn't get the part.

MARK: Mmm.

JILL: It's obviously not the time to bother you, but do you think you could let me know when you make the decision? If you are going to cast her I'd like to go ahead and write the article.

MARK: She'll get the role. I've been sitting here for the last half hour trying to think of someone else for it just to spite her, but I can't. She is very good in this one.

JILL: Yes. Everyone seems to think so.

MARK: I'll tell you what, though. She's just going to have to wait until I start the official casting before anything's confirmed. The other actors have to live with uncertainty so why shouldn't she?

JILL: As far as you're concerned, though, it's definite.

MARK: Yes. There's no one else who could do it as well. You certainly changed my life when you brought her up to meet me. It's good to see you again. We go back a long while.

JILL: Yes, I can still remember the day you and Russell left for the city. You were both going to start your university courses.

MARK: Yes.

JILL: I was shedding a quiet tear and you were assuring Mum and Dad that Russell would come to no harm because you knew the ways of the big city. You'd visited your aunt three times.

MARK: I went to the city twice a year from the time I was eleven.

JILL: I was exaggerating. You cut a very commanding figure. Russell was in awe of you. I think he still is.

MARK: I wouldn't say that. He's just the sort who needs a bit of guidance from time to time. Is he still . . . drinking?

JILL: No. He's coping very well.

MARK: I could never understand why he did. Everybody liked

106

him. I should have the drinking problem, not him.

[WENDY *and* RUSSELL *enter from the kitchen-dining room.*
RUSSELL *carries a coffee tray, with cups and a pot on it.*]

WENDY: Coffee?

JILL: No thanks, Wendy. I'm just going. Goodbye, Mark.

MARK: Good to see you again.

RUSSELL: Where's your car?

JILL: Just around in the side street.

RUSSELL: I'll walk out with you.

[*They start to move towards the door.*]

Listen, when is Mum's birthday?

[*They exit, still talking.*]

JILL: [*off*] The twenty-third.

RUSSELL: [*off*] Of what? January? What in the hell will we get her?

[WENDY *looks across at* MARK, *who is sitting there looking sullen.*]

WENDY: Coffee?

MARK: That damn taxi's taking its time. Thanks, Wendy. I will.

WENDY: One sugar, isn't it?

MARK: [*surprised*] You've got a good memory.

WENDY: Unfortunately, I tend to remember the details and forget the substance.

MARK: Wendy, you really are looking wonderful. Seven years has only made you more stunning. I'm not just saying that. It really has. How do you do it? I've practically become a geriatric and you're just approaching full bloom.

WENDY: I don't think you're geriatric. You're looking very well.

MARK: Well I'm not. I'm practically crippled by arthritis and half of the other diseases of senility to boot.

WENDY: [*handing him the coffee*] It's not terribly strong.

MARK: Good. Apart from everything else I think I'm getting ulcers. It's really quite depressing to think that the only thing functioning efficiently these days is my brain and I'm even beginning to wonder about that.

WENDY: I, er, heard Sally leave earlier.

MARK: It would have been difficult not to.

WENDY: I like her.

MARK: You like her? My God, you're the second woman who ever has. The first was her mother and that only lasted three months.

WENDY: No, really. She's got amazing vitality.

MARK: That's one way of putting it. No. Joking aside, I do love her very much but it's very wearing. [*Pause*] Has, er, anyone told you much about my film?

WENDY: The, er, last one? [*As* MARK *nods*] Yes, a few friends have mentioned it.

MARK: It's quite personal in some ways. I'm steering clear of that sort of thing in the future. It's a bit of a strain making sense of the, er, patterns of life you see around you. I hope you like it.

WENDY: It should be very interesting.

MARK: Did anyone mention that one of the characters is an, er, History academic?

WENDY: Mmm.

MARK: The character's not really Russell. It just incorporates some of the external circumstances.

WENDY: Mmm.

MARK: Yes. It's not Russell. You can't lift characters straight from life. It just doesn't work that way.

[*Pause.*]

You might use aspects of people you know but it's never a real person up there on the screen.

[*Pause.*]

WENDY: Someone said that the academic has a drinking problem.

MARK: Yes. I was worried about that. Was Russell upset?

WENDY: A little. He's got it under control now.

MARK: That's great. I tried to make him a drug addict but it didn't seem to work. I'm sure he won't be so annoyed when he sees the film. The character really is quite different. The suggestion in the film is that the academic turns to drink because he doesn't live up to his early promise, but that's hardly Russell, is it? Back after seven years as a full professor. Los Angeles must have been good for him. Did you like it over there?

WENDY: Not really. It's overwhelmingly hospitable but that's mainly a surface. I'd rather have a handful of good friends.

MARK: I was a little surprised to hear that he got the job here. I realise that it's just a new university, but I wouldn't have thought that anybody could get a professorship these days without a PhD.

WENDY: He had excellent references. You knew he worked with

Mitchell Ayres over there, didn't you?

MARK: No, look. Don't get me wrong. I know he deserves the job. I'm just glad that they were far-sighted enough to dispense with nominal qualifications when they appointed him. Who's Mitchell Ayres?

WENDY: One of the world's most distinguished historians. He offered Russell a job in his department at Berkeley after he heard him speak at a seminar.

MARK: He can be very impressive.

WENDY: He's got a fine brain.

MARK: Yes, he has. It's just that I always felt that because he did so well as an undergraduate there was an undue weight of expectation placed on him. Don't you think that was a part of his trouble?

WENDY: I'm not sure. Some friends of ours tell us that the academic character in your film has aspirations as a novelist?

MARK: Oh. That. No, look, that's a very minor area of the characterisation. Almost insignificant.

WENDY: Russell did feel that it would be something of a betrayal —

MARK: No, really. It's only mentioned in passing.

WENDY: We were told that the central character thumbs through the manuscript and laughs at it.

MARK: Laughs? No. Not at all. He mentions that the manuscript needs more work but I can't recall that he laughs.

WENDY: Our friends were pretty sure that he laughed.

MARK: That's nonsense. Who are these friends of yours? He might give a bit of a chuckle but I would have thought that that's more a comment on his lack of feeling than on the quality of the manuscript. [*Irritated*] These friends of yours must be pretty simple-minded if they think that because a character in my film laughs at a manuscript it means that I, personally, am laughing at Russell's work. I thought the manuscript he sent from Los Angeles had real promise. It did need work in my opinion but I'd be the last person to laugh at anyone else's creative efforts.

[*Pause.* MARK *rises.*]

Is that the taxi? Have your friends told you anything about the academic's wife?

WENDY: Yes, they did mention her.

MARK: I think you'll find that a very sympathetically written role.

Sally played it. Again, I had to come up with a pretty over-simplified thesis to explain her to the audience. She, er, neglects her own development and devotes herself to her husband — that sort of thing. Nonetheless it's a very moving part. A lot of women cry. So do I, to tell you the truth.

[*Another pause.*]

I really regret that time we . . . all got involved in that unfortunate . . .

WENDY: Oh that.

MARK: I didn't ever get around to apologising.

WENDY: I'd put it out of my mind, it was so long ago.

MARK: I still feel ashamed about it all . . . It was mainly Russell's fault but I still feel I was very irresponsible.

WENDY: So was I, but I think it was all pretty unimportant in retrospect.

MARK: Just as long as it didn't leave any scars. I think we were all skating on pretty thin ice.

[RUSSELL *comes back through the front door.*]

RUSSELL: Your taxi's arrived, Mark.

MARK: Ah. About bloody time. [*Putting down his coffee cup*] Thanks for the meal, Wendy. I'll give you a ring and we'll all, er, meet again soon. I'm sorry about Sally. She's a bit tense at the moment. Thanks again.

RUSSELL: Pleasure.

[MARK *nods and leaves.*]

I know he's a bastard but I'm still fond of him in an odd sort of way.

WENDY: Sometimes I get an image of you standing in a paddock in the path of an oncoming bull, saying to yourself: 'I know he's going to gore me but I can quite understand why he's doing it. After all it is his paddock and he probably was beaten by the farmer this morning and I am wearing a red tie, and incidentally I can't help admiring all that energy and drive.'

RUSSELL: Don't you think we should have much to do with him in future?

WENDY: I don't particularly want to. Do you?

RUSSELL: [*shrugging*] I've known him a long while.

WENDY: Do you like him? Now?

RUSSELL: I don't really know. I must admit he's not nearly as impressive as he used to be.

WENDY: Was he ever really impressive?

RUSSELL: Oh yes. There was a whole circle of us at university who used to follow him around as if he was the messiah. He used to make definitive pronouncements on any subject you'd care to name: 'There are three and only three recurrent themes of History. The fall of kings, the rise of kings and the fall of the kings who have risen.' I guess we must have been pretty naive if we found that sort of stuff impressive. But he did have a certain charisma.

WENDY: Like Mitchell Ayres.

RUSSELL: Yes. In a way. Yes.

WENDY: Sometimes, Russell, you remind me of Goebbels.

RUSSELL: Goebbels.

WENDY: A rather benign low-key Goebbels blundering through life in search of his Hitler.

RUSSELL: That's a bit much.

WENDY: You trotted around behind Mark for years.

RUSSELL: I didn't.

WENDY: You did. You used to do everything you possibly could to please him. Including inviting him to sleep with me.

RUSSELL: Which you did.

WENDY: Yes I did, but I didn't want to go through it all again with Mitchell Ayres.

RUSSELL: You still think I was setting something up, don't you?

WENDY: I know you were setting something up. So did Ayres.

RUSSELL: The car broke down. I had to check into a motel.

WENDY: But it started again the next morning. When you arrived back I was so angry I could have happily shot you.

RUSSELL: The car broke down. I rang you.

WENDY: Russell.

RUSSELL: All right. I'm sorry. I do get a bit odd from time to time but you didn't sleep with him so it's all right. Isn't it?
    [*There is a long pause.*]
    You did sleep with him, didn't you? Hah. I knew you weren't upset when I rang.
    [*Pause.*]

WENDY: They laugh at you, darling. You're not a Goebbels, you're a clown. I've seen that film of Mark's. I went yesterday afternoon. He's made an absolute fool of you.

RUSSELL: Really. Oh.

WENDY: He's made you a doomed sycophantic alcoholic clown sliding towards social extinction.

RUSSELL: Don't say sycophantic. I'm not sycophantic.

WENDY: Russell. How do you think you got your job with Ayres? You didn't have impressive qualifications, you'd published practically nothing. All you seemed to be doing at the time was drinking. I'm sorry I'm being so brutal, but going through tonight was like reliving a nightmare.

RUSSELL: Ayres gave me that job because he was impressed by the paper I delivered at that Minnesota conference.

WENDY: Of course he was impressed by it. How could he help being impressed by it? It was a thinly disguised love song to Mitchell Ayres.

RUSSELL: Darling, that's really nasty.

WENDY: It's true. Goebbels was courting his new Hitler.

RUSSELL: Darling, you're making me really upset.

WENDY: I'm sorry, but it's true. While you were delivering it the man in front turned to his companion and said: 'He'll be on Ayres' staff within a month.' You mentioned Ayres illuminating insights about twenty times. The two men in front were keeping a scoreboard.

RUSSELL: Darling, you're being really unfair. Why are you being so vindictive?

WENDY: Because I felt I was living through a nightmare here tonight. Didn't you?

RUSSELL: I suppose it was pretty rugged.

WENDY: It was more than rugged.

RUSSELL: Well maybe it was, but that's no excuse for you to say that the only reason I got my job was because I flattered Ayres.

WENDY: [angry] Russell. You were finally so embarrassing to him he had to get rid of you!

RUSSELL: He didn't get rid of me.

WENDY: Russell, he did. Raging egotist though he is, he did! It would take fairly massive doses of flattery to embarrass a man as egotistical as Mitchell Ayres, but you managed to do it.

RUSSELL: [upset] Wendy, he didn't get rid of me.

WENDY: If someone wants to keep you on his staff he doesn't make a practice of showing you advertisements for jobs in other countries.

RUSSELL: He was unselfish enough to realise that this was a good opportunity for me. He's that kind of man.

WENDY: You were embarrassing him, Russell. Discerning people were becoming disgusted at your continual undue deference to him to the point where even he became embarrassed. I'm not a fool, Russell. I could tell.

RUSSELL: On the day we left he told me I'd been the most valuable member in his department. He had tears in his eyes and he meant them. You saw the tears. He meant them.

WENDY: Russell. I overheard him talking to Ed Bartoli at that party at the Brackners' place a few weeks before he showed you that advertisement and they were laughing about you. I'm sorry, but they were. Ayres said, 'With friends like that who needs enemies?' and the two of them roared laughing. How do you think that made me feel?

[*Pause.* RUSSELL *looks shattered.*]

You're a clown, Russell. I love you, but you're a clown.

[*There is another silence.*]

RUSSELL: I'll fix him.

WENDY: Calm down.

RUSSELL: I'll fix him. His last book is a mess. In fact it's worse than that. It's a load of bloody garbage. I was completely loyal to that man. Right. Well he's going get a hell of a letter from me. One hell of a letter. By the time I get through with what I think of him and his last book he won't be laughing. Mark either. He's going to hear what I think of his film right to his face. I'm no clown, Wendy.

WENDY: Well, you have been. I'm going to bed.

[WENDY *leaves.* RUSSELL *stands muttering curses.*]

RUSSELL: I'm no clown. No I am not. Clown. Shit. That's a bit rough.

[*He reaches for the whisky bottle on the sideboard and with an instinctive action starts to pour himself a drink. Before the liquid leaves the bottle, he stops the pouring action and looks at the glass. He speaks loudly, for* WENDY'*s benefit.*]

That's a bit rough. I'm no Goebbels and I'm no clown. What a hell of a loyal wife you turned out to be. It's not very pleasant when an old friend rips you to shreds in a film and you find out that your professor has been laughing at you. It's the time when a man needs a little emotional support from the woman he loves. Why have you suddenly turned on me?

[WENDY *reappears at the doorway.*]

WENDY: Because I'm sick of being the next thing you turn to after the whisky bottle.

[WENDY *goes back into the bedroom.*]

RUSSELL: That's a bit bloody rough.

> [*He looks down at the whisky bottle that is still in his hand, and speaks loudly to* WENDY *again.*]

You think you've got me over a barrel, don't you? If I start drinking again you'll say I'm only doing it to get attention.

> [*There is no answer. He pours himself a drink.*]

Well, I don't give a damn what you say. I'm drinking.

> [*He pours himself a glass of whisky and drinks it.* WENDY *comes to the door and watches him. She has already begun to undress for bed. He looks at her defiantly. She walks across, takes the whisky bottle out of his hands and pours another glass. She hands it to him. He stares at her in disbelief.*]

WENDY: Go on. Drink it.

> [RUSSELL *continues to stare at her and the glass.*]

Go on. Drink it.

> [RUSSELL *suddenly explodes and lashes out at her in fury. He misses but it is obvious he is in earnest. She scrambles away from him in fear.*]

Russell. Stop it. Please.

> [RUSSELL *catches her and gives her a backhander across the mouth. The blow is powerful enough to draw a trickle of blood from the corner of her mouth. She scrambles away.*]

RUSSELL: Who do you think you bloody well are? You couldn't even teach school.

WENDY: Russell. Stop it.

RUSSELL: I may be weak but you're weaker.

WENDY: Please, Russell. Calm down.

> [*He clutches her and grabs her round the throat.*]

RUSSELL: I'm a clown, am I? A clown. I'll fix you and Mark and Mitchell Ayres. I'll fix the bloody lot of you.

WENDY: Please, Russell. Stop.

> [RUSSELL, *breathing heavily, takes his hands from her neck.*]

RUSSELL: You think I got this job the same way, don't you? You think I spent the whole interview flattering the Dean.

WENDY: I'm sure you didn't.

RUSSELL: Well, you're wrong. I did. I charmed the arse off him, but if he thinks I'm going to be his bum boy he's got another thing coming. I'll fix him. My staff think I'm his bum boy. They voted to declare my position as administrative head of the department vacant yesterday. They're going to elect a departmental chairman. How's that? Yeah, well I'm going to

fix them too. They think I'll be broken and shattered by it all.
Well I won't. I'll accept their decision with dignity and
without alcohol, stand for the election, and if I lose, stand
again next year. I may be a clown, but from now on I'm going
to be a clown with dignity. I'm sorry. That's a nasty cut. Stay
there and I'll get some disinfectant.

[*He exits to the bathroom.* WENDY *sits on the couch.*]

[*Off*] I'm really sorry. I do love you.

[RUSSELL *comes back carrying a bowl of water, some cotton wool
and a bottle of disinfectant. He begins to dab her chin.
Occasionally she flinches as the disinfectant is applied.*]

You're right. That was a shit of an evening.

WENDY: It was more than that. It was a nightmare.

[WENDY *gets up off the couch and moves to the bedroom door.*
RUSSELL *moves to the light switch, looking at her in a worried
and thoughtful manner. He throws the switch.*]

SCENE TWO

*Three or four days later. A room of a large inner-city hotel in
which* SALLY *and* MARK *are staying.* MARK *picks up the phone and
dials.* SALLY *sits on a settee reading a glossy magazine.*

MARK: [*on phone*] Ron. We've just got the last thirty thousand
from Rees. Yep.

[*Pause.*]

Right.

[*Pause.*]

Yes, I know, I know. They can sense the mood.

[*Pause.*]

Yes. Right. No, don't give him a preferential rate. Just straight
investment, and fire the contract off to him today.

[*Pause.* MARK *smiles.*]

Thanks. See you tomorrow.

[MARK *puts down the phone and turns to* SALLY.]

Well, there you are. I told you we'd have it all tied up by the
second week in February.

SALLY: You really didn't believe it yourself though, did you?

MARK: I was reasonably confident, but I must admit it all came together very smoothly.

SALLY: I'll really do that part well, Mark.

MARK: I know you will.

SALLY: I'm sorry that I behaved so outrageously the other night but you really were a bugger, you know. I really did think you were going to ditch me and cast some overseas name. Why did you get me so worried?

MARK: I didn't think we should talk about you doing the part until the film was tied up.

SALLY: It was more than that. You were irritated by the fact that Jill wanted to interview me and not you.

MARK: Not at all.

SALLY: Come on, admit it. You were piqued.

MARK: I must admit that I was a bit surprised to be treated as if I wasn't even there. I've known her since she was a kid and she barely even said hullo to me.

SALLY: She did.

MARK: She didn't. She talked to you non-stop the minute we got inside the door of her flat.

SALLY: She is a bit fascinated by me, poor thing. I can't wait to see the article.

MARK: Was there ever anything . . . physical between you?

SALLY: [teasing] You've been dying to ask that, haven't you?

MARK: Quite frankly, yes.

SALLY: Well, there wasn't. I think she would've liked there to be. She really was terribly kind and generous to me but I just didn't find her attractive. I was a bit awful to her sometimes but she was so determinedly good and kind that she got a little wearing.

MARK: Jill's hero-worshipped Russell all her life. I'm sure one of the main reasons that Wendy got Russell across to the States was to get him away from her.

SALLY: Did they ever actually . . . [She makes a gesture.]

MARK: I'm sure there was nothing . . . physical involved although quite frankly nothing would surprise me about Russell. He's always been a bit odd.

SALLY: Really? What's he done? He and Wendy seemed like a consummately dull domestic couple. I thought that little act we did for them the other night was probably the high point of their life.

MARK: Ah no. Russell's a bit deceptive.

SALLY: Well, he certainly fooled me. What's he do?

MARK: I can't be bothered going into it.

SALLY: No, come on. What's he done?

MARK: I didn't really mean to bring it up.

SALLY: You've got me really intrigued now.

MARK: [*grinning ruefully*] It's just ridiculous.

SALLY: What?

MARK: We must have been mad.

SALLY: Were you involved?

MARK: [*nodding*] Me and Wendy.

SALLY: You and Wendy?

[MARK *nods.*]

   When?

MARK: Oh. Years and years ago. A year after they were married.

SALLY: Did you have an affair with her?

MARK: Sort of.

SALLY: Sort of? What do you mean, sort of?

MARK: Well, it wasn't exactly an affair.

SALLY: It was just a sort of an affair?

[MARK *nods.*]

I've never had one of those. They must be absolutely thrilling.

MARK: I only slept with her once.

SALLY: Well, I can understand that. She's as dull as dishwater.

MARK: Now come on. Don't be bitchy. She's very beautiful.

SALLY: Beautiful?

MARK: She's a beautiful person.

SALLY: She never says anything.

MARK: She's reflective.

SALLY: All I can say is that if Teddy Kennedy talked to her for half an hour he must like to hear the uninterrupted flow of his own voice.

MARK: Now come on. She's not as vivacious and attractive as you are but in her own way she is very beautiful.

SALLY: All right, so what transpired or conspired or expired between you and this beautiful, enigmatic, pastoral woman?

MARK: [*smiling*] Stop it.

SALLY: Well, I've never heard you deliver such a eulogy. It's obvious why Russell married her. It was just to please you. Now come on. I'm all agog. Tell me all. I'm not jealous. She probably had a fresh charm about her in those days that made her quite alluring. Did Russell find out?

MARK: Er, yes. He was there.

SALLY: What do you mean?

MARK: [*grinning despite himself*] He was there.

SALLY: There. In the house?

MARK: In the room.

SALLY: In the room?

MARK: [*laughing*] It was ludicrous.

SALLY: What in God's name was going on? An orgy?

MARK: More or less. It was ludicrous. Russell organised it. He'd just got onto the beat generation stuff and was reading Kerouac's *On the Road* with all those marvellous and improbable orgies, and when I came to stay for a week he got me reading it and Wendy reading it and we all sat around eagerly waiting for it all to happen.

SALLY: And it obviously did.

MARK: Wendy finally got drunk and asked us to get on with it.

SALLY: And an enjoyable evening was had by all.

MARK: [*shaking his head and grinning ruefully*] Dreadful. I can't think how we ever did it. The worst part . . .

   [MARK *shakes his head and decides not to say anything.*]

SALLY: Yes?

MARK: [*shaking his head in rueful shame*] No, no, no.

SALLY: Come on. This is better than this month's *Cleo*.

MARK: No.

SALLY: Come on.

MARK: When Wendy went to sleep, Russell . . .

SALLY: What?

MARK: Propositioned me.

SALLY: [*interested*] Really? Did you . . .

MARK: [*nodding, ruefully*] He talked me into it.

SALLY: Who did what to who?

MARK: Stop it.

SALLY: No, really. I'm interested.

MARK: Stop it.

SALLY: Did you ever want to do it again?

MARK: No.

SALLY: I bet you did.

MARK: I didn't.

SALLY: I wish you'd told me all this before I visited them. I might have found the whole evening much more interesting.

MARK: Yes, well, don't tell anyone anything. Right?

SALLY: Of course I won't.

MARK: Well don't. You're the first person I've ever told about it.

SALLY: I won't say a word.

MARK: I've done my duty and apologised to Russell about the film so we don't have to see them again for years.

SALLY: I won't say a word.

[*Pause.*]

I did sleep with Jill once or twice.

[*Pause.*]

My God, you country boys are pretty deceptive.

MARK: [*getting irritable*] Look, I've told you all about it. I don't want to discuss it any more. Right.

[*Pause.*]

God I'm glad all that finance is sewn up.

SALLY: Talking about sewing up, when can I see Shirley about my costumes?

MARK: Don't call them costumes. Clothes. Any time.

SALLY: You're not dressing me in calico and making me look like a colonial drab.

MARK: No, no, no. Shirley says it was all long and flowing and muslin around about then. You'll look great.

SALLY: It's all looking so good that I'm getting anxious.

MARK: There's nothing to get anxious about.

SALLY: That's why I'm anxious. I had one of my very old nightmares last night.

MARK: What was it about?

SALLY: The house on the cliff. Haven't I told you that one?

MARK: No.

SALLY: The first house that we rented after Mother left Dad was a little shack on the top of a cliff overlooking the sea.

MARK: You've told me about the house.

SALLY: We were as poor as church mice but Mother refused to live anywhere that didn't have a beautiful aspect. The only thing we didn't know was that the cliff was being undermined by the sea and we'd find ourselves a bit closer to the edge after every storm. They were terrible years. I was only eight and Mother cried for hours on end and I had nightmares about us going over the edge.

MARK: Well, there's absolutely nothing to worry about. I'll go down and get the morning papers.

SCENE THREE

Lights come up immediately on JILL*'s flat. It is morning five days later.* JILL *sits by herself on the floor of her flat reading a tabloid-type magazine. In his living room* RUSSELL *does likewise.* SALLY *approaches the door of* JILL*'s flat looking distressed and nervous, and after a momentary hesitation knocks on the door.* JILL *goes to the door, opens it, sees* SALLY, *steps back and beckons her inside.* SALLY *looks at the tabloid spread out on the floor.*

JILL: I thought you might come. Would you like some tea?
> [SALLY *nods and sits down on the couch.* JILL *picks up the offending paper and stuffs it away under a bench as she goes to make the tea.*]

If it's any consolation I feel terrible about it. I wanted to withdraw it a couple of days ago but I'd already signed the release contract.

SALLY: [*bursting out*] Jill, most of it isn't even true! I'm getting that film role because Mark thinks I'm the best person for it. He wouldn't give it to me if he didn't. He's the most utterly ruthless man you can imagine. I could rant and scream until doomsday and it wouldn't make any difference. If he found an actress who was half of one percent better for the role he'd get rid of me without moment's hesitation. He's admitted it.

JILL: I know.

SALLY: My performance is good in his last film, Jill. Mark wouldn't use me again if it wasn't.

JILL: I know. I went and saw the film again yesterday.
> [SALLY *moves across and takes the magazine from where* JILL *has placed it and begins to read.*]

SALLY: 'And while one can only admire the audacity of Marshall in casting his wife Sally as a sensitive, tactful and loyal academic's wife, this is one time when casting against type has come unstuck. And how.' Jill, I may not be as sensitive and tactful and loyal as you'd want me to be but you've made me sound like a monster. [*Reading again*] 'Attraction to other people is often more a matter of style than content, and what Sally lacked in content she surely made up for in style.' Jill, you've made me sound like an absolute monster.

JILL: I'm sorry.

SALLY: Mark wants to sue you and he's got grounds, but the only thing that I want to know is why you did it? I can't understand it. We were sitting here laughing together on this couch only a week ago. Mark really wants to sue you.

JILL: [*bursting out*] Well, Mark's got a bloody nerve after what he did to Russell in his film!

SALLY: Jill, that was a fictional representation that wasn't even accurate. This is a direct and vicious slander.

JILL: [*upset*] I went to Mark's film and people in the audience were laughing at my brother, Sally. It wasn't fictional to me.

SALLY: You realise that I can't possibly do the part in *Richard Mahony* now, don't you? I'd be subjected to utter ridicule. You do realise what you've done to me, don't you?

JILL: Yes.

SALLY: Is it true that you organised getting me fired from the magazine? Did you really go to Iris Burke?

JILL: Yes.

SALLY: I'm a blind fool, aren't I? I was naive enough to think that you would be pleased to have me on the staff because you all knew I was a good journalist. The only reason Iris Burke hired me was because I was good. I got better interviews out of better people than anyone else around and I assumed you'd be big enough to admit that to yourselves and accept it without conspiring behind my back. And all that garbage about sleeping with people to get the interviews is just so much crap. Sure I slept with a few, and so did you if I remember correctly and I still managed to get better interviews. It's just pure spite, Jill, and I've had enough of it. I've had it all my life. When I was twelve a girl I'd known for three years came up to me in the classroom and started stabbing me with a compass screaming: 'She thinks she's bloody fantastic, Miss.' I'm just sick of that sort of envy, Jill, and the last person I expected it from was you. I'm sorry I didn't ring you after I moved in with Mark but I always sensed there was something wrong when I was living here . . .

JILL: No there wasn't, Sally. I wanted you here . . .

SALLY: You must have felt terribly smug seeing me reduced to a nonentity and knowing you were responsible for it.

JILL: Sally. That's not true. Really it —

SALLY: You took me out to lunch two hours before I was fired.

Do you remember that?

JILL: You were really arrogant then, Sally. You really —

SALLY: I can remember it so clearly. You were chirpy and smiling and friendly and all the time you knew I was going back there to get fired. I don't understand that sort of personal treachery, Jill. It's foreign to me. And you had the gall to give me all those lectures. 'Sally, you must learn not to hurt other people's feelings. Return that phone call of Martin Sludge's or he will be desperately unhappy.' 'Sally, you mustn't say things like that about him. It's very funny but it's very cruel and malicious.' Malice? What have you got to say about malice now, Jill? You've just written the most malicious piece of journalism it would be possible to write. Your whole soul's steeped in malice and it always was because you're nothing but an unattractive, untalented nobody and you always were and you always will be. You destroyed me, then imprisoned me here for eighteen months and tried to drag me down to your own level of nothingness. No wonder I didn't ring. My instincts were perfectly valid.

[SALLY *storms out of the flat, leaving* JILL *desolate. After a few seconds* JILL *begins crying quietly on the couch.*]

SCENE FOUR

RUSSELL *'s living room. He has cast aside the paper and is sitting there thinking. The room is a little untidy.* RUSSELL *gets up and goes across to the phone. He is just about to start dialling when* MARK *enters.*

MARK: Russell. Wendy.

RUSSELL: I thought you'd be back in Sydney.

MARK: [*tight-lipped*] We're going this afternoon.

RUSSELL: Would you like a drink?

MARK: No thanks. You've seen the article, I presume?

RUSSELL: Yes, I was just about to ring Jill. I think she's been very foolish.

MARK: I suppose she realised what effect it would have on Sally?

RUSSELL: Is Sally all right?

MARK: Of course she's all right. She'll survive. She's a fighter.

When you see Jill next time tell her that it's only because Sally
doesn't want me to that I'm not suing. And let me tell you
something. If you think that I'm going to go around for the
rest of my life feeling guilty about what I'm supposed to have
done to you in my film then you're mistaken. This atrocity of
Jill's makes anything I've done seem completely insignificant.

RUSSELL: Well, it's not insignificant. I'm not condoning what Jill
did, but you had no right to make fun of me and my novel, no
matter how bad it was, and to make fun of my drinking
problem.

MARK: Your drinking problem was nothing but a cheap
attention-getting device.

RUSSELL: Crap! I drank because I felt nervous at three o'clock
every afternoon. That's why I drank.

MARK: You drank to draw attention to yourself. It wasn't enough
to be idolised by your students, you had to be mothered by all
your friends as well.

RUSSELL: Now come on —

MARK: And quite frankly we all got a bit sick of it. I'm glad you
got your professorship. It's more than I thought you'd ever
achieve. Obviously your old ploy of working on people's
sympathies has paid off for you in the long run. Personally, I
prefer to do it the hard way.

RUSSELL: Jesus, Mark, what kind —

MARK: Yes, well, you might have got all the first class honours at
university but I was the one who knew how to run my life. Just
remember that I had the decency to leave a lot out of that film
that I could've put in. No wonder Wendy is having a hard time
of it now. It's a wonder she's not in a mental home. There's
something really warped about a man who encourages his best
friend to make love to his wife and himself in the one night.

RUSSELL: And there's something pretty warped about a best
friend who does it.

MARK: You're warped, McAlister. You're completely unbalanced
and you always have been. Married less than a year to one of
the finest women alive and you start that sort of stuff. I could
have had her for myself, you know. The only reason I didn't
move in on her was out of some misguided loyalty to you. If I
had've known how you were going to treat her I wouldn't have
had a moment's hesitation.

[RUSSELL *looks wearily dubious.*]

You can look as sceptical as you like but it's true. I asked her out months before you got engaged and she wanted to accept. I decided not to at the last moment because I didn't want to hurt you.

RUSSELL: Oh, for Christ's sake. She was just trying to be tactful. She had to drop a dozen hints about loyalty before you finally woke up that she didn't want to go.

MARK: You remember it your way and I'll remember mine, but whatever the truth of the situation, all that I can say is that she got a bloody bad bargain. You're warped, McAlister. All that kinky sex stuff does is destroy people. Wendy was suicidal after that little episode.

RUSSELL: She was depressed and so was I. The only one who wasn't was you. I'm glad you're showing some retrospective sensitivity because at the time you were as gleeful as a satyr in the Palace of Virgins.

MARK: All right. I wasn't as sensitive as I could have been at the time, but when I did realise the implications of it all I was disgusted with the whole sordid episode. It's a wonder Wendy's still sane. Where is she?

RUSSELL: Living by herself for a while.

MARK: Living by herself?

RUSSELL: [tersely] Yes. She's walked out on me.
    [Pause.]

MARK: Yes, well, look, I'm sorry but you've only got yourself to blame. She's much too good for you and always has been. In the middle of her personal grief —

RUSSELL: [angrily] Our personal grief, Mark. Hers and mine.

MARK: She still found time to organise your exit to the States because you were so heavily into the bottle that another year here would have finished you. Are you drinking again? Is that why she's left?

RUSSELL: No. Now will you please go?

MARK: I'm going. Just tell your sister that the most prominent, if not the most talented, film director in the country thinks she's beneath contempt, and that she won't stop Sally doing that film. Sally will do it and Sally will triumph!
    [He leaves.]

RUSSELL: [to himself] Triumph of the will.
    [MARK re-enters, looking a trifle awkward.]

MARK: Try and sort this thing out with Wendy. I'm not the most altruistic person in the world but on the day that you two were married I was genuinely elated to see two people who were so obviously in love, and it might be selfish of me but in a world where rampant disintegration is the norm, your marriage is the one image of permanency that I'd like to retain.

RUSSELL: I'll tell her that. I'm sure that if she realises that your image of permanency was at stake she'd come back to me tomorrow.

[*Pause.* RUSSELL *nods.* MARK *leaves.* RUSSELL *moves across to the telephone and dials.* JILL *has stopped crying and sits on the floor staring straight ahead. Her phone rings. She picks it up.*]

JILL: Yes.

RUSSELL: It's me.

JILL: Hi. Have you read my article?

RUSSELL: Yes. How are you feeling?

JILL: Terrible. Sally's just been. How are you feeling?

RUSSELL: Pretty bad. Mark's just been here.

JILL: Would you like me to come over?

RUSSELL: If you'd like to.

JILL: Could you stand another casserole?

RUSSELL: Fine. We'll watch some television. Have you had any reaction to your article?

JILL: Nine people have rung me to tell me that they think it's the best thing I've done.

RUSSELL: A pleasant little society we live in, isn't it?

JILL: I'll be there in ten minutes.

[*Slow fade to black.*]

THE END

THE CLUB

Gerard Maguire as Gerry, Frank Wilson as Jock and Frank Gallacher as Ted in the premiere production at the Russell Street Theatre, Melbourne, 1977. Photo: David Parker.

The Club was first performed by the Melbourne Theatre Company at the Russell Street Theatre, Melbourne, on 24th May 1977 with the following cast:

GERRY	Gerard Maguire
TED	Frank Gallacher
LAURIE	Terence Donovan
DANNY	Harold Hopkins
JOCK	Frank Wilson
GEOFF	John Walton

Setting designed by Shaun Gurton
Directed by Rodney Fisher

CHARACTERS

GERRY COOPER
TED PARKER
LAURIE HOLDEN
DANNY ROWE
JOCK RILEY
GEOFF HAYWARD

SETTING

The action of the play takes place in the committee room of a top professional football club. There is a formal committee table surrounded by chairs. Lounge chairs and a coffee table dominate the downstage area. It is in this area that most of the action takes place. Large, framed head-shots of former club champions adorn the walls. A door on the left leads to the general and recreational areas of the club building, while to the right a door leads to a private bar used by committee members.

ACT ONE

GERRY COOPER, *lean, alert, in his middle thirties, sits on the table smoking, a folder in one hand.* TED PARKER *enters from left. He is small, pudgy, manic, nervous, in his early forties.*

TED: Good.

GERRY: Good what?

TED: Good that you're early.

GERRY: Always early.

TED: Going to be tough.

GERRY: What?

TED: [*more clearly*] Going to be tough.

GERRY: Who? Laurie?

TED: No. The whole business. Going to be awkward. It'll have to be handled carefully. My first impulse is to blast hell out of him. Really blast hell out of him. He's hurt me, Gerry, and I'm angry. Really angry, but I think it's much better if I stay cool. Don't you think so? Better to stay cool?

GERRY: If you stay as cool as you are now we're all in trouble. Calm down.

TED: Sometimes it takes more courage to hand out the olive branch than to jump in boots and all. I'm not going to smile and pretend that it didn't happen, mind you, but I'm going to stay cool.

GERRY: Calm down.

TED: I could use a drink.

GERRY: Grab a bottle of Scotch from next door.

[TED *nods and goes out, right.*]

TED: [*off*] How's June?

GERRY: Sick.

TED: [*off*] That's great. Sick?

GERRY: Mmm.

[TED *re-enters with a bottle of Scotch and two glasses.*]

TED: What's she got?

GERRY: 'Flu.

TED: There's going to be a new 'flu strain in the next ten years that's going to wipe out nine tenths of the world population.

131

GERRY: Yeah ?

TED: I read it in the Sunday papers.

GERRY: That'll test Medibank.

[TED *pours them each a whisky. The left door opens and* LAURIE HOLDEN *comes in.* LAURIE *is a tall well built man in his middle forties. There is an awkward silence.* TED *declines.*]

TED: I'm sorry it's come to this, Laurie.

LAURIE: So am I.

[*There is another awkward pause.*]

June better yet, Gerry?

GERRY: Improving, thanks, Laurie.

LAURIE: Give her my love.

GERRY: Will do.

TED: Thanks for coming, Laurie. The Committee thought it might be better if we tried to thrash this out privately before tonight's meeting.

LAURIE: Fine.

TED: The Committee wants to see if you and I can settle our differences, Laurie. They don't want to accept your resignation.

GERRY: I thought I'd come along to see if I can act as an impartial sounding board for you both. Jock was going to come along and lend a hand too, but as usual he's late.

LAURIE: Jock? Lend a hand?

GERRY: His idea, not ours, but once he gets an idea in his head he's a little hard to discourage. We'll go if you two get to a point when you'd rather talk things through yourselves.

TED: The Committee's unanimously of the opinion that they don't want to lose you, Laurie. You're one of the best coaches we've ever had and you've given the Club great service.

GERRY: We'd find it very hard to replace you, Laurie.

[*There is another pause.*]

TED: The Club's going through a slump but nobody blames you.

LAURIE: I should bloody well hope not.

TED: [*exploding*] Holy Jesus, Laurie. There's no need to be totally self righteous. When a football club performs as badly as ours has over the last five weeks, most coaches would be honest enough not to try and absolve themselves of all the blame. It really makes me wonder whether there's any point to this exercise when I come to you in a spirit of conciliation and you jump down my throat at the first opportunity. I was hurt by what you said about me in the press, deeply hurt. It took all my self-control to be pleasant to you when you walked in that door.

GERRY: I think I should tell you that the Committee took a pretty dim view of your press statements, Laurie. If you had any grievances you should have come to us.

LAURIE: The press asked me if it was true I was handing in my resignation, so I said yes, and they asked me why, so I told them.

GERRY: How did they know about your resignation before we did?

LAURIE: I don't know.

GERRY: Did you tell the players you were about to resign ?

LAURIE: Yes. I felt I owed it to them.

TED: You must have known they'd take it to the press.

LAURIE: I thought it was a possibility. I didn't ask them to.

GERRY: It puts the Committee in a hell of a position when you criticise the Club President in the press, Laurie.

TED: What's my sin, Laurie? What's my crime? All I could get out of the article was some vague accusation that I was autocratic. What exactly were you trying to say? That I have opinions? All right. I'm guilty. That on occasions I express them? All right. Guilty again. Just what am I expected to do, might I ask ? Go away and hide in a corner? I'm the Club President, Laurie. I was elected by the members to lead this Club and I'll bloody well lead it, and if anybody tries to stop me I'll crush them. No, Gerry. I'm sick of pussyfooting around. I'm going to speak my mind. He's called me autocratic so he just better come up with some evidence.

LAURIE: I wouldn't know where to begin.

[*There is a knock at the door and* DANNY ROWE *enters. He is twenty-eight, small and nuggety.*]

TED: What do you want?

DANNY: I want to know what's happening.

LAURIE: It's all right, Danny. I can handle it.

DANNY: [*to* GERRY] The players want their point of view heard before the Committee makes any decision about Laurie.

TED: The players can go to hell.

DANNY: They always could as far as you were concerned, Parker, but we'd just like the Committee to know that we're a hundred percent behind Laurie.

TED: Well, you can just go and tell the players that the Committee are a hundred percent behind me.

DANNY: Then perhaps the Committee had better roll up and play tomorrow's match.

TED: What's that supposed to mean?

DANNY: It means that if that bloody Committee of yours gives Laurie the boot tonight, then we don't play tomorrow.

LAURIE: Come off it . . . [*Danny*].

TED: This is lovely. Really delightful. A strike threat.

LAURIE: Danny. Go home and calm down.

TED: A strike threat.

DANNY: It's no threat. We mean it. You sack Laurie tonight and you won't have a team tomorrow.

TED: Sack him? What do you mean sack him? He's bloody well resigned. We're not sacking anyone. Did you hear that, Gerry? A strike threat? [*to* DANNY] You won't find me bending under that sort of pressure, my boy.

LAURIE: There'll be no strike whether I'm here or not.

TED: I should bloody well hope not. There's more than enough industrial anarchy in the community at large without us copping it on the football field. Next thing you know they'll be holding a stopwork meeting every time the umpire blows his whistle.

DANNY: Very funny. You'll be sneering on the other side of your face tomorrow.

GERRY: Danny, if you'd just clear off we'll get this whole thing sorted out.

TED: Laurie offered his resignation and we're treating it seriously. What else do you expect us to do?

DANNY: He only offered to resign because you bloody well drove him to it. How could any coach run a team with you sticking your nose in everywhere?

TED: Sticking my nose in?

LAURIE: I appreciate this, Danny, but you're doing me more harm than good. Go home and calm down.

DANNY: Someone's got to tell him.

TED: What do you mean sticking my nose in?

DANNY: It's not your job to pick the bloody team.

TED: I don't. I'm not even on the Selection Committee.

DANNY: No, but you take two thirds of 'em up to the bar and talk for four hours every Wednesday night.

TED: Jock and Tony? So what? The team is barely discussed.

DANNY: That's not what I heard.

TED: Then you'd better rap your spies over the knuckles because the team is barely discussed. Laurie, have you ever thought I've tried to influence the selection of the team ?

LAURIE: Yes.

TED: When?

LAURIE: This week.

TED: That's a lie.

LAURIE: You told Jock and Tony that Geoff Hayward wasn't to be dropped.

TED: I didn't tell them any such thing. I expressed an opinion that he shouldn't be dropped and they happened to agree with me. Aren't I allowed to express an opinion? Am I supposed to go around this place with adhesive tape over my mouth? I might have known that Geoff Hayward was at the bottom of all this. What have you all got against him? He's struggling for form at the moment but he's an absolute champion. What have you got against him ?

LAURIE: Nothing. He's playing badly and should be dropped to the reserves.

TED: That's your opinion, but the other two selectors happen to agree with me. Tough luck. Don't try and make a conspiracy out of that. In my opinion it's no wonder the lad's a bit out of touch. The team's made him feel as welcome as a blowfly at a butcher's picnic.

DANNY: I'm sorry. We were all going to give him a big kiss, but we thought he'd be in a hurry to get home and count his money.

TED: We're not still back on that issue, surely? The Club did not pay a hundred thousand for him as reported in the press —

DANNY: I know. You paid eighty.

TED: How did you know?

LAURIE: I told him.

TED: Thanks. That was meant to be confidential. Geoff didn't get it all. His club got the bulk of it. My God, if what you're trying to tell me is that the team's playing badly because it's still sulking over a little bit of money that went into the pocket of a legitimate champion then I'm disgusted.

DANNY: There are a lot of legitimate champions in this club, Parker, and all we got for joining was a guernsey and a pat on the back. I've given the Club ten years of my life and all I've got in the bank is eighty dollars.

TED: Well, you must be a hell of a fast spender, Rowe. You're on a bloody good contract and you're due for your provident fund when you retire.

DANNY: I can hardly wait. I'm taking my two best friends out to a Pizza Palace and putting the other half in the bank.

TED: You've done pretty well out of the Club, Rowe. If you can't organise your finances then that's your fault.

DANNY: What's that meant to mean, Parker?

TED: Nothing more than what I said.

GERRY: This is all beside the point. We've spent the money on Hayward and there's nothing much we can do about it. If you don't think he's worth his place in the team you're entitled to want him dropped, Laurie, but if Jock and Tony vote against you it's scarcely a reason to go running to the press.

LAURIE: The press came to me. I didn't go to them.

GERRY: All right, but you didn't have to talk to them. Could we steer this discussion back to more fruitful areas? Danny. I think we've got the players' point of view now, thank you.

DANNY: We want to know the outcome.

GERRY: All right. Wait outside.

[DANNY *moves reluctantly to the left door and goes outside, closing it after him.*]

Right, well it seems we've got a bit closer to the real seat of the problem. You think Ted's been interfering in team selection and more specifically that he's been protecting Geoff Hayward?

LAURIE: No, it's not just that. I resent the fact that he's come into the Club with no background and no experience and carried on as if he's God almighty.

TED: I was elected by the members of this Club on a platform of reform and I intend carrying it through.

GERRY: In what other ways has Ted interfered, Laurie?

TED: I haven't interfered in any bloody way!

GERRY: I'm just trying to get at the facts, Ted.

TED: I know what he resents. He resents the fact that I've brought a level-headed business approach to the Club, and that that approach is going to bear fruit. That's what he resents. He'd like to take us back to the days of the glorious Club tradition.

LAURIE: Rubbish.

TED: We might have the proudest tradition in the League but we haven't won a premiership in nineteen years. Tradition, tradition, tradition. We've been strangled by it. The days when recruits would flock to the Club from all over the country simply because of its name are long since gone. It's no good waiting for players to come to you; you've got to go out there into the marketplace and fight for them.

LAURIE: I've been asking the Committee to buy players for years and you know it. Don't give me a lecture on tradition.

TED: All right. So why are we fighting? I've gone in there and battled with the bloody diehards and for the first time in the Club's history we're buying players.

LAURIE: You're buying the wrong bloody ones. I could have bought three players for the money you spent on Hayward, and every one of them would've been more use to the team than he is.

GERRY: [*looking at his watch*] We're getting nowhere. Could I have a word to Laurie alone, Ted?

TED: Sure. I want this thing sorted out as much as you do, Laurie. I'll go and get some cigarettes.

[*He goes to the door on the left, opens it, and turns to them.*] Where's all that spirit we had when I was elected last year. It can't have evaporated. Remember my election slogan? The great leap forward — boom or bust. What happened?

DANNY: [*off*] We bust.

TED: [*turning to him, heatedly*] We came seventh and if we had've had Geoff Hayward in the team we would've made the finals. You've all been against Geoff from the minute he came here, but his first two games this year were brilliant, Laurie. You can't deny that. Absolutely brilliant.

LAURIE: And his last five have been ratshit.

TED: Give him a chance, Laurie, and give me a chance too.

[*He leaves through the left door, glaring at the unseen* DANNY.]

GERRY: [*tersely*] What the hell did you go to the press for?

LAURIE: I got fed up. I've had enough of that clown.

GERRY: I've been at my wit's end trying to contact you. Tony said he found you at home.

LAURIE: I was.

GERRY: I've been phoning you all day. Didn't you hear it ring?

LAURIE: Yeah. I sat there listening to it while Helen made me cups of tea. It was the most relaxing day I've had in years.

GERRY: Well it wasn't for me, cobber. Not at all. You're the type who gives administrators nightmares. You bottle up your grievances for months and don't say a word and suddenly I pick up my morning newspaper and bang, it's all there on page one.

LAURIE: I've had enough, Gerry. That little cretin's been trying to tell me how to do my job ever since he was elected. I'm a professional and I shouldn't have to put up with it. Not from the owner of a meat pie factory who's never played a game of football in his life.

GERRY: He was elected by the members and so were four of his cronies. They've got the numbers and we're stuck with them.

LAURIE: He's got to go and that's final.

GERRY: You're scarcely in a position to be delivering ultimatums, Laurie. The Committee are on the point of accepting your resignation.

LAURIE: Then they'd better accept it. I can't go on this way. Geoff Hayward turned up three quarters of an hour late for training last night, I told him to do twenty push-ups and he told me to get stuffed. Three hours later, courtesy of Ted Parker, he's picked in the team.

GERRY: Ted's not on the Selection Committee and you are. Did you tell Jock and Tony that Geoff had defied you?

LAURIE: No, but I told them I wanted him dropped. That should've been enough.

GERRY: They're not just your puppets, Laurie. They've got minds of their own. Why didn't you tell them that the lad had defied you?

LAURIE: Because it isn't easy to admit that you can't control one of your players. It shouldn't have been necessary in any case. He's been playing atrociously. Did you see last week's game?

GERRY: Yes.

LAURIE: He ignored all my instructions, wandered down to the forward line, and stood there staring out into the crowd. And when the ball came downfield he just stood there watching it go past. I'm not exaggerating, Gerry. He stood there and watched it go past.

GERRY: Yes, I did see that incident. What's wrong with him?

LAURIE: I don't know, but it might help if he didn't feel that he had the unconditional support of the Club President.

GERRY: Yeah, well Ted does feel pretty committed to him.

LAURIE: He was the one who authorised us spending all that money on him.

GERRY: It goes a bit deeper than that. Keep this absolutely confidential, but Ted kicked in with an extra ten thousand out of his own pocket.

LAURIE: He must have money to burn.

GERRY: He hasn't now. His firm's about to go bankrupt.

LAURIE: Don't expect me to cry. He came down from the grandstand last week and tried to tell me how to run the game.

GERRY: Really? That's a bit much.

LAURIE: He's never played a game of football in his life.

GERRY: He is a problem.

LAURIE: I thought the stuff I said in the press might have embarrassed him into resigning.

GERRY: Embarrass? You couldn't embarrass Ted Parker. I lost my temper the other day and told him he was a cunning little rodent and he took it as a compliment. I wish you had've come to me instead of going to the press, because none of this need have happened. He's going to have to resign soon in any case.

LAURIE: Ted?

GERRY: Mmm. There's a storm coming up and I doubt whether he'll weather it.

LAURIE: What's he done?

GERRY: Got himself into real trouble. It's dynamite. I can't tell you anything else and I won't, but I can pretty well guarantee that he won't be around in a month or two, and you'll just have to take my word for it.

LAURIE: This is not some kind of trick?

GERRY: It's no trick. I want him out as much as you do, so patch it up, withdraw your resignation, and in a month's time or even less, he'll be gone.

LAURIE: This puts a different light on things.

GERRY: I want the clown out as much as you do.

LAURIE: What in the hell's he done?

GERRY: I can't say, Laurie, and that's final, but take my word, he'll be gone in a month. Withdraw your resignation.

LAURIE: I won't apologise. Verbally or in print. I meant what I said about him.

GERRY: Yeah, well he's pretty agitated at the moment, but let me have five minutes with him and I'm sure he'll be reasonable.

We'll get a joint press statement out from the two of you saying that you've patched up your differences and you've withdrawn your resignation.

[GERRY *goes towards the door, looking at his watch.*]

The meeting's starting in an hour and a half. Just give me five minutes with him.

[GERRY *opens the door and indicates to* TED *that he should come in.* LAURIE *goes out of the door after* TED *comes in. They look at each other as they pass but don't speak.*]

TED: You know what I've been thinking? We should stop bending over backwards to placate him and accept his bloody resignation.

GERRY: It's a tempting thought.

TED: Why don't we?

GERRY: It's difficult to replace a coach halfway through a season, Ted, and he knows it.

TED: We're not going to renew his contract at the end of the year. Let's get rid of the bastard now.

GERRY: We're going to try and not renew his contract at the end of the year. He's very popular with the supporters and the players and the Committee knows it.

TED: To hell with the players and the supporters. The Committee's where the power is and we've got the numbers. Last Saturday's game clinched it. Blind Freddy could have seen that Danny was being beaten pointless, but Laurie refused to shift him until the last quarter. It lost us the game. Ian and Kevin were disgusted. They said that tradition can go to hell, that they're right with us and that Laurie is definitely getting the axe.

GERRY: I know, I had a long talk with them after the game; but they can change their minds again.

TED: They won't change their minds. Laurie is a dead duck.

GERRY: I never count anything as certain until it happens.

TED: Look, the supporters will be ecstatic when they find out who we're getting to replace him, and the players only like Laurie because he pampers them like babies. As far as he's concerned they can't do a thing wrong. Second from the bottom and five straight losses and the only explanation he can give us is that they're a bit upset, poor darlings, because Geoff Hayward got a little bit of money. It's just not good enough. They need a tough bloody hand and they're going to get it. Laurie is a dead duck.

GERRY: That blunder last week was pretty obvious.

TED: Blind Freddy could have seen it.

GERRY: They say he was a great player.

TED: Yes and my aunt makes great scones, but it doesn't mean she should run a cake factory.

GERRY: We can't sack him in the middle of the season.

TED: Well if he stays, he's going to have to apologise. In the press.

GERRY: He won't. Be reasonable.

TED: Why shouldn't he? He's held me up to ridicule. I'm the President, Gerry. He can apologise or resign.

GERRY: [irritated] Be reasonable, Ted. It's going to be nasty enough at the end of the year when we don't renew his contract. He hasn't exactly been a failure here. We've only been out of the finals once in eight years and we've been runner up twice.

TED: What's the good of being runner up? We want the premiership.

GERRY: And we'll get it, but don't make things difficult right now. Let's just issue a press statement to the effect that you've patched things up.

TED: That's not good enough. He's got to apologise.

GERRY: [irritated] Well he won't, so let's just be sensible.

[The right door opens and JOCK RILEY enters. He's a large, big-boned man in his late sixties, shrewd and tough, with a battered yet expressive face.]

JOCK: Sorry I'm late. [Indicating the bottle] Ah. Scotch.

GERRY: Get yourself a glass.

[JOCK retreats through the right door.]

JOCK: [off] Thrashed it out yet?

GERRY: Almost.

JOCK: [off] Bad business. [Re-entering] Where's Laurie?

[He pours himself a stiff drink.]

GERRY: Outside.

TED: Danny's there too.

JOCK: Danny? What's he doing here?

TED: He just popped in to tell us that if we sack Laurie the players'll go on strike.

JOCK: [amazed] Strike? When?

TED: Tomorrow. They've threatened to refuse to take the field.

GERRY: Come on, Ted. They're not serious.

TED: I thought they were.

JOCK: Strike? I'll give the bastards strike!

GERRY: It's not a serious threat. Don't bring it up again.

JOCK: Strike, eh?

[JOCK *moves across to the right door and opens it.*]
Danny!

[DANNY *enters, followed by* LAURIE.]

DANNY: What?

JOCK: What's this bloody business about a strike? Did you threaten this Club with a strike?

DANNY: I told . . . [*Gerry that if*]

JOCK: I've never heard anything like it in my life. Who's involved? Give me their names. You're not indispensable, Rowe. No one's going to hold this Club to ransom. I'll suspend the lot of you. Who else is involved?

DANNY: The whole team. Except Geoff Hayward. It'll give him a chance to show what a real champion he is.

JOCK: This is a disgusting and despicable threat, Danny. I never thought I'd live to see the day. I played two hundred and eighty-two games for this Club and every time I ran onto the ground I felt as honoured to be out there wearing the Club colours as I did the first time.

GERRY: Calm down. We're just on the point of getting this all resolved, Jock.

TED: The Club won't tolerate threats, Rowe.

JOCK: By God it won't. If you're looking for a scrap, Rowe, you won't find me shirking the issue. What role have you been taking in this, Laurie? Have you been stirring the lads?

DANNY: No he hasn't.

LAURIE: They'll be out on the field tomorrow no matter what happens tonight.

JOCK: My God, I never thought I'd live to see the day when I'd hear the word 'strike' uttered in this room. Look at those pictures on the wall, Danny. Cheeta Ryan, the greatest centreman of all time, Warren Oates, only five foot seven but with a heart as big as a pumpkin. Mike Lenehan, Terry Dunstan, Sandy Forbes. Great names from a great club and you've got the honour and the tradition they created resting right there in your hands.

DANNY: Yes, and the shit from the present administration right up our nostrils.

JOCK: Don't get too cocky, Rowe. You're not indispensable.

TED: Just remember that any player found guilty of a gross misdemeanour can lose every cent of his provident fund.

DANNY: Bullshit.

TED: That's true, isn't it, Gerry?

GERRY: No. Look can we . . .[*get back to the*]

JOCK: Do you know what I want to do? I want to turn all those photographs around so they don't have to look down on this shameful scene. How would Harry Payne feel if he knew that the word 'strike' was being bandied around in this hallowed room? Just tell me that. How would he feel? The man who kicked three superhuman goals in the dying minutes of the '23 grand final and won us the flag. He'd think it'd all been for nothing. I wouldn't be surprised if he's turning in his grave right now.

DANNY: He isn't even dead.

JOCK: Harry? I went to his funeral last year.

GERRY: That was Harry Treloar.

JOCK: Shit yeah. There's so many of 'em dropping off I get confused, but it doesn't alter my argument. Dead or alive, what's happened here today is an insult to their memories. Those fellas up there on that wall are worth ten of your modern bloody player. All we hear from today's lot is whinges. About the administration, about money, about every bloody thing. In my day the greatest honour a man could ever have was to pull a purple and gold guernsey over his head. Those men up there didn't think about money. They got two and six a match during the depression and would have played for nothing.

DANNY: Jesus, Jock.

JOCK: Well maybe not two and six, but not very much more and they would have played for nothing.

DANNY: Well, they were stupid. If I'm out there risking a fractured skull or a ruptured spleen for the amusement of a pack of overweight drunks in the grandstand bar then I want to get paid for it.

TED: That's what you think of —

JOCK: Overweight drunks?

TED: That's what you think of your supporters, eh? The lifeblood of the Club. Overweight drunks? Let me tell you something, Rowe. Watching the game every week up there in the grandstand is more financial and business expertise than you're ever likely to meet in your lifetime. Last week I had Sir Richard Tanner on one side of me and Arthur Mowbray on the other, and for your information they were both drinking tomato juice.

DANNY: If you'd been there since morning it's probably all that was left.

TED: That's a pretty low sort of crack, Rowe. I've never been drunk to the point of social embarrassment in my life.

DANNY: Not much you —

GERRY: Come on, fellas. This is getting . . . [us nowhere]

TED: When have you ever seen me drunk, Rowe?

DANNY: The fund-raising dinner for a start.

TED: I was sober all the evening.

GERRY: Fellas, this is . . .[really quite beside the point]

DANNY: You couldn't get out to that stripper fast enough.

TED: She asked me to take off her garter.

DANNY: She didn't ask you to fall flat on your face after you'd done it.

TED: You're very smart, aren't you, Rowe? Very, very smart. You just might need my signature on a clearance form one day soon. Just remember that.

DANNY: Why would I want a clearance?

TED: Because some interstate club might offer you money.

DANNY: I wouldn't take it. I'm staying here.

TED: What if you can't hold your place in the team?

LAURIE: Ignore him.

DANNY: Hold my place? What are you talking about? I'm fitter now than I ever was.

TED: You're nearly twenty-nine, Rowe, and you're slowing down and we can keep you here as long as we like, playing out the rest of your football in the reserves. Remember that.

LAURIE: Any more of this and I'm leaving.

TED: Well, damn him. He comes barging in here uninvited, threatening strikes and calling me a drunk. It's about time someone brought him to his senses. He only got twelve kicks last week. I saw the statistics.

LAURIE: The number of kicks means nothing, it's the — [way he]

DANNY: It's the first time I've dropped under twenty since the start of the season, Parker.

TED: It's the first time you've found yourself playing against a classy opponent.

GERRY: [*irritated*] For God's sake. None of this is relevant.

LAURIE: The number of kicks means nothing. It's the way he disposes of them that counts.

DANNY: He wouldn't have taken his eyes off his grog for long enough to see what I did with 'em.

TED: I watched the match from start to finish and Wilson was beating you pointless whether Laurie realised it or not. You should have been shifted off him after the first ten minutes.

LAURIE: I'll deal with strategy, Parker.

TED: The team hasn't got any to deal with.

GERRY: Stop it, will you? All of you.

DANNY: [*upset, angry*] Everyone gets beaten once in a while, Parker. Wilson's a hell of a good footballer.

TED: Just remember what I said, Rowe. When you decide to go interstate and make some money you'll need our signature.

[DANNY *looks ready to smash* TED. LAURIE *calms him.*]

JOCK: Don't stretch a point, Ted.

TED: They threaten us. Why can't we threaten them?

DANNY: [*flaring*] Wilson's one of the best players to take the field since the war, Parker. It's easy for you and your business mates to sit up there and pour shit on me from behind the glass in your air-conditioned bar. Wilson would've beaten anyone in the country on the day. He was firing. No one could've stopped him.

LAURIE: You played a good game, Danny. Don't let him needle you.

DANNY: I've got twenty-five kicks a match for ten years. Game in, game out, and the first time I have a bad day he's onto me. What right have you got to sit in judgement on me, you fat turd? Get back to your pie factory.

JOCK: That's enough, Danny. Come on. You've given the Club great service and only a fool'd deny it.

TED: It's all right for him to call me a drunk, but I'm not allowed to tell him he played a bad game.

LAURIE: Shut up, Ted, or I'll thump you.

GERRY: Yes. For Christ's sake could we make a start on the real business of the evening? The Committee's meeting in under an hour and a half and we've got to have this whole thing resolved. Danny. Could you wait outside? You've left us in no doubt about the players' position. It will be taken into account.

DANNY: I'm not leaving until I hear something definite. The players want to be notified.

GERRY: All right. Play some pool downstairs. As soon as anything happens I'll let you know.

[DANNY *moves to the left door, but just as he opens it he turns to fire a last salvo.*]

DANNY: You watch the way you talk to me in future, Parker, or you'll end up getting flattened.

[DANNY *leaves.*]

TED: That's lovely. A player threatens the Club President with physical violence and nobody says a word.

JOCK: Ah shut up! You're lucky he didn't flatten you. You've got to be bloody tactful when a player's getting on in years, Ted. It's a hell of a shock to the system when a player you could have matched when you were younger turns round and takes you apart. I got angry about the strike stuff too, but you've got to be tactful about things like that. Tubby Robbins took me apart in the '39 Grand Final and when I got home Rosemary said, 'I think you met your match today,' and I thumped her one. She apologised later but by that time the damage was done.

GERRY: Has Danny's domestic life smoothed out yet, Laurie?

LAURIE: He's back with Raylene, but I don't know if it'll last. I hope it does. He's very fond of his kids.

JOCK: Raylene's a hell of a nice girl but the word is she's not real keen on hiding the sausage.

GERRY: Jock. Ted and Laurie are prepared . . . [*to work out*]

JOCK: Domestic strife's ruined many a great footballer. Donny Joseph's wife went off with a real estate agent the night before the '47 semi-final and he only got three kicks. What's happened to that Avis girl Danny shacked up with?

LAURIE: I wouldn't know.

TED: He's probably still paying the rent on her flat. No wonder he's only got eighty dollars in the bank.

GERRY: Jock. Ted and Laurie are prepared to work out a joint press statement to the effect that they feel they can work together and that Laurie is withdrawing his resignation.

JOCK: Good.

TED: I expect the statement to say a little bit more than that we can still work together.

GERRY: Well, that's for you two to work out. We all know that there are still some unresolved problems. Geoff Hayward being the most immediate.

JOCK: What's the problem with Geoff?

GERRY: He's giving us a bit of trouble.

JOCK: What sort of trouble?

GERRY: His attitude leaves a lot to be desired.

JOCK: Has he been getting uppity?

GERRY: Yes.

JOCK: He's got no reason to be. He hasn't been playing all that well. What's he been doing?

GERRY: Turning up late for training and disobeying Laurie's instructions.

JOCK: Has he now? [*to* LAURIE] Is that why you wanted to drop him? Too embarrassed to tell us you couldn't handle him?

LAURIE: I can handle him.

JOCK: Well, if he's being a young smart-arse he'll just have to cool his heels in the reserves for a few weeks. You should have told me he was playing up, Laurie. I would have gone along with you.

GERRY: Laurie thought that you and Tony and Ted had some sort of permanent conspiracy not to drop him.

JOCK: Christ, no. If he's been playing up we'll put him down like a shot.

GERRY: There you are, Laurie. You couldn't get much plainer than that.

TED: In all fairness I think I should point out that there's another side to all this. There's no excuse for Geoff turning up late to training, but it's a bit degrading for a footballer of his calibre to be asked to do twenty push-ups in front of the whole team.

JOCK: Rot. When I coached this team they did twenty push-ups and if they asked why they did another twenty. Jesus Christ, do you mean to tell me we've got to have a whole drama in the press before I get to find out that Geoff Hayward's playing up? You could have told me, Laurie. It's no sin to have one of your men play up on you. You ought to have known that. I had to lay you out behind the lockers in your first year before I got any sense out of you.

LAURIE: Those sort of methods don't work any more.

JOCK: Nonsense. A good thump never hurt anyone. Let's get the lad in here and thrash this thing out.

GERRY: We don't have to solve everything now.

JOCK: Strike while the iron's hot. I've been very worried about the lad's form recently and I'd like to get him in here and have a bit of a yarn.

LAURIE: I can handle him myself thanks, Jock.

JOCK: Maybe something's worrying him. Have you talked to him lately?

TED: Yeah, he told him to do twenty push-ups.

JOCK: Shut up, Ted. I used to talk to my boys and it always used to pay off. Remember Lofty Bluett? He was the worst tempered man I've ever seen when he first came to the club. He talked back to me, wouldn't do what he was told on the field or off — a real nightmare. One day I sat down with him and looked him in the eye — you had to sit him down to look him in the eye and I said, 'Righto Lofty, what's worrying you, son?' and he just broke down and cried. True. Lofty Bluett cried. Nobody had ever talked to him like that before. Turned out the problem was really simple. He hadn't got a good night's sleep since he was sixteen 'cause his legs were too long for the bed. We bought him a king-sized bed and he won the Club best and fairest the very next year. Maybe Geoff just needs something simple like that.

LAURIE: Yeah. A king-sized pillow for his swelled head.

TED: It's no use, Jock. He's got it in for the boy.

JOCK: You'll talk to him if I get him in, won't you, Laurie? I feel a bit responsible for all this because I was on the sub-committee that decided to get him. Will you have a talk to him and try and thrash it out?

LAURIE: I don't see what good it will do.

JOCK: Now don't be stubborn.

GERRY: We don't have to have him in tonight.

JOCK: Strike while the iron's hot. I'll call him.

[JOCK *leaves through the left door.*]

GERRY: When Jock gets his mind set on something, there's no stopping him. I'll just go next door while you two draft your press statement. Give me a call when it's finished.

[GERRY *leaves through the right door.*]

TED: You should be a bit more tolerant of young Geoff, Laurie. He's going to he a great asset to us sooner or later.

LAURIE: Can we leave Geoff Hayward and get on to this press

statement?

TED: Sure.

LAURIE: One thing I want to make perfectly clear before I agree to sign anything is that I won't have you coming down to the bench and trying to tell me how to run the game like you did last week.

TED: Danny was getting thrashed. I thought you mightn't have noticed.

LAURIE: What do you think I am? An idiot?

TED: Why didn't you shift him?

LAURIE: Who would I have put on Wilson? The obvious choice would have been pin-up boy Hayward but he was playing like a slug on tranquillisers.

TED: What about Holford?

LAURIE: Holford? Holford was holding our whole back line together. If I had've moved Holford their forwards would have run riot.

TED: Well, I still think you should have done something. And there was no need to bellow at me. I was only saying what everyone else at the ground was thinking.

LAURIE: It's easy to see things wrong from up in the grandstand, but I'm the one who's down there on the spot and I'm the one who knows exactly what my men can and can't do, and I don't appreciate interference from amateurs.

TED: I was only trying to help, Laurie. Your reputation suffered quite a bit of damage over that mistake.

LAURIE: It wasn't a mistake.

TED: All right. Let's forget the whole business and get onto the press statement. I was . . . [hoping that]

LAURIE: One more thing. Next time the negotiating sub-committee thinks of spending money on a player, I'd like to be consulted.

TED: You will be. We just didn't have time.

LAURIE: Bullshit. You and Jock and Gerry got your eighty thousand and you weren't going to let anyone else in on the act, despite the fact that you were specifically instructed by the full committee to consult me before any purchases were made.

TED: We were scared that the committee might reverse its decision to give us the money so we did things in a hurry.

LAURIE: I'll say you did. You spent the whole eighty thousand on a dud.

TED: You're wrong, Laurie. That boy's a champion.

LAURIE: It doesn't matter how much natural ability he's got. If his heart's not in it he's a dud. Why didn't you go for Fulton Masters and Andy Payne? You could have got both of them for that price.

TED: I did at first. Masters at any rate. I didn't think of Payne. I was going to couple him with Franky Davis.

LAURIE: Davis is a bit past it but even that combination is a hell of a lot better than splashing it all on Hayward.

TED: I think you're wrong. I thought the same way as you do at first, but I suppose it came down to quality versus quantity in the end.

LAURIE: Who stuck out for Hayward?

TED: Jock. We couldn't shift him. He wanted Hayward and that was it.

LAURIE: Jock. Do you want to know something? Jock is an old bastard. Two years ago he was thumping the table in Committee meetings and yelling at the top of his lungs that the Club would never stoop to buying players.

TED: I know. I fought the election against him on the issue.

LAURIE: When it happens he's in there organising it. Why in the hell did you offer him the vice-presidency? All his cronies got beaten and he only scraped back in by two votes.

TED: I intended it as a gesture of reconciliation.

LAURIE: More fool you.

TED: Yeah. More fool me. The very first thing I did after the election was to go out and buy the Club the best administrator in the business, and now, eighteen months later, Jock is in cahoots with my administrator and the two of them are running the Club.

LAURIE: He's a great survivor.

TED: I don't know why you spend all your time gunning me down. They're the ones with the real power.

LAURIE: I hear you put up ten thousand of your own money?

TED: Yeah. They pulled a last minute bluff and upped the price to ninety. I didn't mind really. I felt as if I'd contributed in a very concrete and personal way to what I thought was a very important step in the Club's history. I still think we've done the right thing. The lad'll do great things for us one day.

LAURIE: I hope you're right.

TED: What're we going to say to the press?

LAURIE: Just that we're prepared to keep working with each other and that I've withdrawn my resignation.

TED: I'd like a bit more than that, Laurie. You called me autocratic in the press this morning. Don't you think that calls for some sort of retraction?

LAURIE: The fact that I've said we can still work together will be more or less a retraction.

TED: No it won't. All that means is that you still think I'm autocratic but you've decided to grit your teeth and sit it out.

LAURIE: That's not too far wide of the mark.

TED: Yes, well I want a bit more. I've got my pride. I want to say that we've had discussions, that several misunderstandings have been ironed out, and that we're sure we can re-establish a fruitful and harmonious working relationship.

LAURIE: I'll say that we've talked with each other and found that we can still work together. That's all.

TED: We shouldn't be fighting like this, Laurie. It's all so ironic. I've always been one of your greatest admirers. Do you remember the day you played your first game?

LAURIE: Of course.

TED: You'd just turned seventeen three days before. Or was it eighteen?

LAURIE: Seventeen.

TED: There was a real sense of occasion and anticipation right around the ground. We all knew already that you weren't just another recruit. We all knew we were going to see the first game of a great new champion and I don't think anyone was disappointed. Do you remember your first kick?

LAURIE: Not all that well. I know I booted a goal, but there was so much adrenalin pumping through me in the first half, that when I came off the field I could hardly remember a thing.

TED: It was magic, Laurie. It really was. I was only fourteen at the time but I can still see it as clearly as if it was a video replay. You read the play and started sprinting for the goal, picked up a long low pass from Wally Baker, steadied, did a beautiful blind turn around Stan Jackson, and slammed it through the centre. I've seen every game we've played since I was six and I remember that one better than most.

LAURIE: Yes, it was a good game. I settled down in the second half and everyone seemed pretty pleased when I ran off the ground.

TED: Pleased? They went bloody wild. Do you know that right up until the time I was twelve I used to cry every time we lost. If we won I went home and booted a football around our back yard in the dark trying to remember every kick of the match and pretending I was in the side. Hah! By the time I was sixteen I could barely hold my place in the school thirds.

LAURIE: We've all got different talents.

TED: I would like to put harmonious somewhere in that press statement, Laurie.

LAURIE: You're a trier, aren't you?

TED: It would make me feel a lot better.

LAURIE: Say we've had a long talk and have resolved our differences. That's as far as I'll go.

[JOCK *comes in the left door.*]

JOCK: I got on to Geoff and he's on his way in.

TED: You're a hard man, Laurie. I'll write it out and give it to Gerry.

LAURIE: I want to check it before it's released.

TED: Don't worry. I won't slip anything in.

[TED *leaves through the right door.*]

JOCK: Geoff's on his way in.

LAURIE: Ted tells me that you were the one who held out for him.

JOCK: Yeah, I did. He is good, Laurie. He's got so much talent he's a bloody freak. He just needs to be motivated properly.

LAURIE: What's this I hear about Parker resigning?

JOCK: Parker resigning? Is he?

LAURIE: Come on, Jock. I'm not an idiot. Gerry said there's some sort of storm blowing up that's going to force him to resign.

JOCK: Yeah, I did hear a whisper to that effect.

LAURIE: Come on, Jock. You don't hear whispers, you start 'em. What's going on?

JOCK: He's got himself into some sort of trouble but I don't know the details. Thank Christ is all I can say. I mean let's face it. The man's a buffoon. He's got to go.

LAURIE: And when he goes you'll be standing for President?

JOCK: If it's the wish of the Committee. I'll tell you something, Laurie. With Parker out of the way things'll start ticking over smoothly again and we'll come out of this trough. You wait and see. Gerry's got some great ideas for next year.

LAURIE: Oh he has?

JOCK: Yeah. A great administrator, that lad. Getting him's one of the smartest things the Club ever did.

LAURIE: You were the one man on the Committee who voted not to appoint him.

JOCK: A man can be wrong.

LAURIE: Not many can manage it as often as you.

JOCK: I'm glad I laid you out behind the lockers.

LAURIE: What are some of these great ideas of Gerry's?

JOCK: We're going to buy up big.

LAURIE: Buy more players?

JOCK: No, sheep. We're going to graze 'em on the oval and save on lawn mowing costs. Of course we're going to buy more players. We're going to go on the biggest buying spree in the history of the game, and what's more it's good economics.

LAURIE: Why?

JOCK: If we win a premiership it'll arrest the membership decline and members mean money. As a businessman myself I can see the logic of it.

LAURIE: As a businessman yourself. God help us. I was one of the mugs who invested in your import business. A hundred dozen pop-up Taiwanese toasters that burnt the bread then fired it like mortar shells. Then we had the forty gross of Russian alarm clocks that ticked so loudly that the alarm wasn't needed because there was no bloody way you could get to sleep, and the eighty dozen pairs of toy handcuffs from the Philippines that had to be withdrawn from sale after three days because forty-seven kids had to be hacksawed out of them.

JOCK: I'm glad I laid you out behind the lockers.

LAURIE: Well, you haven't exactly distinguished yourself in your business career.

JOCK: You won't make fun of me when you hear some of the names we're negotiating.

LAURIE: [sharply] Negotiating? Who's negotiating? Listen Jock, I'm supposed to be consulted . . . [when there's]

JOCK: Not negotiating. I didn't mean negotiating. All we've done is started to think of some names.

LAURIE: Who has?

JOCK: Gerry and I.

LAURIE: What names?

JOCK: Try these for size. Cam Donaldson, Mickey Dimisch and Andy Payne. How'd you like that lot on your goal-to-goal line?

LAURIE: I'd love 'em on my goal-to-goal line but I'd like to be consulted.

JOCK: You are being consulted. Right now. Cam Donaldson, Mickey Dimisch and Andy Payne. Good enough?

LAURIE: Are they available?

JOCK: No, but they will be. Gerry's amazing, but for Christ's sake keep those names under your hat. There's half a dozen clubs after all of 'em. Next year's going to be a good one, Laurie. With you at the helm and players like that in the team there'll be no stopping us.

[GERRY *enters through the right door holding a notebook in his hand.*]

GERRY: Is this all you're prepared to say to the press, Laurie?

[LAURIE *reads the statement.*]

LAURIE: Yes.

GERRY: You're not very generous. Ted's pretty upset.

LAURIE: Tough. What's this I hear about Donaldson, Dimisch and Payne?

JOCK: Sorry, Gerry. It just slipped out.

GERRY: [*coldly*] The rate at which things slip out around here makes me wonder if members of this Club aren't fitted with a special circuit that goes straight from ear to tongue and completely bypasses the brain.

LAURIE: What's the meaning of starting to plan next year's team without even consulting me?

GERRY: I was going to talk to you about it today, only you went and got yourself into this mess with Ted.

LAURIE: Where are you getting all the money for this spending spree?

GERRY: We'll get it.

LAURIE: How?

GERRY: Leave that to me.

LAURIE: Be buggered I'll leave it to you. Listen. I've been around here for twenty-seven years and I'm coach of this bloody Club, not the office boy. How are you getting the money?

GERRY: Keep it quiet, then. It's all touch and go at the moment. We had two of the biggest property developers in the country in the members bar last Saturday —

LAURIE: Arthur Mowbray and Dick Tanner?

GERRY: Yeah, and despite what Ted thinks they didn't get there by accident. I fossicked around and found out that they're both old supporters so I've been courting them, and doing it pretty well even if I do say so myself. Most guys of that age and in their position are looking for an interesting sideline, pastime, hobby, and these two are no exception, except that they won't have anything to do with us while Ted is President. They haven't said anything directly but it was quite obvious what they were feeling and I can't say I blame them. He was fawning on them like a drunken toad on Saturday.

LAURIE: What sort of role in the Club are you planning for them?

GERRY: If we get rid of Ted we can put Mowbray in as Vice-President and make Tanner an honorary lifer.

LAURIE: Where's his twenty-five years active service?

GERRY: We'll get around that. Shit, Laurie, let's not be bush lawyers where there's this sort of money involved.

LAURIE: What sort of money?

GERRY: Two hundred thousand each for starters. If we can't buy ourselves a premiership with that nobody can.

JOCK: We'll collect a bit of cash from our sales as well.

LAURIE: What sales?

GERRY: [glaring at JOCK] I was going to discuss the possibility of offloading one or two of our older players who are still looking good but who are just about over the hill.

LAURIE: Such as?

GERRY: I don't know. I'm just an administrator, you're the expert. Given that we get Donaldson, Dimisch and Payne, who could we do without?

LAURIE: Tony Harper, I suppose.

GERRY: Hardly worth the effort. His market price is somewhere under five thousand.

LAURIE: Market price?

GERRY: I've been making a few enquiries.

LAURIE: They're men, not pigs.

GERRY: All right. If you want to mince words we'll call it something else, but the fact remains that there is a market mechanism operating, there is a price on every player and the price on Tony Harper is so low it's not worth negotiating his sale. The only player we've got that has big money on his head is Danny.

LAURIE: We're not selling Danny.

GERRY: Why not? With the players we're getting do we really

need him?

LAURIE: [*angry*] Yes

GERRY: It's a question. I wouldn't know whether we need him or not. I'm just the administrator and you're the expert. There's no need to get angry. I'm merely posing a question.

LAURIE: We need him.

GERRY: Fine. A few of the wise heads around here seem to think he's looked better than he really is for years because he hasn't exactly been playing in a team full of champions. They're worried that if he plays too many more games like last Saturday a lot of people will start to realise it and his market price, or whatever you like to call it, will plummet.

LAURIE: Which of the 'wise heads' around here believe that little theory?

JOCK: I do. I say sell him while he's still worth something. Let's face it, Laurie, when we were winning our medals it was in a team full of champions. Danny's little more than a talented hack.

LAURIE: Come off it, Jock. He's bloody near as good as either of us were in our day. I know what's worrying you. If he stays around for another couple of years he'll beat your two hundred and eighty-two games.

JOCK: Yeah, well you couldn't beat it and he's not going to either. Bloody leaves his wife and kids for an Avis girl. When my record goes it'll be to someone with a bit of moral fibre.

LAURIE: Moral fibre? I don't seem to recall that you were famous for your celibacy in the old days Jock. In fact if my memory serves me —

GERRY: That's enough. Laurie, what if I told you I could swap Danny for Tony Marchesi?

[LAURIE *looks at* GERRY.]

That's made you stop and think, hasn't it?

LAURIE: Can you?

GERRY: No, but it made you stop and think, which goes to show that the central assumption of the science of economics that we'd all sell our grandmothers if the price is right isn't all that far wide of the mark.

LAURIE: [*defensive, irritated*] The only reason I'd want Danny to go is if Danny wanted to go. I don't care if you could swap him for Jesus Christ.

JOCK: With the team we'll have next year, Jesus Christ will be pushing to make the reserves.

[*There is a knock at the left door.*]

That's probably Geoff. How do you want to handle this, Laurie? I'll have a chat to him first if you like.

LAURIE: I'll talk to him, if you don't mind.

JOCK: Suit yourself. I just thought that a fresh viewpoint might help break the deadlock. I was a coach for fifteen years myself and I have had the odd bit of experience with troublesome recruits.

LAURIE: [*tersely*] Clear out and let me talk to him.

JOCK: Suit yourself.

[JOCK *goes to the left door and brings in* GEOFF HAYWARD, *who is medium to tall and looks and moves like an athlete in top condition.*]

Come in, Geoff. Sorry to interrupt your meal. Gerry and I are just going next door to have a drink so that you can have a little chat with Laurie. Feel free to call me if you need me, Laurie. Sometimes a fresh viewpoint can break a deadlock.

LAURIE: Thank you, Jock.

[JOCK *and* GERRY *leave through the right door.*]

You've read the morning papers, I suppose?

GEOFF: Yep.

LAURIE: The Committee are meeting in just over an hour to decide whether they're going to accept my resignation. I think they're going to ask me to reconsider it but it's hardly worth my while if you're going to keep defying me.

GEOFF: So what are we supposed to do? Kiss and make up?

LAURIE: I don't want you to defy me in front of the players again.

GEOFF: I don't want to be told to do push-ups again.

LAURIE: If you break discipline you do push-ups. Everyone does.

GEOFF: I don't.

LAURIE: Nobody else objects to push-ups.

GEOFF: That's because most of them have got ear to ear bone.

LAURIE: I see. You've done a few subjects at University so you're out of our class.

GEOFF: If they like doing push-ups I must be.

LAURIE: All right. Point taken. You don't like push-ups, but it goes deeper than that, doesn't it? Why are you playing so badly?

GEOFF: I'm doing my best.

LAURIE: No you're not. You played two good games at the start of the year, you went to pieces in your third game and you've got progressively worse ever since.

GEOFF: I've lost form.

LAURIE: It's more than that. You're not even trying. Is it just that you object to me personally or is there some other reason?

GEOFF: I've lost form. That's all.

LAURIE: Look, I know there's some degree of antagonism from the other players. You came to the Club with a big reputation and a lot of money so there's bound to be, but it's not going to help matters if you lay down and stop trying.

GEOFF: You're reading too much into it. I've lost form.

LAURIE: It's more than that. Last week you stood down on the forward line staring into the crowd for over a minute. The ball came and you let it go right past you. Look, level with me, Geoff. That's more than being out of form. What's going on?

GEOFF: All right. If you really want to know, what's going on is that I'm sick to death of football and I couldn't care less if I never played another game in my life. It's all a lot of macho-competitive bullshit. You chase a lump of pigskin around a muddy ground as if your bloody life depended on it and when you get it you kick it to buggery and go chasing it again. Football shits me.

LAURIE: I wish you'd let us know your attitude to the game before we paid ninety thousand dollars for you.

GEOFF: If you think you can buy me like a lump of meat then you'd better think again.

LAURIE: You took our money with your eyes open, Geoff. Don't you think you owe us something?

GEOFF: If you're stupid enough to offer me that sort of money I'll take it, but all you've bought is my presence out on an oval for two hours every Saturday afternoon.

LAURIE: We thought we were buying a lot more than that.

GEOFF: Took your money? It was practically thrown at me. You weren't there at that final sign-up session?

[GEOFF *shakes his head ruefully.*]

It was a joke. There were three of my guys on one side of the table and Gerry, Jock and Ted on the other. Jock was looking at me, and I'm not joking, as if I was a giant pork chop. He was almost salivating. I felt sure that any moment he'd bring out a little hammer and test whether my reflexes are as good as they're cracked up to be. I couldn't believe that those three goons were for real. By the time we'd got ourselves through the pleasantries I was getting pretty crapped off and I decided to make myself a bit difficult, so when they shoved the form in front of me to sign, I read it through four times, put down the pen, shook my head and said I wanted more money. I didn't really expect to get any more — I just wanted to establish myself as something more than a tailor's dummy — but it was marvellous. All hell broke loose. Your guys called my guys cheats, Jock thumped our President on the snout, and Gerry sat there stirring his coffee with a retractable biro. I was just about to burst out laughing when I looked across and there was Ted Parker sitting in the middle of all this pandemonium, his face as white as a sheet, scribbling frantically in his cheque book. 'Ten thousand,' he yelled. 'I'll go an extra ten thousand, but that's my limit.' Everyone had a ball.

LAURIE: Are you still living with that girl?

GEOFF: Susy? Yes. Why? Do you think she's a corrupting influence?

LAURIE: She didn't seem very interested in your football career when I met her.

GEOFF: She's not.

LAURIE: She thinks it's macho-competitive bullshit too?

GEOFF: You can't exactly blame her, when it gets to the point where we start coming to blows behind the lockers.

LAURIE: How's your jaw?

GEOFF: Still sore. How's your gut?

LAURIE: Likewise.

GEOFF: Push-ups are one thing but slugging me into submission just isn't on.

LAURIE: I know. I'm sorry. I love football and I love this Club and it's a bit hard for me to understand someone who holds both of them in contempt.

GEOFF: Love the Club? Jock, Ted and Gerry?

LAURIE: The Club's not Jock, Ted and Gerry. It's nearly a hundred years of history.

GEOFF: Yeah. Well I missed the history and copped Jock, Ted and Gerry. Honestly, what's an old fool like Jock doing in a position of power?

LAURIE: He was a great player, and whether he deserved to or not he won four premierships when he was our coach.

GEOFF: Didn't he deserve to win them?

LAURIE: We're not here to talk about Jock.

GEOFF: Was he a bad coach?

LAURIE: Yes.

GEOFF: How come he got those premierships then?

LAURIE: [*irritated*] He got them in his first six years, in the days when the best talent in the country was fighting to get a purple and gold guernsey. By the time I took over all of that had long finished.

GEOFF: Someone told me that you were responsible for getting him the sack.

LAURIE: I thought he was coaching disgracefully and I did some lobbying. I'll admit that to anyone. He dosed himself up with whisky before the '67 Grand Final and halfway through the last quarter he took Benny McPhee out of the centre where he was really firing and put him at full forward, where he was never sighted. It cost us the premiership. Why are you so interested in Jock?

GEOFF: I'm not. It just amuses me to see you guys sticking around in this Club for years, having your little power battles, cutting each others throats and filling up your lives with petty nonsense.

LAURIE: I might be old fashioned but it seems important to me to step in and do something when a great Club's going downhill because of incompetent coaching.

GEOFF: I don't want to play the devil's advocate but you've done some pretty bad coaching yourself lately.

LAURIE: Such as?

GEOFF: Such as not shifting Danny off Wilson last week. He was getting thrashed.

LAURIE: I know.

GEOFF: Wilson was leaving him for dead.

LAURIE: [*irritably*] I know.

GEOFF: Then why didn't you shift him?

LAURIE: Because he was desperate to keep trying. He's never been that badly beaten before. I know it was the wrong thing to do but Danny's been the backbone of my team for eight years and I felt I owed him something. Besides, I doubt whether there's anyone in the team who could've done any better.

GEOFF: I could beat Wilson.

LAURIE: You? You were down the other end of the ground staring into the crowd!

GEOFF: I could beat him.

LAURIE: [*angrily*] I'm getting pretty bloody fed up with your arrogance, Geoff. You've been paid a fortune and you won't even try, and when I try and talk to you about it you give me a lecture about how petty my life is, and to cap it all off you nonchalantly tell me you could beat Wilson when in the last five weeks you've hardly got a kick. I was watching you carefully last week and you couldn't even outrun Butcher Malone.

GEOFF: I was stoned.

LAURIE: Drunk?

GEOFF: Stoned.

LAURIE: Marihuana?

GEOFF: Hash.

LAURIE: Why?

GEOFF: Because it feels fantastic. Five minutes after you smoke it your head lifts right off your shoulders. I wasn't looking out into the crowd, incidentally, I was watching a seagull. Not just an ordinary seagull. It was the prince of seagulls, dazzling me with blasts of pure white everytime its wings caught the sun. The roar of the crowd paid homage to its grace and beauty. You ought to try some, Laurie. It alters your whole perspective on things.

LAURIE: Are you stoned now?

GEOFF: [*nods*] I had a smoke before I came.

LAURIE: Are you addicted?

GEOFF: You don't get addicted to hash, Laurie. Hey, did you see me fly for the ball in the second quarter? I was so far up over the pack I felt like Achilles chasing the golden orb.

LAURIE: Jesus, Geoff. How am I supposed to deal with this?

GEOFF: Just don't ask me to do push-ups.

[JOCK *pokes his head through the right door. He is smiling affably.*]

JOCK: Sorted things out yet?

GEOFF: Not quite.

JOCK: Would you like me to have a talk to the lad, Laurie? Sometimes a fresh viewpoint can help in these sort of situations.

LAURIE: [*irritated*] No.

JOCK: Just give me a few minutes, Laurie. I've got something I want to say to him.

> [LAURIE *gets up, looking at* JOCK *in an irritated way, and leaves through the left door.*]

He's got it in for you, I'm afraid, Geoff. Not to worry. We'll sort it out. You did some nice things last week. Not one of your best games but you did some nice things. Glorious mark you took in the second quarter. You just seemed to go up and up.

GEOFF: I felt like Achilles.

JOCK: Who's he?

GEOFF: A Greek guy who could really jump.

JOCK: [*nods*] Some of our new Australians could be champions if they'd stop playing soccer and assimilate. Why did Butcher Malone take a swing at you when you hit the deck? Did you give him an elbow in the gut?

GEOFF: No, I blew him a kiss.

JOCK: That's good. That's subtle. I was a bit more direct in my day, although I did have a little trick that used to throw 'em out of their stride, come to think of it. You know those times when you're half a yard behind your man and he's going for the ball and there doesn't seem any way you can stop him?

> [GEOFF *nods.*]

Well, the thing in your favour is that everyone, including the umpire, is looking at the ball, right?

GEOFF: Right.

JOCK: Right. Well as soon as your man leaves the ground, get your thumb and ram it up his arse. Works every time.

GEOFF: Sounds effective.

JOCK: It's a beauty. Wait here while I have a piss.

> [*As* JOCK *moves to the door he notices that* GEOFF *has taken out a pouch of tobacco. He stops.*]

Roll your own?

GEOFF: Mmm.

JOCK: I used to roll my own.

GEOFF: Would you like me to roll you one?

JOCK: Yeah. Thanks. I'll be back in a minute and we'll have a nice quiet smoke and a little chat.

> [GEOFF *nods his head as* JOCK *goes out the door. He fishes in his back pocket and takes out a tin. He looks at the door through which* JOCK *has gone, looks at the tin, nods his head and smiles.*]

END OF ACT ONE

ACT TWO

JOCK *re-enters. A minute or two has elapsed.* GEOFF *has rolled two cigarettes. He smokes one and hands the other to* JOCK.

JOCK: [*coughing*] Hope you don't smoke too many of these?

GEOFF: Eh?

JOCK: Makes you short of breath. How many do you have a day?

GEOFF: Three or four.

JOCK: Ah, that's no problem. [*Inhaling*] Quite strong. You get a bit used to having it filtered. Laurie's a bit worried about your form lately. I think you're playing well but Laurie thinks you could do better. I do too. I don't think you're playing as badly as Laurie thinks you are but I think you could do better. What do you think?

GEOFF: I think I could too.

JOCK: Good lad. Puts me in a bit of a spot if you're down on form because I was the bugger that stuck me neck out and said we had to get you. The first time I saw you play I knew you were a freak. One in a million. I still think I'm right. Nothing's worrying you, is it?

GEOFF: No.

JOCK: No problems with women?

GEOFF: No.

JOCK: Don't screw too many or you'll get the jack.

[*There is a pause.*]

I get the feeling something is worrying you, Geoff.

GEOFF: You could be right.

JOCK: I've got an instinct about problems. Do you want to talk about it?

GEOFF: I don't know whether I can.

JOCK: It won't get any further than this room if you do. You know that.

GEOFF: Thanks.

JOCK: Have you been able to talk about it to Laurie?

[GEOFF *shakes his head.* JOCK *looks pleased.*]

Yeah. It's hard to talk heart to heart with Laurie. He lacks that little human touch. When I was coach I used to spend hours with my men — joking, chatting, horsing around — but

163

Laurie's a bit stand offish. Not really one of the boys, don't you think? Bit remote.

GEOFF: Well, he hasn't told me too many jokes.

JOCK: That's right. No sense of humour. None at all. Bit of a fanatic, don't you think?

GEOFF: He lives for football.

JOCK: Right. I used to take the boys up to a country race meeting sometimes in the middle of the week to break the tension and we'd have a few beers and a laugh and it was great. But Laurie would never come. He'd stay back and train by himself in the middle of the oval for hours and hours. Bloody fanatic even then. Do the players really like him?

GEOFF: They seem to.

JOCK: I can't understand that. He seems too stand-offish. I was one of the boys when I was coach and they'd do anything for me. Of course, you'll hear some stories that my men weren't fit but that's all bullshit. I didn't make a god of fitness and overtrain my men like Laurie; but they were fit, and if you hear any stories that my discipline was lax and that I played favourites, don't believe that either. If someone didn't do what I told 'em I tore strips off them whether they were my drinking mates or not. Laurie started all those stories. He's always had it in for me. From the minute he joined the Club he's made it his business to rewrite the Club's history with him as its biggest shining star. He was obsessed with beating my record of two hundred and eighty two games. Absolutely obsessed. He had a bad groin injury and a dicey hamstring and he was in agony every time he went out onto the field but there was no stopping him.

GEOFF: He didn't beat it though, did he?

JOCK: No, he tripped over little Rabbit Rutherford coming out of a pack and did his cartilages with three games to go, and I can't say I was sorry; in fact to tell you the truth, I laughed me bloody head off. No, I'll make no bones about it. I've got no love for Laurie. Not after the way he took over as coach. I know the style of game had changed and I was making a few mistakes — I was brought up on a different brand of football, not this modern play on, killer instinct, steamroller, win at all costs stuff — and if anyone had have put it to me straight and open that I was getting a bit past it I probably would've agreed and stepped down like a man. But that's not Laurie's style. He

went around to the members of the Committee behind my
back and told them I was drunk during the '67 Grand Final. I
had a cold and I had a few sips of whisky, but I wasn't drunk.
He'd had his eye on the job for years. He just waited till I
made one little mistake and went in for the kill. He'll keep.
He's going to get his. He promised that Committee the world
and he hasn't won them one premiership. Not one bloody
premiership and I've won four. I don't wonder that you're
having trouble with him, Geoff, and I don't blame you at all
because you've got real ability and you can see through him.
He can't command the respect of anyone of real ability and he
never will. What we need around here is a man of authority
who can command, because these days it's fear that wins you
premierships, Geoff, I'm afraid. These days the game is so
bloody tough that you've got to get your players so scared of
making a mistake that they go out there and play the game in a
state of fucking terror. Fear's what wins you premierships and
Laurie couldn't scare a field mouse.

  [*There is a pause.*]

Yes, I can understand why you can't discuss anything with
Laurie and I just wanted you to know that I'm on side. What's
your problem?

GEOFF: It's a bit difficult to know where to begin. It is to do with
  women.

JOCK: Usually is. Are you going with anyone in particular?

GEOFF: No.

JOCK: What about that tall sheila I saw you with at the Club ball?

GEOFF: She's just a friend.

JOCK: Jesus, I'll tell you what. I wish I had a few friends like that.
  I don't mind admitting, Geoff; I was having a bit of a perve.
  Did she know you could see straight through that thing she
  was wearing?

GEOFF: I think that was the idea.

JOCK: Marvellous looker, Geoff. Couldn't keep my eyes off her.

GEOFF: She's a beautiful girl.

JOCK: So what's your problem?

GEOFF: It's so bloody embarrassing.

JOCK: Get it off your chest.

GEOFF: You'll keep it absolutely secret, Jock. It'd destroy me if it
  ever got out.

JOCK: It won't get past this room, lad.

GEOFF: It's not that I'm not attracted to women, Jock. I am. Desperately attracted. But when it gets to the vital . . .
[*Pause.*]

JOCK: Can't you get your act together?
[GEOFF *shakes his head morosely.*]
Hell.

GEOFF: For Christ's sake keep that to yourself, Jock.

JOCK: Maybe you're training too hard. I could never get it up on Saturday night after a match. Have you er, always had, er, this sort of problem?

GEOFF: No. At one stage of my life I had no problem at all.

JOCK: Mind you, you're not the only one. There was an article in the Sunday paper that said that the young men of the nation were being swept by an epidemic of impotence. Woman has become the hunter and man the hunted. Bloody unnatural.

GEOFF: I don't think it's that.

JOCK: Have you seen a doctor?

GEOFF: Yes. There's nothing wrong with me physically. It's up here.
[GEOFF *taps his head.*]

JOCK: Yeah, well I'm a bit suspicious of these psychological explanations. Nothing up there [*tapping his head*] could've stopped my old trooper rising to the occasion. Are you sure you're not training too hard?

GEOFF: It's not that. It's my family.

JOCK: Your family?

GEOFF: They've screwed me up. In more ways than one.

JOCK: Yeah?

GEOFF: You don't mind me telling you this, Jock?

JOCK: No, not at all.

GEOFF: It gets pretty sordid.

JOCK: Fire away.

GEOFF: It won't get past this room?

JOCK: Certainly won't.

GEOFF: Have I ever talked to you about my sister?

JOCK: No. I didn't know you had one.

GEOFF: I don't speak about her very often. She was in a serious car accident the night before her eighteenth birthday. I was only fourteen.

JOCK: Badly hurt?

GEOFF: Very. Both legs were amputated above the knee.

JOCK: Hell.

GEOFF: It would've been tragic for anyone — but for someone as young and beautiful as Gabrielle it was shattering. She wasn't just beautiful either, Jock; she was intelligent, warm, cheerful, popular — she had everything going for her. We tried to keep a stiff lip but I was distraught and so were my parents. Every time I looked at her I had to turn my head away so that she wouldn't see me cry, because the last thing she wanted was pity. I just can't tell you how brave she was, Jock. Don't be sad, she'd say. I'm still alive and I've still got my family. I mean Jesus, is that courage, Jock? Is it?

JOCK: That's courage.

GEOFF: One night I heard her crying in the dark in the next room and it became too much for me to bear — is this all too much for you, Jock?

JOCK: No, no, go on.

GEOFF: You're looking a bit pale.

JOCK: No, no. It's just that the tobacco's stronger than I'm used to. Go on.

GEOFF: So I went and lay beside her and held her in my arms and we cried together. For hours. Every night after that I'd comfort her in the same way and we'd lie together crying in the dark, then one night . . . I'm sorry Jock, I shouldn't inflict this story on anyone. You're looking as white as a sheet.

JOCK: It's the tobacco. Honest.

GEOFF: Are you sure it's not getting too heavy?

JOCK: No. Go on.

GEOFF: Well, without either of us knowing quite how or why, we became lovers.

JOCK: Jesus.

GEOFF: We knew what we were doing was wrong. The surprising thing was that we didn't care. It all seemed so right. Can you understand that, Jock? It was wrong but it was right. Can you understand that?

JOCK: No legs?

GEOFF: It sounds sordid but it wasn't. I loved her, Jock.

JOCK: How long did this go on?

GEOFF: Not long. One night when Dad was away on one of his many business trips the light was suddenly switched on and there was my mother.

JOCK: Hell.

GEOFF: Can you imagine how we felt? Can you imagine how she felt? I can still see her standing there. Still young, and still beautiful in a flowing silk negligee and with a look of utter shock on her face. There was nothing she could say to us and there was nothing we could say to her. She turned off the light and went back to her room and we clung together listening to her sobbing. Finally I couldn't stand it any longer. I picked up my sister and carried her to Mother's room and we all clung together crying like lost souls in the dark. Gradually as the night wore on . . . this is too much for you, isn't it, Jock?

JOCK: No, really.

GEOFF: It gets worse.

JOCK: Go on.

GEOFF: Again, I've no idea quite how and why but my mother and I became lovers too.

JOCK: Hell.

GEOFF: Three nights later my father arrived home early from a conference . . .

JOCK: Hell.

GEOFF: He looked at the three of us and said just one thing. 'You've killed me, son.' Three days later he shot himself. I've been impotent ever since.

JOCK: No bloody wonder.

GEOFF: It's got so bad that every time I run out onto the ground I feel as if everyone's whispering to each other about me. I just can't concentrate on the game.

[JOCK *frowns and takes another puff of his cigarette. He looks at the photos on the walls, blinks his eyes and looks at them again.*]

JOCK: I'm going to have to lay it on the line I'm afraid, Geoff. It wasn't right to get involved with your sister or your mother and I can't pretend I'm not disgusted, but the Club must not suffer because you happen to have no moral bloody sense. The thing in our favour is that no one knows about it, so thinking that anyone's whispering about you is nonsense and you just better get out there and start playing.

[JOCK *turns, looks at the photos again and frowns.*]

That bloody tobacco's made my eyes go funny. I'll swear I saw those photos move. Quite frankly I had my doubts about paying eighty thousand for a Protestant. If a good Catholic lad so much as even thought of screwing his handicapped sister he'd still be down on his hands and knees yelling Hail Marys, but the damage is done. I held out for you and I'm the one that's going to be crucified if any of this ever comes out. I've got all kinds of enemies around this place and most of 'em are up there on that wall.

[JOCK *looks at a particular photo.*]

Look at that frown on Jimmy McPhee. Look at all of them just itching to sit in judgement.

[JOCK *turns back to* GEOFF.]

This is worrying, Geoff. Extremely worrying. They know that I was the one responsible for getting you. The word gets around.

[JOCK *turns again to the photo of McPhee.*]

Wipe that bloody frown off your face, McPhee.

[GERRY *comes in through the right door as* JOCK, *with his back to him addresses the photo.*]

You shouldn't even be up on the bloody wall. You only played eighty-nine games and none of 'em were worth a cracker. Hacks and dead-beats the lot of you. The only photo that should be up there is mine. Two hundred and eighty two games and four premierships!

GERRY: What in the hell are you carrying on about?

JOCK: We're in trouble, Gerry. Big trouble.

GERRY: We will be if you don't pull yourself together.

[*He takes* JOCK *aside.*]

I've just had a phone call from Bob. The whole thing's hitting the press sooner than we expected.

JOCK: The stuff about Geoff?

GERRY: What stuff about Geoff?

JOCK: He's a nut.

GERRY: If he gets too hard to handle we'll sell him. Now pull yourself together. The stuff about Ted is hitting the press on Sunday. What's that smell?

JOCK: Ted?

GERRY: Yes, Ted. You'll just have to cut down on your drinking, Jock. You'll jeopardise our whole plan of operations. The stuff about Ted is coming out on Sunday. We can probably force him to resign tonight.

JOCK: Sunday? That's earlier than we expected.

GERRY: I just said that.

JOCK: We could probably force him to resign tonight.

GERRY: I just said that too. Now get yourself into shape before the meeting. It's going to be a tough night.

[GERRY *storms back through the right door.* JOCK *turns to* GEOFF.]

JOCK: Yeah, well look, my boy. I'm going to put it to you right on the line. Stay right away from your family and concentrate on the Club. There are really exciting things happening here next year and if you want to miss out on it all, then we'll bloody well sell you.

GEOFF: What things?

JOCK: We're getting some great new players and a fantastic coach. Oh shit. I shouldn't've said that . . . What is wrong with my head? Just keep that quiet. Laurie's had his chance and last week was the last straw. He's done his dough. A five year old could've seen that Danny had to be taken off Wilson.

GEOFF: Who's the new coach?

JOCK: The best. The very best. We're throwing out the old tradition that the coach has to have played for the Club.

[*He turns to the photos.*]

Why should these old hacks get first go at a plum job? We're going for the very best. We're getting great players too, so if you pull your socks up and start trying you could find yourself the star in a team full of champions; so stop feeling sorry for yourself and start trying or we'll cut our losses and sell you to a deadbeat team up the Mallee.

[*There is a knock at the door and* LAURIE *enters from the left.*]

LAURIE: Are you finished, Jock? I'd like another word with Geoff.

JOCK: Yeah, I'm finished. You remember what I said Geoff. I'm not joking.

[JOCK *leaves through the right hand door.*]

LAURIE: What was all that about?

GEOFF: Jock got a little bit heavy.

LAURIE: Well, I'm going to get a bit heavy too. I'm not very impressed with your attitude, Geoff. Danny's down below playing pool. He hasn't got half of your natural ability or your brains; he's fucked up his personal life and he's coming to the end of his football career, but he's thrown every ounce of his energy for the last ten years into doing as well as he possibly could for the Club and for me; and I admire that, because if you've got talent you've got a responsibility to use it and not fuck around. So if you're ever out on that field again and you're not a hundred per cent fit, a hundred per cent clear headed and a hundred per cent trying then you'll never play another game for this Club in your life, Selection Committee or no Selection Committee. You look me in the eyes, Geoff, and listen to what I'm saying. You might think it's a big joke to smoke and screw and take Ted down for ten thousand dollars; but I don't think it's all that funny.

GEOFF: I didn't take him down.

LAURIE: You took him down.

GEOFF: He took himself down, the stupid little turd.

LAURIE: All right, he's a stupid little turd. He's also seen every game this Club's played since he was six years old and I know that that's the last thing that'd impress you, but by Christ it impresses me.

GEOFF: What's ten thousand dollars to him? He's rich.

LAURIE: He's not. He's about to go bankrupt. Now maybe I'm just feeling guilty about what I did to him in the press this morning, but I promise you if you don't start playing football then I'm going to make you give him back every cent of his money, even if I have to pound it out of you. Right? Look at me?

GEOFF: Laurie, you're giving me the shits.

LAURIE: And so are you. If you're really on about love and peace and non-competitiveness then pay back your money and get out. Get out for good and don't fuck around. If you hate the game and all it stands for, then get out; but I'll tell you one thing — you'll miss it. I've seen you swelled up with bloody pride out there. I've seen you so bloody pleased with yourself that you've had tears in your eyes.

GEOFF: Bullshit.

LAURIE: It's not bullshit. Don't think I couldn't tell what was going on in your mind when you took the opposition apart in the first match. You thought that you were fantastic. You thought that you were the greatest footballer alive.

GEOFF: It was good. So what. So is being stoned and making love to Susy.

LAURIE: Anyone can get stoned and make love to Susy.

GEOFF: That's a pretty distasteful assertion.

LAURIE: You know what I mean. It's a great feeling when you're out there playing well and you're going to miss it. I ought to know. I've been missing it for fifteen years. If you want my honest opinion, the reason you're into drugs and non-competitiveness is that you tried a few things that didn't come off in your third game and you've been scared ever since.

GEOFF: Scared?

LAURIE: Yes. Scared that you're not half as good a footballer as you bloody well thought you were. You're in the top league now, Geoff, and there's lots of competition. It's no good saying you could beat Wilson, you've got to do it.

GEOFF: Don't try that one on me.

LAURIE: You're scared.

GEOFF: Lay off the primitive psychology, Laurie.

LAURIE: We've got Taylor against us tomorrow. It's no good telling me you could beat him either. You've got to do it.

GEOFF: I've watched these sort of films too, Laurie. What I'm supposed to do now is leap up and say: 'I will. I'll eat that bastard for breakfast,' and go out and play the game of my life. Is that right?

LAURIE: If you're not scared, then why do you have to drug yourself up before you go out on the field?

GEOFF: Because football bores me. I've done it all, Laurie. When I was twelve I was living in a little country town and my ultimate dream was to get a game in the local firsts. Six years later I was picked in the State side. I was an acknowledged champion.

LAURIE: No you weren't. You were just a young kid with a lot of potential and you still are. Anyone who wasn't cross-eyed and bandy-legged could get a game with the Tasmanian State side. When you've got the guts to go out there and take on proven champions like Wilson and Taylor, and when you start to miss the roar of the grandstand, then come back and tell me you're trying. Until then you can sit and rot in the reserves for the arrogant young turd you are.

GEOFF: I'm more than a kid with potential, Laurie. Tasmania's provided this State with more champions than you can name. They don't pay eighty thousand dollars for a kid with potential.

LAURIE: Normal people wouldn't, but as you've pointed out, this Club is run by morons. Now if you don't come to your senses I'm going to drop you to the reserves for the rest of the year, and the year after that and the year after that. As far as I'm

concerned you can play out the rest of your career in the
reserves and be damned to the eighty thousand dollars. Now
get out of here and don't come back until you mean business.

[GEOFF, *who is angry at* LAURIE'*s dismissal of him as a 'kid with
potential', opens his mouth to reply, but sees that* LAURIE *is in a
towering rage, so he shuts it and leaves through the left door.*
LAURIE *takes out a packet of cigarettes and lights one, trying to
calm himself.* TED *enters through the right door looking
agitated and angry.*]

Have you sent out the press statement?

TED: They're trying to force me to resign.

[TED *moves across to the presidential chair at the head of the
committee table.*]

LAURIE: What do you mean, force you?

[GERRY *enters through the right door followed by* JOCK.]

GERRY: I just thought you might want to resign. That's all.

TED: There's no way in the world I'm going to resign.

GERRY: It's up to you, Ted. I'm sure the Committee will back you
if you want to battle this whole thing through.

TED: I'll battle it through and I'll expect a hundred per cent
loyalty from the Committee.

JOCK: You won't get it from me.

TED: I wouldn't expect it from you. Or from Laurie. But I'll get
it from the rest.

JOCK: If you were a man you'd step down right now.

TED: Cowards duck. Men fight.

JOCK: Fight who? Women?

TED: You believe her story, I suppose. Every word.

JOCK: Why shouldn't I? Gerry was there.

TED: I slapped her. That's all Gerry saw.

GERRY: You hit her at least once, Ted.

TED: I slapped her.

GERRY: If it comes to the point of testifying, I'll say that I was
confused and I wasn't sure what you did. But you did hit her.

JOCK: With closed fists too, you mongrel. Don't expect me to be
sorry for you.

LAURIE: What's going on?

GERRY: Ted's in trouble, Laurie. A stripper's sueing him for
assault and the whole things going to be plastered over the
Sunday papers.

LAURIE: The stripper at the fund raising night?

TED: I didn't hit her. It's a load of trumped up garbage. If the Committee sticks with me, we'll see it through.

LAURIE: I thought you only fumbled with her garter?

GERRY: He followed her around backstage.

TED: She egged me on all through her act, Laurie. Eyed me off, stroked my hair, asked me to take off her garter played the vamp for all she was worth, but then when I went around backstage she switched it all off and treated me as if I was dirt under her feet. Nobody treats me like that, Laurie, least of all a little trollop like that. I'm the President of the greatest football Club in the history of the game and I won't have some little slut laugh in my face.

LAURIE: [to GERRY] Was she hurt?

TED: Of course she wasn't. I hardly touched her, but by the time the journalists have got through with me it'll sound like we went fifteen rounds.

LAURIE: How did the press find out?

GERRY: God knows. We've been doing everything possible to keep it quiet at this end.

TED: The Committee's got to support me. If everyone's behind me we can fight it through.

JOCK: I'm not supporting you, you mongrel. The medical report said she had bruises all over.

TED: What medical report?

GERRY: [hastily] Oh the . . . er . . . newspaper rang me to see if they could get a Club reaction to the incident and they mentioned a medical report that's in the hands of the girl's lawyer.

TED: I slapped her, Gerry. You've got to testify that I only slapped her.

GERRY: I'll say that I was confused. I can't say that I definitely didn't see you hit her if they've got a medical report that mentions extensive bruising. I'd go up for perjury.

TED: She must have got one of her friends to slap her around so that she'd get more money out of me. It happens all the time. I gave her twenty dollars and she was quite ready to forget the whole thing. That's how upset she was. She's gone away and thought about it and decided to make some easy money out of me.

GERRY: I wouldn't be surprised if you're right, but the public are going to believe her rather than you.

TED: [*with a touch of hysteria*] Who gives a stuff what the public believes? The facts are that she called me a pig and I slapped her. I'm the greatest President this Club has ever had. I've singlehandedly wrenched it out of the stone age against pressures that would've broken a lesser man. I've fought a pitched battle against the forces of tradition and conservatism and I've won; in fact I've been so bloody successful that those very forces have turned around and adopted my ideas as if they were their own.

JOCK: Are you referring to me?

TED: [*with more than a touch of hysteria*] Yes, I am referring to you. I've changed the whole future course of this Club and because of what I've done the next years are going to be the greatest years we've ever had. We're going to have a triumph that'll make the great years of the '20s look pale by comparison. We're going to dominate the League for the next decade and I'm going to be here while we're doing it. No little trollop is going to deprive me of that! The Committee will stick by me to a man.

JOCK: You want to bet.

TED: I'd stake my life on it.

JOCK: Then you're a dead man. The Club's not going to let its name be dragged through the mud just to save your hide, Parker. I'm going to move that you stand down.

TED: You won't get a seconder.

JOCK: Want to bet?

TED: Even if you do you won't get the numbers on committee.

JOCK: Want to bet?

TED: Who have you got?

JOCK: Tony, Ian, Jack and Kevin for starters.

TED: Bullshit. They don't even know about it yet.

GERRY: They do. I rang around as soon as the paper rang me.

TED: Ian and Kevin are my friends, Jock. If anyone's going to stick with me they will.

JOCK: Want to bet?

GERRY: The one thing you've got to understand, Ted, is that if the consensus is that you do resign, then it's not necessarily because we don't think you're innocent or that we're not your friends, it's just that because we're on the Committee we've got to face realities, and the reality is that it isn't so much whether you're innocent or not that counts — it's whether the public think you're innocent; and in this case, I'm afraid, the public are going to think the worst. We just can't afford to jeopardise the credibility of the Club by retaining a President who's erred in the way that they're going to think that you've erred.

TED: What kind of logic is that?

GERRY: It's the logic of pragmatism, Ted. You ought to know that. You brought it to this Club and you were right. Loyalty to any one individual is a luxury you can't afford in a business with a multi-million dollar turn-over. I'm sorry, Ted, I'll vote to retain you; but if the majority of the Committee ask for your resignation I hope you can understand their viewpoint.

LAURIE: They're going to get you, Ted. Get out gracefully.

TED: Laurie, I've had my differences with you but I've been a good President. Not a great one but a good one. They're not going to sack me if I lay my record on the line.

LAURIE: They don't need you any longer, Ted. If they didn't need me they'd sack me too.

[TED *looks at* LAURIE *knowing that* LAURIE *is in fact to be sacked. He realises that his dismissal is inevitable and gathers the remnants of his dignity together.*]

TED: Nobody's going to sack me, Laurie. I've just resigned.

GERRY: I'm sorry that this has happened, Ted. You've been a good President and you won't be forgotten. You fought to get me my job here and I won't forget that either. I just hope I can go on to do justice to the faith you showed in me.

TED: [*blackly*] I'm sure you will. [*To* LAURIE] I hope that you and young Geoff sort out your differences. I'd like to think that my money was well spent, I doubt if I'll ever be dashing off ten thousand dollar cheques again.

LAURIE: I don't think your money will have been wasted.

[TED *puts on his overcoat and moves towards the left door.*]

TED: [*To* LAURIE] Do you know what I thought was the best game of football you ever played? The day you took on Dick Turner in '55. Mind you, I think he just shaded you. By a whisker.

LAURIE: A lot of people don't.

TED: It was like watching two magicians trying to outdo each other.

LAURIE: I think everybody got their two bob's worth.

TED: [*to* GERRY *and* JOCK] I'm not running away. I could stay here and fight and probably get the numbers but I couldn't be bothered. I've got a bedridden wife to look after and I've run

out of energy and I don't even know whether it's worth fighting when the Club's fallen into the hands of people like you. You've been scheming to get rid of me for six months and the gods have delivered me into your hands, but one day when the true history of the Club is written I'll have pride of place over you two vultures. I'll be amongst the very great ones.
[*He leaves.*]

GERRY: Poor bastard. I feel sorry for him.

JOCK: Sick in the bloody head.

GERRY: He did hit the girl. I had a hunch that something might happen when I saw him head off so I followed him. It was a hell of an ugly scene. The girl was quite hysterical.

JOCK: Mongrel. What kind of man hits a woman?

GERRY: He was screaming out that he was the President of a great club and belting her with closed fists. I put a headlock on him and dragged him off.

LAURIE: Why didn't she call the police?

GERRY: I calmed her down and gave her twenty dollars but the poor kid was only eighteen and had never stripped before and a couple of days later she freaked out and just about went off her head.

LAURIE: What day was that?

GERRY: Last Monday.

LAURIE: Who was the girl you and Jock were talking to on Tuesday?

GERRY: What girl?

LAURIE: In your office. I came to see you and your secretary said you were busy and a couple of minutes later a young girl came out. Jock was in your office too.

GERRY: We must have been interviewing someone for a secretary's job.

LAURIE: Come on. She was no secretary. Was she the stripper?

GERRY: No. Her flatmate.

LAURIE: Why was she there?

GERRY: What is this, Laurie? A Star Chamber?

LAURIE: Why was she there?

GERRY: She came to tell us that the girl who'd stripped was on the verge of a breakdown. She was having bad nightmares and wouldn't move outside her flat.

LAURIE: Did she ask you for more money?

GERRY: Yes.

LAURIE: So what did you do?

JOCK: We told her that if she wanted money she'd better go to Ted. It was nothing to do with the Club.

LAURIE: Ted hasn't got any money.

JOCK: That's not our bloody fault. She wanted the Club to pay a thousand dollars and we weren't going to come at that.

LAURIE: So what'd she do? Go to the papers?

JOCK: We didn't tell her to go to the papers. All we said is that if her flatmate was in a bad way then she should go to a lawyer.

LAURIE: And sue Ted?

GERRY: He's still got property and if the little kid is in a bad way she deserves every penny she can get.

LAURIE: You'd spend eighty thousand dollars for one player but you wouldn't spend a thousand to keep the Club President off the cover of a scandal sheet.

GERRY: If the kid's in a bad way she deserves every penny she can get.

LAURIE: I'm sure she does, but if it hadn't've suited you to get rid of Ted right at that minute you would've written that cheque for a thousand dollars without a second thought. You put the press onto it too, didn't you?

JOCK: So what. He deserves every thing he gets, the bloody little upstart. Comes in here and takes over the Presidency and he's never played a game of football in his life.

LAURIE: I won't hold you up. You probably want to go in there and drink to your success.

GERRY: I can't see why you're getting so bloody moral about all this, Laurie. You carted him into the press yourself this morning.

JOCK: Yeah, he's not exactly your favourite person. I'd pay a thousand dollars to get him in a scandal sheet. What a bloody disgrace to the Club. Hitting a woman. What a bloody disgrace to those champions up there.

[JOCK *indicates the photos on the wall.*]

LAURIE: Do you know what, Jock? .

JOCK: What?

LAURIE: You're a hypocritical old bastard.

JOCK: Well, it is a bloody disgrace.

LAURIE: I would've thought that a man who's given his wife as many black eyes as you have wouldn't be quite so self-righteous.

JOCK: You're too smart for your own good, Laurie. You've needled me and picked at me from the very first minute you came here.

LAURIE: Underneath that rough charm of yours that's served you so well over the years, Jock old mate, there's a cunning and ruthless old turd.

JOCK: You've had it in for me ever since I laid you out behind the lockers.

LAURIE: That certainly didn't help. A tap on the shoulder and a king hit before I could raise a finger in my defence, but I shouldn't've been surprised. I knew what you were all about long before that. I saw the last game of football you ever played.

JOCK: Bullshit. You would've still been in nappies.

LAURIE: I was six, and I'd wormed my way right down to the fence. What was the name of that little guy you flattened?

JOCK: You weren't there.

LAURIE: Yes I was. In fact the whole thing happened only about twenty yards away from where I was standing. You waited until he started to pick himself up off the ground, lined him up, and went straight into him with your knee. He was about five foot seven and ten stone. What was his name again, Jock?

GERRY: That's enough, Laurie.

JOCK: He wasn't as badly hurt as the papers made out.

LAURIE: He did recover. Eventually. Some people think that you retired after that match out of remorse but I know you better. The Club was told by every other club around the League that if you ever took the field again you'd be lucky to get off it alive.

JOCK: They didn't scare me.

LAURIE: Not much they didn't.

JOCK: Nobody's ever called me a coward before.

LAURIE: Well, I'm calling you one now, and if you're going to be our new President then it's my last year as coach.

JOCK: It's going to be your last year in any case, smartarse. We're going to get ourselves a real coach here next year, thank Christ, so stick that in your pipe and smoke it.

[JOCK *storms out through the right door.* GERRY, *furious that this information has been disclosed, glares at* JOCK *as he passes.*]

LAURIE: Am I being sacked?

GERRY: There's some talk that your contract mightn't be renewed. Some of the Committee feel that you've had a fair chance and haven't come up with the goods.

LAURIE: Who are you getting?

GERRY: I don't think anyone's got as far as thinking about that.

LAURIE: [*indicating photos*] There's no one up there who's as good as I am.

GERRY: I think there's some talk of dispensing with the tradition that the coach must have played for the Club.

LAURIE: I see. Just like that. Well, there's no need to ask who you're after.

GERRY: He gets results.

LAURIE: Yes, he does.

GERRY: You've had eight years, Laurie, and you haven't come up with the goods.

LAURIE: I haven't had the players to come up with the goods, and the reason that I haven't had them is that all through those years Jock kept thumping the table, pointing to those photos and shouting that the Club had never paid for its champions in the past and it wasn't going to start now. All right. He won four premierships. With the players he had I could've won ten. You can't do this to me, Gerry. I've worked my guts out for eight years bringing ratshit teams up off the bottom of the ladder. If you give me half of the names that have been mentioned here tonight I'll win you a premiership.

GERRY: I don't doubt it. The irony of this whole situation — and I know that this isn't going to make you feel any better, is that I've done a thorough check around the traps and after Rostoff you're considered the next best coach in the business. Different styles, of course, but no one doubts your effectiveness. The chances are that you could win us that flag, but the Club's been waiting nineteen years and the Committee wants to be absolutely sure. We've got a two-million-dollar annual turnover and you can't afford to risk that sort of money on sentiment. Do you see our point of view?

LAURIE: Yes. Quite clearly.

GERRY: You'll have no trouble finding another team to coach.

LAURIE: I don't want another team to coach.

GERRY: Try not to get too angry, Laurie.

[LAURIE, *in a fury, stares at* GERRY. JOCK *bursts in through the right door.*]

JOCK: I've been called all sorts of things in my time by sports writers, Laurie, but never a coward!

LAURIE: You were a thug as a footballer and a failure as a coach. You're the last person who should be our President.

JOCK: You can call me what you like, Laurie, but the record books are going to show that I played three more games than you did, and won four more premierships, and they're still going to be saying it in a hundred years.

[JOCK *leaves through the right door.*]

LAURIE: I'm going to fight this, Gerry. I'm going to go to every member of the Committee and tell them what an oily little weasel you are.

GERRY: It won't do you any good. They've made up their minds. Their first loyalty is to the thousands of supporters out there who want a premiership: and so it should be. If the Club doesn't think like that, then it won't survive.

LAURIE: If this Club survives by spreading a man over the front pages of a scandal sheet and sacking a man who's never been given a fair chance to prove himself, then its survival isn't of much importance.

[LAURIE *goes to the wall and takes down his own photograph.*]

I love this Club and I love the game, Gerry, and my photo's not going back up there until you and Jock are gone.

GERRY: I don't love the Club and I don't particularly like the game and that might make me an oily weasel in your eyes, but I'm the best football administrator in the country and you're only the second best coach, so don't count on being able to return that photo for quite a long while.

LAURIE: Get out of here, Gerry, or I'll bloody well take you apart.

[GERRY *leaves through the right door.* LAURIE, *with his photo tucked under his arm, picks up his coat and turns to leave.* GEOFF *enters.*]

What do you want?

GEOFF: I'm looking for Ted.

LAURIE: He's gone.

GEOFF: I've written a cheque for him. For ten thousand dollars.

LAURIE: Good for you.

GEOFF: You won't be able to hold that over me again.

LAURIE: I'm not interested in holding anything over you. I just want to know if you're going to start trying, because if you're not, you're going straight down into the reserves. I meant what I said.

GEOFF: I'll do what I've been paid to do. Is that your photo?

LAURIE: Yes.

GEOFF: Have they told you you're getting the sack?

LAURIE: Yes. How did you know about it?

GEOFF: I heard it from Jock.

LAURIE: It seems that everyone's heard about it except me. Look, Geoff. I'm asking you for the first and last time for your help. You're not just a kid with potential, you're an amazingly bloody talented footballer, and I want you to take over the centre from Danny tomorrow.

GEOFF: Danny's not going to like that.

LAURIE: Let me worry about that. You're the only one in the team that can match Taylor so I want you to play centre. I want to win that game very badly and give the Committee a kick in the teeth.

GEOFF: I don't like our chances.

LAURIE: Neither do I if you're going to be a pessimist right from the word go. We can win.

GEOFF: It'd be a hell of an upset if we did.

LAURIE: You did lose confidence after that third game, didn't you?

GEOFF: A little bit.

LAURIE: There's no need to be touchy. It happens to all of us. I only got seven kicks in my third game and for the next four matches I wasn't worth a cracker. Stand away from Taylor at the first bounce and I'll get Alan to knock it to you instead of Keith. If you get that first kick and do something with it you'll be right for the rest of the match. I'm sorry I asked you to do fifty push-ups but if you're playing under Rostoff next year you'll have three assistants noting down every mistake you make and at half time you'll be screamed at and told you're a gutless turd in front of the whole team.

GEOFF: [gloomily] I thought they might be getting Rostoff.

LAURIE: Yeah, well they haven't got him yet. If you play well enough and the team plays well enough for the rest of the year they'll find it pretty hard to sack me.

GEOFF: Do you think?

LAURIE: If we make the finals it'll be pretty embarrassing for them.

GEOFF: Finals?

LAURIE: It's not impossible.

GEOFF: I suppose not.

LAURIE: If we win twelve of the next fifteen games we'd make it.

GEOFF: It doesn't sound so impossible when you put it like that.

LAURIE: It's not impossible.

[DANNY *knocks and enters through the left door.*]

DANNY: Still going. Don't waste your time on him.

LAURIE: It's O.K. Geoff's going to start trying.

DANNY: About time.

LAURIE: They're sacking me, Danny.

DANNY: When?

LAURIE: At the end of the year.

GEOFF: They're getting Rostoff.

DANNY: Rostoff? Like hell they are. I'll call the boys.

LAURIE: No strikes, Danny. If you really want to help me the best thing you could all do is to try like hell for the rest of the year.

DANNY: Try like hell?

GEOFF: They'd find it pretty hard to sack Laurie if we made the finals.

DANNY: Bastards. We'll win the bloody flag.

LAURIE: We won't win the flag but we could make the finals.

DANNY: It'd help if moneybags here got off his arse and started trying. Put him on Taylor tomorrow.

LAURIE: Taylor? [*to* GEOFF] I suppose that if you did go well on him, you'd get your confidence back.

DANNY: Put him on Taylor. Make him earn his money.

LAURIE: I'll think about it.

DANNY: Are you taking your photo?

LAURIE: I don't want it hanging up here.

DANNY: Good idea. Let's take the rest. They wouldn't want to be up here either. [*To* GEOFF.] Give us a hand.

[DANNY *and* GEOFF *start taking down the photos.* LAURIE *watches them. They use chairs to reach the photos high on the walls.* GEOFF *pauses and looks at a particular photo.*]

GEOFF: Did Harry Payne really kick three goals in time on in the '23 Grand Final?

LAURIE: Yeah. Dad was playing on the forward flank and set one of them up for him.

GEOFF: Is your dad's photo up here?

LAURIE: No. He played most of his football in the reserves.

DANNY: He could have been a regular in any other club.

LAURIE: He probably could've but he didn't want to shift. Keep that ten thousand, Geoff. If you start playing well, Ted'll think his money well spent.

[GEOFF *looks at* LAURIE, *obviously a little puzzled by the remark, as he is not aware of its full implications.* DANNY *meanwhile, has stopped in front of* JOCK's *photo. He looks at it, takes it off the wall and calmly drops it to the ground.*]

DANNY: I dropped Jock.

[GEOFF *looks at* DANNY, *who is standing on a chair looking down at* JOCK's *photograph.*]

GEOFF: Don't let it lie there. Jump on it.

[DANNY *descends from the chair and resumes taking down photos.*]

DANNY: We shouldn't be too cruel to Jock. He's always been very good to his mother.

GEOFF: I can imagine.

DANNY: No. Really. On the twenty-ninth of May, no matter where he was or what he was doing, he'd always send her a bunch of flowers and a telegram of congratulation.

GEOFF: Was the twenty-ninth her birthday?

DANNY: No, his.

[GEOFF *and* LAURIE *laugh.* LAURIE *picks up his jacket and turns to go. But before he can leave,* JOCK *and* GERRY, *having obviously heard the noise of the breaking glass, enter through the right door.*]

GERRY: What's going on?

DANNY: I dropped Jock.

GERRY: Where are you taking those photos?

DANNY: We haven't decided.

GERRY: Is this some kind of juvenile protest?

DANNY: Yeah. If the Committee notices that they're gone, they might ask themselves why before they go appointing Rostoff.

JOCK: What're you doing helping this lot, Geoff?

GEOFF: I don't want Rostoff, either.

[GEOFF *and* DANNY, *who have been working away at a fast rate through the preceding dialogue, now have all of the photos off the walls.* LAURIE *opens the door for them as they each carry a stack out.*]

GERRY: I hope this gives you some small satisfaction, Laurie?

LAURIE: Yes, it does.

GERRY: All of them will demand that their photos go straight back up there as soon as Rostoff wins them a flag. Probably earlier.

LAURIE: Possibly.

GERRY: You've got young Geoff back on side, I see?

LAURIE: Yes. Geoff's going to play very well for the rest of the year. We're going to win quite a few games.

GERRY: Don't think that it'll make any difference to your position, Laurie. I thought I'd made that clear. The Committee are certain Rostoff will win them a flag and they're not certain that you will, and in the end that's the only argument that's going to count.

LAURIE: Possibly, but I'm going to put the counter argument to the Committee that a premiership that's won the way Rostoff wins them isn't one that they'll be particularly proud of.

GERRY: Do you really think they'll listen?

LAURIE: They might. Despite what your economics books tell you I'm not convinced that pragmatism is absolutely irreversible.

JOCK: Don't get all excited about getting Geoff onside, Laurie. He's totally bloody erratic. He'll be cutting your throat again tomorrow.

LAURIE: No he won't.

JOCK: Yeah, well I know something about him that you don't.

LAURIE: Good for you. See you at the game tomorrow.

[LAURIE *leaves*. GERRY *turns on* JOCK *in fury*.]

GERRY: You've been a great help tonight. You told them about Rostoff and now they're all prepared to fight, and you go and get Geoff in here and now he's all reconciled with Laurie. What'll happen if the Club starts winning for the rest of the season?

JOCK: It won't matter. Everyone on the Committee wants Rostoff now.

GERRY: I wouldn't trust the Committee as far as I could kick them. I can get rid of a moralistic coach any day, but a moralistic coach who's winning games could be bloody hard.

JOCK: They want Rostoff.

GERRY: What's this stuff you know about Geoff?

JOCK: He's bloody unstable. First thing we do next year is sell him.

GERRY: Sell him?

JOCK: Yeah. He's been up his mum and his legless sister and he thinks he killed his old man.

GERRY: [*staring*] What?

JOCK: He confided in me, so don't tell anyone although hey! If he starts playing too well we can always leak a rumour or two.

GERRY: Jock. Geoff has two brothers, no sisters and his father had his fifty-fourth birthday last Saturday. Now get inside and try and sober up before the meeting.

[GERRY *storms off in a rage, followed by a frowning* JOCK *carrying his broken portrait. They leave a denuded Committee room behind them.*]

THE END

TRAVELLING NORTH

Leo McKern as Frank and Julia Blake as Frances in the film

Travelling North was first performed at the Nimrod Theatre, Sydney, on 22nd August 1979 with the following cast:

FRANK	Frank Wilson
FRANCES	Carol Raye
SOPHIE	Julie Hamilton
HELEN	Jennifer Hagan
FREDDY	Graham Rouse
SAUL	Henri Szeps
JOAN	Deborah Kennedy
CELEBRANT	Anthony Ingersent
GALLERY ATTENDANT	Deborah Kennedy

Set designed by Ian Robinson
Directed by John Bell

CHARACTERS

FRANCES
FRANK
SOPHIE)
                FRANCES' *daughters*
HELEN   )
JOAN, FRANK'S *daughter*
FREDDY WICKS
SAUL MORGENSTEIN
WEDDING CELEBRANT
GALLERY ATTENDANT

SETTING

The action of the play takes place in various locations in North Queensland, Melbourne, an area near Tweed Heads and Sydney, between 1969 and 1972.

ACT ONE

SCENE ONE

Queensland, late afternoon. The atmosphere is warm and tropical. FRANCES, *a slim, attractive woman of about fifty-five, wearing an elegantly casual Balinese dress, stands looking outwards, listening.* FRANK *enters. He is a tall, athletic looking man who, although he is over seventy, still exudes energy and vitality. He is wearing neat shorts, long white socks and a pressed silk shirt.* FRANCES *is absorbed in her thoughts and does not hear* FRANK's *approach. When he speaks she is startled, and her reaction speaks of an underlying tension and anxiety, a characteristic temperamental trait which contrasts with* FRANK's *assertive air of confidence.*

FRANK: Can you hear the little puffing billies out there hauling in the sugar-cane?

FRANCES: I was just listening.

FRANK: They'll keep going all day and all through the night. Sorry I've been away so long, but there's a chap over there with the same model camper-van as ours so I struck up a conversation so I could see how he's fitted it out inside.

FRANCES: Did you see anything interesting?

FRANK: No, and I had to listen to half an hour of homespun wisdom before I could get out again. The number of folk philosophers north of the New South Wales border has almost reached plague proportions.

FRANCES: The man we met yesterday came over and invited us for a meal.

[FRANK *begins setting up two deckchairs.*]

FRANK: Yes, he stopped me just a second ago, but I saw the lump of cold sausage on the table behind him and politely declined.

[*He takes a pencil, a notebook and a small slide-rule from his pocket and begins to make some calculations.*]

Five gallons at Noosa gives us a total of eighty-five gallons over a distance of one thousand five hundred and twenty

191

miles, giving up a miles per gallon figure of . . .[*manipulating the slide-rule and frowning*] just under eighteen. That damn salesmen looked me straight in the eye and said we'd get twenty-three. Naked dishonesty is becoming commonplace.

FRANCES: Still, aside from that it's been a very satisfactory van.

[FRANK *continues to manipulate his slide-rule.*]

And it's been a wonderful holiday. Do you realise we've known each other over a year now and this is the first time we've spent more than a weekend together?

FRANK: Because of this young man's deception, we are running nearly twelve dollars over our petrol budget. I should've checked independent road tests. Why the hell did I ever trust him?

FRANCES: He seemed very honest.

FRANK: A sure sign that he was a crook. It might seem a small matter to you, Frances, but it does take the edge off a trip when you know you've been cheated at the outset.

[*Pause.*]

I've been thinking a lot about where we should settle, and I think we should go right up into the tropics north of Townsville.

FRANCES: Yes, it would be lovely, but I don't know if I'd like to be quite so far away from my family.

FRANK: If you want my opinion, the further you get away from those daughters of yours the better.

FRANCES: I'm sorry they're behaving in such a surly manner. I really didn't expect it.

FRANK: Neither did I. When I came to pick you up they treated me as if I was a travelling rep for the white slave trade.

FRANCES: I think they're a little embarrassed that technically we're living in sin.

FRANK: By whose standards?

FRANCES: Their standards.

FRANK: By their standards we're living in absolute sin, there's nothing technical about it. But I wouldn't be too sure that the moral question is at the core of it. I think the real reason they're annoyed is that you're not down there to do their housekeeping and baby-sitting.

FRANCES: Frank!

FRANK: If there was a law against exploiting parents, your two would get ten years apiece. When they learn that we're going to leave Melbourne and live up here permanently they're going to scream blue bloody murder, so be warned and don't let them intimidate you.

FRANCES: How are your children going to react?

FRANK: Well, Eric hasn't spoken to me for fifteen years so I don't think he's going to care much, and I'm sure Joan won't mind, but for heaven's sake let's stop worrying about what our children think. It's our lives, after all.

FRANCES: The girls have been very kind to me, but I must admit I'm getting a bit tired of all their problems and I'm looking forward to us being together by ourselves.

FRANK: It's going to be wonderful, my dear. We're going to lead the ideal life. We'll read, fish, laze, love and lie in the sun.

FRANCES: You make it sound wonderful.

FRANK: It will be.

FRANCES: But we'll still travel?

FRANK: All over the North. We'll use the cottage as a base.

FRANCES: I always get restless if I stay too long in the one spot, no matter how beautiful it is.

FRANK: We'll travel all over the North. You've had a hard struggle bringing up those daughters of yours and it's time you started enjoying life. I'll go and cook the fish.

FRANCES: I'll do that.

FRANK: Indeed you won't. You're my companion. not my slave, and that's the way it's going to stay.

[*They kiss.*]

SCENE TWO

Melbourne, winter. It is damp and cold. SOPHIE *and* HELEN *are talking. Both are very attractive women.* HELEN *is in her late twenties and* SOPHIE *about thirty. They are stylishly dressed in a conventional middle-class manner.* HELEN *is the more direct and incisive of the two. She has an almost neurotic compulsion to ferret out the facts that suggests an underlying suspicion and resentment of the world in general.* SOPHIE *seems gentler, more well-adjusted, but there is a quality of self-absorption about her that often causes her to lose concentration on the immediate proceedings and withdraw into her own thoughts.*

SOPHIE: It sounds as though it's really what she wants.

HELEN: She wouldn't know what she wants. She's the original reed who's blown around in the wind. Frank has pressured her into it. I knew the old fox was working away at something.

SOPHIE: I still think she really wants to go.

HELEN: He's an old man who needs someone to look after him and she'll just be used up. The trouble with Mother is that she just never, never, never thinks ahead.

SOPHIE: Try and be a bit generous, Helen. They're like two teenagers in love and it's rather sweet.

HELEN: I think it's nauseating.

SOPHIE: They've been sending each other two letters a day. Even at the height of adolescence I couldn't match that sort of enthusiasm.

HELEN: I think the whole thing's sick. Falling in love is what you do when you're eighteen. They should be old enough to know better.

SCENE THREE

The same setting, some time later. FRANCES *is being interrogated by her two daughters.*

SOPHIE: We're very glad for you, Mother. Really.

HELEN: It's your life. You're entitled to do exactly what you want with it.

FRANCES: Frank wanted to go right up north, but we've settled for Tweed Heads so I'll be able to fly to Melbourne. I'll probably be down here as often as I'm up there.

SOPHIE: If that's what you want, then we're very happy for you.

FRANCES: The winter climate is so much better up there and as you get older the climate seems to become more and more important.

HELEN: You realise, of course, that the summer up there is unbearably sticky.

FRANCES: Yes, I do rather prefer our dry summers down here.

HELEN: I'm really very happy for you, Mother, and I don't want you to think I'm playing the devil's advocate, but you have thought all this through, haven't you?

FRANCES: Oh, yes.

HELEN: You do realise that a six-week trip may be a different proposition than living with Frank full time?

FRANCES: What do you mean?

SOPHIE: From what I've seen of him, Frank can be pretty dogmatic and assertive.

FRANCES: I'm aware of his faults.

SOPHIE: And he's nearly twenty years older than you are.

FRANCES: He's very fit and his brain is as agile as a twenty-year-old.

HELEN: He's not going to stay that way forever and we don't want to see you ending up as a full-time nursemaid. He's very sick at the moment, isn't he?

FRANCES: He caught a heavy cold when we came back to Melbourne, but . . .

HELEN: Pneumonia, according to what you told Sophie.

FRANCES: Yes, but he's had penicillin and he's well over the worst of it.

HELEN: I don't want to sound brutal, Mother, but did it ever occur to you that he might be looking for someone to care for him in his declining years?

FRANCES: You always manage to find the most ugly motives in quite wonderful things, Helen. We've fallen in love and we want to live together. I'm sorry I'm leaving you both because I know it's a very hectic time in both your lives and I liked to feel I was helping out in some small way . . .

SOPHIE: We're not upset because you won't be around to baby-sit, Mama, we're upset because we'll miss you. Jim says you're the most un-mother-in-law mother-in-law he could imagine. Quite frankly, I think he enjoys your company better than mine. We just want to be sure you realise the implications of what you're doing because we don't want you to be unhappy.

FRANCES: I appreciate that, dear.

SOPHIE: You have been known to be impulsive and people have taken advantage of you in the past.

HELEN: Is Frank going to marry you?

FRANCES: I don't think so. He doesn't really believe in it.

SOPHIE: How do you feel about that?

FRANCES: I'd be lying if I said I was entirely happy. Logically I can see that if two people love each other a certificate isn't necessary, but I was brought up in a religious family and it's hard to get rid of all the residual guilt.

HELEN: You realise, of course, that if you aren't married you've got no legal protection whatsoever. When he dies you might get nothing in his will.

FRANCES: Those sort of things don't really worry me. Besides, he's got very little to bequeath.

HELEN: What are you going to live on?

FRANCES: Frank's got a little bit of superannuation and we'll have his pension.

HELEN: That won't be enough.

FRANCES: We're going to live very simply.

SOPHIE: Won't you be isolated up there, Mama? You won't be able to go to films, theatre, galleries . . . all the things you love.

FRANCES: We'll be near enough to Sydney to go down there quite often.

HELEN: How will you afford it ?

FRANCES: We'll manage.

HELEN: I think you should absolutely insist that he marries you.

FRANCES: I couldn't.

HELEN: Why not?

FRANCES: He doesn't believe in it and I'm afraid I just don't feel strongly enough about it to make a fuss.

HELEN: Sometimes you should make a fuss, Mama. That's your trouble. You never face things squarely.

SCENE FOUR

The same setting, some time later, SOPHIE *and* HELEN *are alone.*

HELEN: Did you know they had sex the second time they met?

SOPHIE: How did you know that?

HELEN: I read their letters.

SOPHIE: Helen, you shouldn't read Mama's mail.

HELEN: I know, but I did.

SOPHIE: I thought they'd be past all that.

HELEN: You should read them. They're revolting. 'Eager bodies pressing down' and all that sort of nonsense. People of that age ought to have better things to do with their time. Did you know he was a Communist?

SOPHIE: No, he isn't. He resigned from the Party after Hungary.

HELEN: We built that whole new room on to the house two years ago so that Mama had somewhere to stay. It cost us a fortune and it's all totally wasted.

SOPHIE: That's not . . .

HELEN: Well, quite frankly, I'm really irritated. She's acted on impulse and whim all her life . . .

SOPHIE: Helen . . .

HELEN: She has. She's always been erratic and irresponsible.

SOPHIE: Erratic perhaps, but I wouldn't say irresponsible.

HELEN: You weren't shot off to live with your uncle when you were only eight.

SOPHIE: She was having a hard time.

HELEN: There were a lot of other divorced mothers having a hard time who didn't farm out their kids. I'm sorry, but the truth of the matter is that she couldn't be bothered with us then, and she still can't be bothered with us now.

SCENE FIVE

Melbourne. It is cold and wintery. FRANK, *dressed in a neat pullover and slacks, talks to* JOAN, *an attractive and intelligent woman in her early thirties.*

FRANK: I just thought I'd let you know.

JOAN: I'm very happy for you. I like Frances a lot.

FRANK: We're not getting married.
    [*He sneezes.*]

JOAN: That's no surprise.

FRANK: This damn chill, sodden Melbourne wind will kill me if I stay down here another winter. You're not upset at this decision, are you?

JOAN: Why should I be upset?

FRANK: Some children apparently get upset when their parents start a new relationship. They see it as an act of betrayal against the memory of the other parent.

JOAN: Mum's been dead a long while now.

FRANK: I think you're mature enough to realise that nothing will ever tarnish the affection and fond memories I had of your mother. We were in some ways, I think, the perfect married couple.

JOAN: Come on.

FRANK: What's that supposed to mean?

JOAN: I don't know whether Mother would have agreed with that if she was still around.

FRANK: Why do you say that?

JOAN: Just joking.

FRANK: We had our differences, but your mother was a fine woman and I loved her very much. Have you heard from your brother recently?

JOAN: Very little.

FRANK: I presume he still has no desire to communicate with me, so you'll tell him about this, will you?

JOAN: I will.

FRANK: Are you still friendly with that self-opinionated popinjay who talks too fast and hasn't got a brain in his head?

JOAN: Yes I am, and I think I should tell you that he's got a similarly high opinion of you.

FRANK: Are you living with him yet ?

JOAN: No.

FRANK: He doesn't deserve you. How are things at work?

JOAN: Good. The school's swung over to open-classroom teaching and I'm enjoying it.

FRANK: Is that the system where the kids do what they like?

JOAN: They work on projects of their own choice.

FRANK: Doomed to failure. You'll turn out a mob of anarchist illiterates.

JOAN: I thought you were supposed to be a progressive thinker.

FRANK: Socialism and discipline aren't incompatible, my dear.

JOAN: Well, we can forget socialism now that Gorton's in.

FRANK: Don't give up. We'll win in seventy-two. That terrible daughter of Frances's is coming to see me.

JOAN: Sophie? She's quite nice.

FRANK: No, the tough one with the sharp tongue and a mind like a steel trap.

JOAN: Oh, Helen. Yes, she is pretty formidable.

FRANK: She's coming to blast me for spiriting off her mother, and quite frankly I'm terrified.

SCENE SIX

Melbourne. It is cold and bleak. HELEN *is talking to* FRANK. FRANK *is clearly nervous.*

FRANK: More tea?

HELEN: No, thanks.

FRANK: Biscuits?

HELEN: No, thanks.

FRANK: So your mother's told you about our plans?

HELEN: Yes, she has.

FRANK: Very good of you to come and discuss things.

HELEN: I thought perhaps we should talk to each other before you left.

FRANK: Frances is very sad to be moving away from you.

HELEN: It's going to be a wrench for us all.

FRANK: It's just, I suppose, that she's reached the time of life where she wants to put her own interests first.

HELEN: I'm not quite sure that she knows what her own interests are.

FRANK: I think you do her an injustice.

HELEN: I just wondered if you were fully aware of just what exactly she is giving up by this move.

FRANK: She's been very happy down here. There's no doubt about that, and she's become very, very fond of all your children. How is young Tarquin, by the way?

HELEN: Tarquin is one of Sophie's children.

FRANK: Of course, how stupid of me. Yours is, er . . .

HELEN: I've got three.

FRANK: Yes but, er, isn't there one with a name like Tarquin?

HELEN: No, nothing like Tarquin. In my opinion Tarquin is a pretentious, dated and rather stupid name, but that's Sophie's business. The child you're probably referring to is called Tobias.

FRANK: Ah yes. Tobias.

HELEN: I just wondered if you were fully aware, for instance, that Mother has a fully furnished room set aside for her at both of our houses, that she is free to come and go at any time, that she is never allowed, although to her credit she tries, to pay any money towards her upkeep, and that aside from a little babysitting here and there she is able to see as many concerts, plays, films and exhibitions as she needs.

FRANK: She's been very happy down here, but she feels now . . .

HELEN: The Melbourne weather apparently doesn't meet with your approval, but this is, for all its faults, the cultural capital of the nation, a fact that Mother, with her plethora of cultural interests, has relished, so you see when you said that she's putting her own interests first, and when you suggest travelling up north to a steamy, isolated, little shack with someone who, to be polite, has seen the best years of his life, I wonder whether you have really seriously considered what it is you're doing?

FRANK: Are you suggesting that I'm spiriting her up there against her will?

HELEN: Mother is a very impressionable woman. In any given situation she tends to follow the loudest voice.

FRANK: In that case she would certainly stay down here with you. Now if you've finished your tea I'd like to go on my daily walk.

SCENE SEVEN

The new cottage. We know immediately we are near the tropics by the changes in lighting and scenery. A first glimpse of the place shows it to be a wreck. FRANCES *is cleaning rubbish from the cupboards and piling it on the floor. The door opens and* FRANK *enters in a shirt and shorts. Vivaldi is heard on the radio in the background.*

FRANK: This bedroom is a hideous mess. I asked the agent to have the place cleaned out.

FRANCES: I couldn't care if it was ten times as bad. We're here and we're together and I'm very happy.

FRANK: So am I. It's like a junk-yard after a cyclone. How could anyone have lived in this?

FRANCES: The garden is wonderful. Hibiscus, frangipani, poinsettias and there's even a marvellous little banana plant, and there are pink angophoras by the thousands on the hill behind us.

FRANK: Yes, it's a good little spot.

FRANCES: I've never heard so many bellbirds.

FRANK: Yes, it's a regular little paradise. The edge of the lake is thick with black swans and ibis.

FRANCES: It's very, very beautiful.

FRANK: And the best part about it all is that there isn't another house in sight.

FREDDY: [off] Anyone at home?

[FRANK goes to the door. FREDDY, a jovial man in his sixties enters, wearing a bright shirt and shorts.]

G'day there. Am I intruding?

FRANK: No. I, er, don't believe we've met?

FREDDY: Freddy Wicks, your neighbour. I saw you'd arrived so I came across to see if I could lend a hand.

FRANK: That's very kind of you. I'm Frank and this is Frances.

FRANCES: I didn't realise we had a neighbour, Mr Wicks.

FREDDY: Freddy, please. No, you can't see me from here. I'm up the back there into the trees, so cheer up, you're not on your own after all.

FRANK: [dully] What a surprise.

FRANCES: Are you there by yourself?

FREDDY: Yeah. Ever since I lost the wife eight years ago.

FRANCES: I am sorry.

FREDDY: Yeah. A happy marriage. A blameless life. Snuffed out like a candle. Makes you wonder.

FRANCES: Have you any children?

FREDDY: Yep. Two boys and a girl. They've all done well: one's a teacher, one's a lawyer and m'daughter married a Qantas pilot, but it gets a bit lonely up there all by m'self. But let's not be morbid. Would you like an ale?

[He deposits two beer bottles on a table.]

FRANK: Well, perhaps a bit later. We're trying to clean this rubbish out.

FREDDY: I've got a ute up there. I'll bring it down and help you cart the stuff to the tip. I don't want to sound like a snob, but it's a great relief to have an educated couple like yourselves in here. I'm not saying anything against old Sam, God rest his soul, but he wasn't the sort of neighbour you could have an informed discussion with.

FRANK: He died here, I take it.

FREDDY: Yes, right there where you're standing. I was the one who found him. The poor bugger drank himself to death. The climate here's fine, but I find that if you don't keep your mind active you can get a bit morbid. Where do you two come from?

FRANK: Melbourne.

FREDDY: I had a cousin from Melbourne. Poor fellow shot himself.

FRANK: It can have that effect on you.

FREDDY: How long have you two been together?

FRANK: If you mean under the same roof, about an hour and a half.

FREDDY: Have you just married?

FRANK: No. We're living in sin.

FREDDY: Go on.

FRANK: You've got a ute, you say?

FREDDY: Yes, I could back in up the drive.

FRANK: That's very kind of you. The sooner we shift this junk out the better.

SCENE EIGHT

FRANK *and* FRANCES *sit in the cottage garden at twilight.*

FRANK: Well, my love, we've got no water supply other than the rain, no sewerage, no mail, milk or paper delivery, no rubbish collection, no bitumen on the road and Freddy, but we are right in the middle of sub-tropical splendour at its very best and we have got each other.

FRANCES: You've been a bit cruel to poor Freddy. He seems a good soul at heart.

FRANK: He is, he is. A no-nonsense, salt-of-the-earth, plain-speaking, straight-talking, nosy, interfering, moralistic, insensitive . . . Do you find the township depressing?

FRANCES: No, I think it's lovely. I didn't expect so many trees.

FRANK: No! The people! Bald, sunburnt heads, pink faces and fat bellies. they look as if they've been interbreeding with the local crayfish.

[FREDDY *comes down into the garden.*]

FREDDY: Evening.

FRANCES: Hello, Freddy. Thanks for helping us clean everything up.

FRANK: [*reluctantly*] Yes, thanks.

FREDDY: No worries. If you can't help your neighbours now and then you might as well live in a cave. You weren't a serviceman by any chance, Frank?

FRANK: I was, as a matter of fact. In both wars.

FREDDY: There's one of the best RSL clubs along the coast down in the township. Why don't you and Frances come down with me and I'll introduce you around?

FRANK: Not just tonight, thanks all the same, Freddy.

FREDDY: You can get a solid three-course meal and a floorshow straight up from Sydney for just over five dollars.

FRANK: Sounds very good value, but not just tonight.

FREDDY: It's not just a boozers' club. We have discussion nights and everything.

FRANK: Discussion nights?

FREDDY: We had the federal vice-president up last Friday night tearing strips off those Vietnam protesters.

FRANK: Why was he doing that?

FREDDY: Because they're marching in support of the enemy while our lads are out there dying in the jungle and that's near enough to treason in my book.

FRANK: Have you ever asked yourself what our lads are doing out there in someone else's jungles, Freddy?

FREDDY: They're trying to stop a Communist takeover.

FRANK: That's a load of twaddle, Freddy.

FRANCES: I know how you feel, Freddy, but I really don't think this is a war we should be proud of.

FRANK: There's no war anyone can be proud of.

FREDDY: I fought against Hitler and I'm proud of that.

FRANK: This war is different, Freddy. Use your brains, man. Think! Don't go around parroting platitudes like, 'My country right or wrong.' It's nonsense!

FREDDY: Everyone's entitled to their opinion, Frank.

[*Pause.*]

I'd better be making tracks.

FRANCES: Thanks again for your help, Freddy.
FREDDY: If you need me again, just call. We mightn't see eye to
    eye on everything but I think you'll find I'm a good
    neighbour.

SCENE NINE

A doctor's surgery. SAUL MORGENSTEIN, *sallow, lugubrious, manic
depressive, wry, in his sixties, sits behind his desk.* FRANK *enters.*

SAUL: Mr Frank Brown?
FRANK: That's right.
SAUL: My name is Saul Morgenstein. You're new to the district.
FRANK: Comparatively. I've been here two months.
SAUL: I've been here eight years and I'm still regarded as a
    newcomer. Do you like the area?
FRANK: It's very beautiful.
SAUL: It is, isn't it? And very peaceful. I've had an interesting
    life, Mr Brown. In fact my life has been so interesting that I
    can scarcely believe I've had it, but at this end all I want is
    tranquillity. What's your problem?
FRANK: No real problem. I'd just like a check-up.
SAUL: You have a check-up regularly?
FRANK: Not really. I just thought it was about time I did.
SAUL: When some people ask for a check-up it usually means
    that something more specific is worrying them.
FRANK: As far as I know I'm in excellent health.
SAUL: [*taking* FRANK's *blood pressure*] Do you like fishing?
FRANK: Yes, I love fishing.
SAUL: Did that crooked estate agent Foulmouth tell you that the
    fishing in the lake was excellent?
FRANK: Falmont? Yes, he did.
SAUL: He's a liar. He did the same thing to me. The lake looks
    magnificent, but the bottom is choked with weed. If he ever
    gets piles I'll prescribe mustard-coated suppositories. What
    do you do for a living, Mr Brown?
FRANK: I was a civil engineer. I also led an active life in politics.
SAUL: Did you ever run for office?

FRANK: Yes, I did.

SAUL: Did you win?

FRANK: No. It's quite hard when you're the Communist candidate in Toorak.

SAUL: When did you do this?

FRANK: In the thirties.

SAUL: Not a very popular time to be a Communist, I imagine.

FRANK: No it wasn't, and I paid for it.

SAUL: How?

FRANK: In cash. The construction firm I worked for sacked me at fifty-nine and I only got a fraction of my superannuation entitlements.

SAUL: Stand up, please.

FRANK: Have you any scruples about examining an ex-Communist?

SAUL: Not at all. I'm much more worried about the lack of superannuation.

FRANK: I'm insured.

SAUL: I saw you in the township yesterday with a lady. Was that your wife?

FRANK: Yes.

SAUL: There's some talk in the township that she isn't. Legally.

FRANK: She isn't, legally.

SAUL: She's a very attractive woman.

FRANK: [a trifle tersely] Yes, she is.

SAUL: I'm sorry about all the questions, Mr Brown, but I think we'll be seeing a lot more of each other in future so I'd like to get past formalities.

FRANK: Why will we be seeing a lot more of each other?

SAUL: When you were walking down the main street yesterday you stopped and leaned against a post.

FRANK: I had pneumonia in Melbourne last year and ever since I often get short of breath.

SAUL: After exercise?

FRANK: Yes.

SAUL: A tightening of the chest?

FRANK: Yes.

    [Pause.]

Is it anything to do with my heart?

SAUL: Yes it is. You're getting mild angina.

FRANK: What does that mean exactly?

SAUL: It means that your heart muscle and arteries have deteriorated to some degree and can't supply the heart with enough blood during and after exercise. Hence the chest pains and breathlessness.

FRANK: Can you be certain that's what it is?

SAUL: No. I can send you to Sydney for a cardiograph if you like, but the symptoms are very clear.

FRANK: What are my long term chances?

SAUL: You're not going to make a hundred, Mr Brown. Can I call you Frank?

FRANK: Please do.

SAUL: But if you take the right drugs and take things easily then there's every chance you'll go on for years and years.

FRANK: How many years?

SAUL: I can't give you an exact figure. It could be three, five, ten, even longer.

FRANK: As little as three?

SAUL: Look, you could drop dead tomorrow. I don't think you will, in fact I wouldn't mind betting you'll outlive me, but in a case like this there's no way of knowing.

FRANK: I see.

SAUL: We are very imperfect machines, Frank, and we wear out. If there is a creator somewhere I can't help feeling he went on to better things on some other planet. My problem is ulcers. I have to live on biscuits and milk.

FRANK: Better those than a weak heart.

SAUL: You'd feel differently after a few weeks of biscuits and milk. There's very little joy in growing old.

FRANK: What does this illness mean in terms of alteration to my life patterns?

SAUL: I've told you already. You take things easy.

FRANK: What about the, hmm, intimate areas?

SAUL: Intimate areas? Are you still . . . ?

FRANK: I am old, but I am not defunct.

SAUL: Well, er, if you've been managing up to now, by all means keep trying. Angina in a sense is like having your own built-in doctor. Whenever you feel pain, stop what you're doing and try again later. This may prove disconcerting to your good wife, but remind her of the words of Lord Wellington: that a strategic withdrawal is often the first step towards a forward thrust of renewed vigour. I'll write you out some prescriptions.

SCENE TEN

The cottage interior. It is night. FRANK *is reading the paper.* FRANCES *is restless.*

FRANK: Are you going to church again this Sunday?

FRANCES: I'd like to.

FRANK: You puzzle me, Frances. You're obviously an intelligent woman, and your political stance, while not being terribly radical, is at least decently progressive, but your respect for religion has me puzzled.

FRANCES: I'm sorry, Frank, but I just can't shake off my belief that there's a God.

FRANK: How can there by a God, my love? This world is so full of misery and injustice that it's beyond credulity to think that it was all organised by a loving Father.

FRANCES: It might be illogical but I just believe in him, Frank.

FRANK: Do you pray?

FRANCES: Yes. Quite often.

FRANK: Do you think he objects to us not being married?

FRANCES: I think he'd prefer it if we were.

FRANK: My dear Frances, whom I love dearly, do you really think that God, with billions of people to look after on this planet alone, is really losing sleep over the fact that an old geriatric on the New South Wales coast is cohabiting out of wedlock with a much younger lady?

FRANCES: It isn't logical or rational, but I just feel that he knows and cares.

FRANK: Then he's an old busybody.

[*Pause.* FRANCES *paces restlessly.*]

FRANCES: Do you think it's time we loaded the van and went up north?

FRANK: We've hardly settled in here.

FRANCES: We've been here over six months.

FRANK: The fish are really biting in the lake at the moment. Why don't you come out with me in the boat?

FRANCES: I don't really enjoy it, Frank.

FRANK: Well, stay here and read a book.

FRANCES: I can't concentrate. I know it's silly of me but I just can't concentrate. I have to put the book down and go for a walk. Can we go down to Sydney?

FRANK: Sydney? What do you want to go to that polluted hole for when we're up here in one of the most beautiful places on God's earth?

FRANCES: I'd like to see some exhibitions and some theatre.

FRANK: It's such an exhausting business organising the whole thing that it's hardly worth doing. Who was the letter from?

FRANCES: Helen.

FRANK: How is she?

FRANCES: Fine. Sophie is going to have a baby.

FRANK: Another one?

FRANCES: It's come at a very bad time for her because of her studies.

FRANK: Hmm.

FRANCES: I thought perhaps we could go down to Melbourne then.

FRANK: When's it due?

FRANCES: August.

FRANK: August. That's in the middle of winter. I'm not going down there in August.

FRANCES: It's a little hard to reschedule the baby at this stage. If you feel you don't want to come, I can go by myself.

FRANK: If you go down there by yourself those damn daughters of yours will chain you up and not let you back.

FRANCES: Don't be silly.

FRANK: Why are you so edgy lately?

FRANCES: Well, my daily routine is not all that exciting. I watch you out on the lake all morning, I get a lecture from Freddy on why our boys should be in Vietnam in the afternoon, I cook the evening meal then get a lecture from you on why they shouldn't be in Vietnam at night. You've changed, Frank. You used to love to travel.

FRANK: You're right. We mustn't stagnate. As soon as I've got this lung trouble under control we'll go down south for the baby.

FRANCES: The lung trouble is nothing serious, is it ?

FRANK: No. It's just an aftermath of the pneumonia.

FRANCES: If it was something more serious, you wouldn't try to hide it from me, would you?

FRANK: Why would I try and do that, my love?

FRANCES: Because you don't want me to worry about you, and I appreciate that, but really I'd rather know than not know.

FRANK: I've got a slight problem with my heart.

FRANCES: Your heart?

FRANK: It's just a slight deterioration of the heart muscles. It's not really serious at all. Saul says I could live for another fifteen years.

FRANCES: Perhaps we shouldn't drive down to Melbourne.

FRANK: It really isn't all that serious, my love. [*Seeing something in the paper*] Damn! Graham Byford died.

FRANCES: Graham Byford?

FRANK: You wouldn't know him. He had a property up on Tinaroo Lake. I used to call on him every time I went up there.

FRANCES: How old was he?

FRANK: Seventy-two. The last time I saw him he was fighting fit and walking five miles a day. He should have lived to ninety-five, damn it. He should have lived to ninety-five!

SCENE ELEVEN

SAUL's *surgery.* FRANK *and* SAUL *are talking.*

FRANK: I'd like to know a bit more about these tablets I'm taking, Saul.

SAUL: Have they helped the chest pains?

FRANK: In general, yes, but I've had some pretty sharp ones over the last couple of weeks. I've been writing to one of my old friends with a similar condition and the tablets he's taking seem to be quite different from mine.

SAUL: That's quite possible. There are a lot of alternative medications.

FRANK: Just exactly how do the tablets I'm taking at present operate and how do they differ from the other prescriptions available?

SAUL: The Anginine relieves the immediate symptoms during an attack and the Lanoxin tones up your heartstrings.

FRANK: Tones up my heartstrings?

SAUL: In a manner of speaking.

FRANK: Saul, I hope you don't feel I'm being excessively demanding, but I'm starting to find the level of your medical explanation a little unsatisfactory.

SAUL: You don't need to know the details.

FRANK: Listen, Saul, I'm the one who's going to die of this condition, not you, so if you don't mind I'll decide what I need to know and what I don't. How exactly do the two drugs operate, and how do you know that the ones you've chosen are the best in the available range?

SAUL: I don't know exactly how the drugs operate. I'm a general practitioner, not a biochemist.

FRANK: Why did you choose Lanoxin and Anginine?

SAUL: Because they've worked with other patients.

FRANK: Where are all the available drugs listed?

SAUL: In the manuals.

FRANK: Where can I get copies?

SAUL: You can't. They're only available to qualified medical practitioners.

FRANK: That's ridiculous.

SAUL: Why is it ridiculous? If they were freely available every Tom, Dick and Harry would think they knew more than their doctors.

FRANK: If 'toning up the heartstrings' is the best explanation their doctors could offer to explain the effects of a toxic drug on a complex system of musculature, then who would blame them?

SAUL: You can be a very arrogant and irritating man, Frank.

FRANK: I ran a firm which employed seven hundred people, Saul. I won't be treated like a moron. I want a copy of those manuals.

SAUL: Then you'd better go and qualify as a doctor.

FRANK: It's a ridiculous and criminal state of affairs when a man is denied access to information about drugs that are vital to his survival.

SAUL: Frank, will you please go?

FRANK: Why is it that you medicos are so scared of letting your patients know what's going on? Do you just like the sense of power and authority or do you think we'll discover you're a pack of frauds? I want those manuals, Saul, and I'm not leaving here until you tell me how to go about getting them.

SAUL: Calm down or you'll have an attack!

FRANK: Then give me the manuals or I'll have it right here in your surgery and completely foul up your morning!

SAUL: I've got fifteen patients waiting out there.

FRANK: Exactly, so don't let's have a fuss.

SAUL: [*grabbing books from the shelf*] There you are. Take them! Drug manuals, reference books on heart disease, and if there's anything else you want, take that too. Just take them and get out. You're having an extremely bad effect on my ulcers.

SCENE TWELVE

Melbourne. HELEN *speaks to* SOPHIE *on the telephone.* SOPHIE *is looking very pregnant.*

HELEN: Have you had a letter from Mother?

SOPHIE: Yes, I got one today.

HELEN: She hasn't written to me for two weeks. You got one last week too, didn't you?

SOPHIE: Yes, but that was because she'd just read some article about healthy diets during pregnancy.

HELEN: Did she say when she was planning to come down?

SOPHIE: Yes, in about three weeks. Frank's coming with her.

HELEN: Why?

SOPHIE: He wants to see his daughter.

HELEN: I thought he was supposed to be sick?

SOPHIE: He is and Mama sounds a little bit worried about bringing him on the trip, because she's found out that he's got some sort of a heart condition.

HELEN: Heart condition. I thought it was lungs?

SOPHIE: Apparently it's heart.

HELEN: Lovely! So she's got a permanent invalid on her hands for the rest of his life. How's the little one? Kicking?

SOPHIE: Like a mule. You're very good sending her money.

HELEN: She sent the first one or two cheques back. But I knew she needed it. That old bastard took the bulk of his super-annuation in a lump sum, so he could buy himself, a yacht, which he sails around the lake while she peels the spuds. Might be twins. You're very big.

SOPHIE: Don't say that. I couldn't bear the thought.

HELEN: It runs in the family. Our great-uncle was a twin.

SOPHIE: Don't.

HELEN: Eileen Hanrahan had twins and she said it wasn't too bad. She put one on each breast.

SOPHIE: Oh God!

HELEN: I think I might have another bub.

SOPHIE: Are you serious?

HELEN: Yes.

SOPHIE: You said you'd never even consider it. Why have you changed your mind?

HELEN: Moya Simpson's just had another one and it's made me clucky.

SOPHIE: That's not a very good reason.

HELEN: It's not the only one. I actually get a little bit of attention when I'm pregnant. Martin's parents are almost friendly to me from seven months through to the first viewing, and Martin comes to see me in the hospital every second day, which means I see him far more often than normal. He even flew home early from a conference in Surfers Paradise after I had Janessa. The cyclone alert probably had something to do with it too, but I like to think the best of people.

SOPHIE: So I've noticed. Is Martin keen on the idea?

HELEN: Who can tell? He just grunted: 'Fair enough, what's for dinner?' Now it's just a matter of letting nature take its course, which can mean quite a wait in Martin's case. He's quite virile when the firm's sales figures go up, but they're having a very bad year.

SOPHIE: [laughing] Stop it.

HELEN: No, it's true. A five percent rise in sales and it's like a second honeymoon, but right now . . .

[She shrugs.]

SOPHIE: Count your blessings.

HELEN: If you hear from Mama, tell her I'm still here and still waiting for a letter, will you?

SOPHIE: I'm sure there's one in the post.

SCENE THIRTEEN

The cottage, day. FRANK *and* FRANCES *prepare to leave on their journey to Melbourne.* FRANK *checks off items packed in a box against a list.*

FRANK: Shaving gear, mirror, towels, track suits, medicines, pills, cash, transistor, torch, hot water bottles, mosquito coils, camera, double adapter, scissors, whetstone, maps, list of caravan parks, insect repellent, teapot, tin opener, safety pins, sunglasses and slide-rule — and, of course, my tablets.

FRANCES: You seem to have an extraordinary number of pills and tablets.

FRANK: I'm testing which ones are the most effective.

FRANCES: Does Saul let you have as many as you want?

FRANK: We have an understanding. I test the samples the reps leave.

[FRANCES *brings out a suitcase ready for loading into the van. There is a knock at the door and* FREDDY *enters.*]

FREDDY: You're off, then?

FRANK: Yes, we've finally made it.

FREDDY: Have a good trip. Hope everything goes well with the baby.

FRANK: Keep an eye on the place for us, Freddy.

FREDDY: Yeah, I will, and I might just have a little surprise for you when you come back.

FRANK: A surprise?

FREDDY: Yeah. You've got a lovely little garden out there but there's one essential item missing.

FRANK: There is?

FREDDY: How'd you like a barbecue down by your banana plant?

FRANK: A barbecue. By our banana plant. Well, er, that sounds wonderful but we, er, don't eat all that much meat.

FREDDY: You've got to have a barbecue, Frank. Everyone does up here. It's part of the outdoor living.

FRANCES: It's very kind of you, Freddy, but we really wouldn't want you to go to all that trouble.

FREDDY: It's no trouble, really. I enjoy building things, in fact I've drawn up a plan of it already. If you hang on here a second I'll go and get it.

FRANK: How big is it going to be?

FREDDY: I was thinking of a fairly simple one about so high [*indicating chest level*] but I can make a big one if you'd rather.

FRANK: No, please . . .

FREDDY: Hang on while I get the plans.

    [*He goes outside.*]

FRANK: We've got to stop him. We'll load the things in the van so we can say no and run.

    [*He picks up the case and heads for the door, but stops short.*]

FRANCES: Another pain? [FRANK *nods*] Sit down. It's a bad one, isn't it?

FRANK: Damn thing. It must have been the thought of Freddy's barbecue.

FRANCES: I'll run up and get Freddy to go for Saul.

FRANK: If this proves serious, there's a letter of instructions in my top drawer.

FRANCES: Frank, you're going to be all right.

FRANK: The first thing I want you to do if I die is to break open a magnum of champagne and share it with Saul and Freddy. Not a bottle, a magnum.

    [FRANCES *runs out, leaving* FRANK *alone.*]

For all my faults I'm damn well worth a magnum.

END OF ACT ONE

ACT TWO

SCENE ONE

The cottage, a short time later. FRANK *lies in bed propped up by pillows.* FRANCES *brings him a cup of hot beverage.* FRANK *sips it and grimaces.*

FRANK: What's this?

FRANCES: Promite. Saul recommended it.

FRANK: I might have known. It tastes like drain water.

FRANCES: He said it was good for you.

FRANK: What did he tell you when you went outside?

FRANCES: He said you'd have to take things very easily.

FRANK: What else did he say?

FRANCES: He said it was a heart attack but not a very severe one.

FRANK: He told me I could either regard it as a very severe bout of angina or a small heart attack, whichever made me feel happier. He's got a very fatalistic sense of humour. I am afraid, though, that whatever we choose to call it, there's no escaping the fact that it signals the beginning of the end.

FRANCES: Drink your Promite and don't be morbid.

FRANK: I'm just being realistic, and we've got to be, because it does mean that we've got to take stock of our relationship.

FRANCES: No philosophising, Frank. Just rest.

FRANK: We must face up to it. Saul says that what I need to do from here on in is to lead a life of indolence and ease, be thoroughly pampered and have every whim instantly satisfied and I could live for ever, but the point is that while that's going to be fine for me it's going to be hell for you, and if you felt like reneging on our pact I wouldn't blame you or be the least bit surprised.

FRANCES: Frank. you're the first man I've ever really loved in my life, and I'm not about to run out on you. Now please drink your Promite and relax.

FRANK: At the very least you mustn't abandon your plans to go down for the birth of the baby.

215

FRANCES: Stop it.

FRANK: No, really. I can look after myself.

FRANCES: Saul says you're not allowed to move for a week, let alone look after yourself. I can see the baby when it's a bit older. They're ugly little things when they're first born, in any case.

FRANK: They are, I must admit. Red, wrinkled, squawking little sods, and anyone who claims they can tell who the poor thing resembles is either lying or being very insulting to the chosen forebear. Nonetheless, it's something grandparents don't like to miss and I'm sorry you can't be down there, and in all seriousness, when and if looking after me becomes too arduous, I expect you to go.

FRANCES: If you don't stop talking, I'll go straight away.

FRANK: Seriously, though, you're not bound by any marriage vows so I expect you to cry 'Enough' when the time comes.

FRANCES: [agitated] Frank, please stop urging me to run out on you. I dodged my responsibilities when I was younger but I'm not going to do it now.

FRANK: I'm not your responsibility.

FRANCES: [agitated] You are, so please, please stop talking about it!

FRANK: When did you even run out on your responsibilities in the past? You ran a boarding-house, you cooked, you cleaned, you did everything you damn well could to keep those kids of yours clothed and fed.

FRANCES: And when the pressure got too much for me I gave them away. I sent Helen off to my brother's for four years when she was only eight. And I don't think she's ever forgiven me.

FRANK: You're the most guilt-prone woman I've ever met. You were under a lot of pressure and you did the best you could.

FRANCES: It wasn't really the financial pressure, Frank. I sent the children away because I simply wanted some time to do the things I wanted to do.

FRANK: Good for you, and when you need some time to do the things you want to do again, then you mustn't hesitate to leave me.

FRANCES: Please stop it, Frank.

FRANK: All right. If you're going to use me as a guinea pig to test your powers of endurance, then your first task is to tip the rest of this indescribable muck down the sink.

FRANCES: It's rich in Vitamin B.

FRANK: You could at least stir it properly.

FRANCES: Sorry.

FRANK: Frances, sometimes I'm an old bastard.

FRANCES: [*ironically*] No!

SCENE TWO

Melbourne, winter. SOPHIE *is visiting* HELEN. *The new baby is in a carry cot.*

HELEN: He's gorgeous, Sophie, but I'm afraid he's the image of Jim.

SOPHIE: I know. It's totally unfair.

HELEN: It's a pity Mama couldn't come down.

SOPHIE: Mmm. It wasn't a heart attack, apparently. It was just severe angina.

HELEN: And milked for every last ounce of drama, I'll bet.

SOPHIE: And you're definitely pregnant?

HELEN: Yes.

SOPHIE: How is Martin reacting?

HELEN: With unusual indifference, I'm afraid. Mind you, nothing much raises Martin out of his torpor, but there's normally a bit more reaction than this.

SOPHIE: I read somewhere that there's a male menopause which is supposed to happen when they realise that they're never going to achieve what they thought they were going to achieve.

HELEN: He had his at twenty-three.

SOPHIE: Are his parents showing any interest?

HELEN: No. It's all a bit depressing. How's Jim taking to his new son?

SOPHIE: Oh, he's wildly enthusiastic. He just hates me. He's furious that I haven't stopped working on my thesis and become a 'good' mother.

HELEN: Where's all this study going to get you in the end?

SOPHIE: It's going to get me a decent job.

HELEN: Don't you think that looking after your children is your most important job?

SOPHIE: No.

HELEN: Why are you so desperate to embark upon a career?

SOPHIE: Because I'm sick of being treated like a mental defective by Jim and all his big-shot academic friends. I'm just as intelligent as they are but none of them take you seriously until you've got a string of degrees after your name.

HELEN: If you ask me they're a lot of intellectual snobs. Martin says his firm has stopped hiring graduates because they're arrogant and lazy and they haven't got any common sense.

SOPHIE: Martin's a graduate.

HELEN: They're a different type these days.

SOPHIE: Are the neighbours still giving you trouble?

HELEN: Yes. It's worse than ever. The ones on the left have stopped burning those huge mountains of leaves since I called the fire brigade, but now they ring the RSPCA every time our dog's water dish is empty.

SOPHIE: What about the other side?

HELEN: I'm winning that one. They confiscated three of Tobias's footballs so I've started him on the trumpet. Are you still planning to go up and show Mama the baby?

SOPHIE: Yes. If you can mind my kids for a day or two.

HELEN: Sure, what's another half dozen?

SOPHIE: When I'm up there I'll see if I can persuade her to come down.

HELEN: I wish she would. For the first time in my life I'm beginning to feel really low.

SCENE THREE

The cottage garden. A beautiful sunny day in early spring. A Schubert concerto is playing softly in the background. FREDDY *is barbecuing meat on his newly completed edifice, a large, misshapen eyesore. He has had a few glasses of flagon red and is waxing eloquent.* FRANCES *is staring out onto the lake and pretending to listen.* FRANK *is further away, reading medical books and casting an occasional baleful eye at* FREDDY *and the barbecue.*

FREDDY: It was the most terrifying moment of my life. There I was with a hundred demoralised Australians behind me — and I'll tell you what: the Australian soldier is a fighter to the last, but when he does get demoralised he really goes and does the job properly — and behind us in hot pursuit the whole of the Japanese Imperial Army. And there in front of me was this Pommy colonel saying: 'I'm frightfully sorry, old chap, but there's absolutely no room on board for any of you.' I just saw red. Without even thinking I whipped out my pistol, stuck it in his gut and said: 'There's a hundred men behind me who aren't going to get shot to pieces because of some bloody obscure regulation that's floating around in your skull, mate, so you can either step aside or I'll pull this trigger.' He stepped aside.

FRANCES: Goodness. Were there any repercussions?

FREDDY: Yeah, I went up on a charge, but I had a hundred mates who would've shot the Colonel if anything had happened to me and they knew it. I should stop boring you with this sort of stuff. I never let you talk about yourself.

FRANCES: There's not all that much to tell. I've led a very boring life compared to yours.

FREDDY: Mine was pretty boring too. I've just got a knack for picking out the interesting bits.

[FRANK's look indicates that he doesn't think much of FREDDY's supposed knack.]

What sort of background did you come from, Frances?

FRANCES: My parents owned a modest property in the Western District of Victoria.

FREDDY: And they sent you to a good school. I can tell.

FRANCES: A very boring school, I'm afraid. I used to climb out of windows at the weekend and go riding horses. I was finally expelled.

FREDDY: Is one of your brothers running the property now?

FRANCES: We lost it in the Depression.

FRANK: [to FRANCES] I've read all I can on this cholesterol business and the circumstantial evidence seems pretty strong, so I'm cutting out all meat.

FREDDY: Nice time to tell me that. Just when I finish your barbecue. [To FRANCES] You think it turned out all right?

FRANCES: It's a very impressive structure, Freddy.

FREDDY: Yeah, it's not too bad.

FRANCES: Did you work strictly to your plan?

FREDDY: Funnily enough, no. I just sort of let myself go and it came straight out of my head.

FRANK: Frances and I feel it's got a strange, haunting aura about it, Freddy. There's something of the Aztec, or perhaps it's Druid; we're not quite sure, but whatever it is we think it has enormous potential as the focal point for a new religion.

FREDDY: Stop pulling m'leg.

FRANK: No, seriously. We could all make a fortune.

FRANCES: It's a wonderful structure, Freddy, and it was very kind of you to do it.

FRANK: It was, Freddy, and the meat smells so good I think I'll wait till tomorrow to get onto my new regime. [*To* FRANCES] Apparently you can eat very well without meat with a little forethought and preparation. I'll get you a vegetarian cooking manual. Oh, and this theory that large doses of Vitamin E are beneficial seems worth a try. I'll put that on your shopping list for tomorrow, and in the afternoon, if you don't mind, you could drive me over to Saul's. My experiments with the various drugs are starting to come up with some answers. How long will the meat take, Freddy?

FREDDY: Five minutes or so.

FRANK: Good. I'll just go for a little stroll. Contrary to Saul's advice, there's a growing body of evidence that suggests that exercise, not rest, is the best thing for an ailing heart.

[*He walks off.* FRANCES *and* FREDDY *watch him go.*]

FREDDY: He takes his illness pretty seriously, doesn't he?

FRANCES: Yes, he does.

FREDDY: Look, er, Frances. If anything does happen to Frank, and I sincerely hope it doesn't, I just want you to know that you have someone around here who you can turn to.

FRANCES: Oh, er, thank you, Freddy. That's very sweet of you.

FREDDY: I've got this great big house up there on the hill and no one in it but me.

SCENE FOUR

SAUL's *surgery.* FRANK *reads a report to* SAUL *from a folder.* SAUL *is looking at the ceiling and fiddling with a ball-point pen.*

FRANK: And the interesting thing is that I'm getting the same results after the attack as I was before. For instance, when I tried Aprinox for a month and switched to Lanoxin to Isordil . . .

SAUL: Perhaps we could have your conclusions.

FRANK: The conclusions are simply that the anginal pain is less frequent and less intense when I take three Lanoxin daily and when I use Anginine for immediate relief.

SAUL: That's exactly what I prescribed for you in the very beginning.

FRANK: Yes, but you were just guessing. I've confirmed it all scientifically.

SAUL: Well, I'm glad it's all over. I've taken so many samples for you lately that the reps think I'm running a health racket.

FRANK: There is one problem with the Lanoxin that you didn't tell me about.

SAUL: What?

FRANK: Its side-effects. It's got a tendency to cause agranulocytosis, which in simple terms is a lack of white blood cells . . .

SAUL: In simple terms?

FRANK: Sorry, I keep forgetting who's the doctor.

SAUL: So do I.

FRANK: I do think you should have warned me. I could be left without my first line of defence against trivial infection.

SAUL: It would be a reckless germ who tangled with you, Frank, but if you're worried I'll give you a blood test.

FRANK: I think you should.

SAUL: But not today. I have patients waiting.

FRANK: Saul. There is one other thing.

SAUL: What?

FRANK: I've always thought that a persistently morbid outlook on life is a sign of character weakness, but I'm afraid that lately I've been feeling a little depressed.

SAUL: My dear Frank. You have a serious heart condition, your hearing is getting worse, you are starting to have trouble with your vision . . . you'd be a mental oddity if you weren't a little depressed. You've got a lot of life left. Live it for its good moments.

FRANK: Frances' daughters are trying to take her away from me.

SAUL: Nonsense.

FRANK: I've got nothing to offer Frances any more, Saul. I'm a sick old man and I'm going to get sicker, but I love her and depend on her and she loves me . . .

SAUL: Of course she does. It's obvious.

FRANK: But those two daughters of hers are luring her down south with an endless succession of babies.

SAUL: I'm sure that's not the only reason they're having them.

FRANK: Maybe not, but you put a squawking brat in front of a grandmother and her head goes soft, and those two down there know it.

SAUL: She's not going to leave you, Frank. I'd put money on it.

FRANK: I haven't told you the whole truth, Saul. There's another reason I'm depressed.

SAUL: What's that?

FRANK: I can't manage to do something I've always managed to do and it's giving me a bloody inferiority complex. I'd like you to prescribe a stimulant.

SAUL: A stimulant?

FRANK: Yes.

SAUL: Frank, you are nearly seventy-six, you have a weak heart, you have, I suspect, had more than your fair share of erotic satisfaction in life, so for heaven's sake grow old gracefully.

FRANK: I take it that means you won't.

SAUL: Certainly not. It'd kill you.

FRANK: Then give me some Tryptanol for my depression.

SAUL: [*reaching wearily for his prescription pad*] How do you spell it, Y or I?

SCENE FIVE

The cottage garden. Sunlit day. FRANCES *leans over* SOPHIE's *carry cot and looks at the baby.* FRANK *listens to Mozart in the cottage.*

SOPHIE: Everyone says he looks like Jim.

FRANCES: He doesn't look like anyone. You were very brave bringing him all the way up here.

SOPHIE: I didn't think there was any other way you were going to see him. How is Frank's health now?

FRANCES: He's quite well, really.

SOPHIE: Why do you have to drive that big camper-van around everywhere.

FRANCES: He's not supposed to do anything strenuous, and apart from that, the vision in his right eye has started to go.

SOPHIE: His eye?

FRANCES: And his hearing's deteriorating too.

SOPHIE: Is that why the music is so loud?

[FRANCES *nods*.]

So what does he do? Listen to music all day?

FRANCES: Sometimes he just thinks. Occasionally he even talks to me.

SOPHIE: What does he think about?

FRANCES: His past life. Apparently he's trying to make sense of it.

SOPHIE: How nice for him. Can he look after himself yet?

FRANCES: Yes. He's quite capable.

SOPHIE: So you will be able to come down and see Helen before the baby.

FRANCES: Yes. I've made up my mind.

SOPHIE: That's good. Helen's been quite depressed lately.

FRANCES: Why is she depressed?

SOPHIE: Apparently Martin and his parents are taking no interest in her pregnancy or in her.

FRANCES: I can't stand Martin's parents, I'm afraid.

SOPHIE: I can't stand Martin.

FRANCES: My mother would have called them the vulgar nouveau riche.

SOPHIE: Your mother would have been right.

FRANCES: I often wonder why she ever married into them.

SOPHIE: She wanted a husband, a home and security.

FRANCES: I don't suppose I can blame her. You both grew up through all those dreadful years of penny pinching.

SOPHIE: They were quite exciting years in a way.

FRANCES: I'm afraid they were very grim. It would have been easier to have stayed with your father. but after six years of marriage I just had no respect for his intelligence or integrity, and it's awful to live with someone you basically despise.

SOPHIE: Stop agonising, Mother.

FRANCES: You should have gone on to university. Your teachers all told me you should, but I would have had to borrow from your uncle and he'd just had Helen for four years . . .

SOPHIE: Stop agonising. I got there eventually.

FRANCES: You're kind to say those years were exciting.

SOPHIE: They were. We were always going on walks and hikes and trips on the train . . .

FRANCES: I could never stand sitting around in the one place for too long.

SOPHIE: One day you even took us off to a bushfire.

FRANCES: [smiling] I couldn't have been that silly, surely . . .

SOPHIE: You did. I can still remember the smell of the smoke and eucalyptus and I can remember men with black faces beating out the flames with wet bags.

FRANCES: Yes, you're right. I volunteered to go and make the men black tea. I must have been totally stupid. What if the wind had changed?

SOPHIE: I used to love those adventures.

FRANCES: Yes, you did, but Helen always wanted to go home. She liked order and stability and everything in its place.

SOPHIE: She'll be very glad to see you. I've never seen her quite so low.

SCENE SIX

SAUL's surgery. SAUL sits at his desk. There is a knock at the door. FRANCES enters.

FRANCES: Sorry I'm late. Are you sure I'm not taking up your time?

SAUL: It's more than a pleasure.

FRANCES: I just wanted to talk to you about Frank.

SAUL: Sit down.

FRANCES: Thank you. He wants to come with me to Melbourne. He said that you told him it would be perfectly all right.

SAUL: I told him that it would be most unwise.

FRANCES: It's terrible to say this, but I'm afraid I just don't want him to come.

SAUL: It's not a terrible thing to say. A man in his condition can be very demanding. You need a rest.

FRANCES: Yes I do.

SAUL: Then tell him straight out you don't want him to go.

FRANCES: He'll transform himself into a wounded martyr and I'll spend all my time down there feeling guilty. He's certain that my daughters are trying to lure me away from him.

SAUL: Are they?

FRANCES: Of course not. Do you think he definitely shouldn't go?

SAUL: It's one of those awkward situations where I can't give any definite advice. I'm sure the journey and climate will be bad for him if he goes but if he stays behind he'll worry, and worry isn't good for him either.

FRANCES: Mmm.

SAUL: I'm afraid it's your decision. One thing before you go, Frances, and this is a little embarrassing. I, er, don't think you should expect too much of him these days.

FRANCES: I don't. I do everything for him.

SAUL: I, er, was talking about the, er, private areas. Which again is the wrong choice of words. What I am trying to say, and saying it very badly, is that I think it's unwise to think of him engaging in intimate activity in his present condition.

FRANCES: Of course.

SAUL: He asked me to prescribe him a stimulant.

FRANCES: Not at my bidding, I can assure you.

SAUL: I tried to tell him that in the twilight years one should be content to reflect on past glories, but he wasn't impressed.
    [*Pause.*]
    Frances, if anything does happen to him, and I sincerely hope it doesn't, I'd just like you to know that there is someone around here who would do anything he could to help you for as long as you'd like to be helped.

FRANCES: I'm, er, very touched, Saul. Thank you.

SCENE SEVEN

Melbourne. FRANK *strides up and down* HELEN's *living room with a big rug wrapped around him. He now wears a hearing aid. The radio is playing Beethoven very loudly, and* FRANK *conducts as he strides.* HELEN, *heavily pregnant, enters with* JOAN.

HELEN: Here he is, if you can get him to notice you.

JOAN: Excuse me, maestro.

FRANK: Joan! Wonderful to see you.

JOAN: Hope I'm not interrupting?

FRANK: No, it's just Malcolm Sargent making a mess of Beethoven as usual. How are you, my dear? You're looking well.

JOAN: So are you.

HELEN: [*with a forced smile*] I'd appreciate it if you could keep the volume down just a little, Frank. You've woken Janessa.

FRANK: Hmm. [*Going to turn it down, muttering*] A bit of Beethoven won't do her any harm.

HELEN: Are you cold, Frank?

FRANK: No. I'm pretending to be an Indian.

HELEN: Turn on the heater, for heaven's sake.

FRANK: I'm fine.

HELEN: Well, it's your own fault if you don't.

[HELEN *leaves.*]

JOAN: It really is cold, Dad. Turn on the heater.

FRANK: If I do, the subject of fuel bills will wend its way into the dinner-table conversation tonight with all the delicacy of a draught-horse's fart.

JOAN: Like that, is it?

FRANK: Like that? It's a thousand times worse. That woman has done a five-year course in how to make guests uncomfortable and graduated with first-class honours. I'm still under heavy suspicion of having damaged a geranium during my morning stroll.

JOAN: You should make allowances for the fact she's pregnant, Dad. When's she due?

FRANK: Two weeks ago. At this rate, the bloody thing'll be three years old before it's born. Frances is being worked like a slave. She's just an unpaid domestic servant. At any rate, enough of my problems. How are you ?

JOAN: Fine.

FRANK: Eric is too busy to come across and see me, I presume?

JOAN: That's what he says.

FRANK: Why does he hate me so much?

JOAN: Mum said you were at each other's throats almost from the minute he was born. It was a case of two dominant personalities meeting head on.

FRANK: I did everything a good father is supposed to do — took him fishing every school holidays . . .

JOAN: He hated fishing.

FRANK: Well, that's his problem, the snotty little twerp. Is he still president of his local Liberal Party branch?

JOAN: I think so.

FRANK: He became a conservative just to spite me. It's a terrible thing to think that my genes are being handed down to future generations via a right-wing real-estate swindler.

JOAN: Come on, Dad. He's not as bad as that.

FRANK: I hope you're going to have children some day and redress the balance.

JOAN: I'm a little bit hesitant to become a wife and mother right at the moment.

FRANK: Don't get too obsessed with this new wave of feminism, Joan. Socialism is the only important path to the future. Feminism is just a sidetrack.

JOAN: [smiling] Having known some of the men intent on leading us to the Socialist future, I think I'll stick to the sidetrack.

FRANK: Hmm. I'm spending an increasing amount of my time these days reviewing my past life, Joan — trying to make sense of it all. I've thoroughly gone into my relationship with Eric and come to the conclusion that his deficiencies are his own fault. I'm not to blame. But certain things you said at our last meeting about the way I'm supposed to have treated your mother puzzled me. I did, I admit, become embroiled in certain romantic dalliances which caused your mother pain and were probably unwise, but there were extenuating circumstances which you probably don't know about . . .

JOAN: I wasn't referring to . . .

FRANK: Let me finish. I want to explain something to you so that you don't judge me too harshly. I married your mother at twenty-two when she was only nineteen, and we were both very much in love, but unfortunately we were both almost totally naive, so that when I grabbed her passionately and, I must admit, clumsily, on our wedding night, she was so shocked that she turned to me and said, 'Don't ever do that again,' and unfortunately she meant it. Now it wasn't my fault and it wasn't hers, it was due to the general ignorance of the times . . .

JOAN: Dad, I really wasn't referring to your romantic dalliances.

FRANK: What were you referring to?

JOAN: Let's talk about something else.

FRANK: No, please. I must know what you're referring to.

JOAN: You assumed that the whole purpose of her life was to wait on you hand and foot. You scarcely ever spoke to her except to issue commands, and you had no respect for her sensitivity and intelligence.

FRANK: That's not true.

JOAN: Let's change the subject.

FRANK: Give me one example of when I ever treated your mother with less than total respect.

JOAN: There were so many, Dad.

FRANK: One. Give me one!

JOAN: If you must have an example the one that springs most vividly to mind is the time when you and Eric were arguing politics over one of Mum's excellent but rarely noticed meals, and she offered one of her rare opinions — a quite reasonable opinion if I remember correctly — and you turned to her and said: 'Stick to your cooking, Eve, you haven't got the brains of a gnat.'

FRANK: [*stunned*] I would never have said that.

JOAN: Maybe it wasn't quite as blunt.

FRANK: I would never have said that. If I did it's unforgivable.

JOAN: I'm sorry, Dad. I shouldn't have mentioned it.

> [*Pause.* JOAN *looks away.*]

FRANK: One thing I'll have to face about myself, I suppose, is that while I've always loved mankind in general, I have been less than generous to some of those I've been involved with in particular. Didn't Eric send any message at all?

JOAN: Yes. He said that if Whitlam ever gets into office, the private sector of our economy is going to be irreparably damaged.

FRANK: Well, you just tell him that Whitlam is a man of enormous political and intellectual stature, who, despite the basic conservatism of his political stance. makes our more recent Prime Ministers look like parliamentary pygmies. What a line-up. Flippers Holt, Shagger Gorton and Twinkle-Toes McMahon. And God help us if we ever get Snedden. Tell him I had a collie dog who had more brains than Snedden!

SCENE EIGHT

Melbourne. FRANCES *talks with* SOPHIE *and* HELEN. HELEN *is no longer pregnant.*

FRANCES: She's a lovely baby, Helen.

HELEN: Do you like her name?

FRANCES: Most distinctive. I shouldn't drink any more. I'm getting quite drunk.

SOPHIE: Why not get drunk? It's a rare occasion that we're all together. Here's to Oriana.

ALL: [*toasting the name*] Oriana.

HELEN: Are you sure you like that name?

FRANCES: Is it too late to change it?

HELEN: No. I just thought of it today.

FRANCES: Well, it does have a familiar ring. Isn't it an ocean liner?

HELEN: Oh, migod. So it is. We can't have that.

FRANCES: How about something simple? You've both got so many exotic names that a family gathering is getting to sound a bit florid. Call her Jill.

HELEN: Jill? Jill? Yes, why not?

ALL: [*toasting the name*] Jill.

HELEN: Mother, don't go back up north straight away.

SOPHIE: Come and stay with us for a while.

FRANCES: Frank's very keen to get moving again and he really isn't very well.

HELEN: Stay a bit longer, Mama. You're just starting to enjoy yourself.

FRANCES: Yes, I am. Thank you for that wonderful night out, Sophie.

HELEN: Did you enjoy the play?

FRANCES: Yes. Sophie, you really shouldn't have taken me to that grand restaurant. It must have cost Jim a fortune.

SOPHIE: He can afford it now that he's a professor.

FRANCES: You must be glad that you've nearly finished your thesis. Are you going to try and find a job?

SOPHIE: I've been offered some part-time tutoring but I don't think I'll take it.

FRANCES: Why not?

SOPHIE: It all seems so futile. I have to start at the very bottom rung and Jim's a bloody professor.

FRANCES: You've got to start somewhere.

SOPHIE: I just don't know whether I've got the energy.

FRANCES: That doesn't sound like you, Sophie.

SOPHIE: What am I supposed to sound like?

FRANCES: When you were a child you were always so positive and adventurous. You mustn't let yourself become morose.

SOPHIE: I'm sorry we had that argument in front of you last night, Mama, but Jim just wants me to shut up and let him get on with his career.

FRANCES: Do you both want a word of advice? I'd normally never try and give any, but I'm drunk and rather worried. I think you should take that job, Sophie, even if it's nothing much to start with, because if you don't you're going to end up one of those bitter, unpleasant wives who drink too much.

SOPHIE: That's not fair. Mama. I don't usually drink as much as I did last night.

FRANCES: I should hope not.

SOPHIE: Was I very embarrassing?

FRANCES: Well, I don't think Jim appreciated it when you stood up and told the restaurant that if they formed an orderly queue he'd autograph their menus. I think you should take that job.

SOPHIE: I know, but I just can't stand the thought of starting at the very, very bottom.

HELEN: In my opinion you should just concentrate on being a good mother.

FRANCES: Different people need to do different things, Helen. [*To* SOPHIE] I used to watch you running down the hill to the beach with your hair streaming behind you and I used to think that you were the very epitome of freedom and exuberance and zest.

SOPHIE: And now I've lost it all. Is that what you're saying?

FRANCES: I just hate to see that bitterness and sense of defeat creeping in. I know that if you had gone on with your studies and become qualified when you were younger then you might have had an established career by now, so I blame myself for a lot of what's happened, but if you take that job you've still got a chance.

SOPHIE: Yes, you're right. There's no sense whining. If that's what

I want, I've got to start at the bottom and battle my way up.

HELEN: It's obvious why I was never the favourite. I didn't spend enough of my youth running down hills with my hair streaming behind me.

SOPHIE: Shut up, Helen. You're paranoid.

HELEN: Well, tell me one thing I did when I was young, Mama. I bet you can't even remember.

FRANCES: You used to sit on the beach making sandhouses for soldier-crabs and give them a tonguelashing if they didn't behave.

SOPHIE: So what's changed?

HELEN: Shut up.

FRANCES: The positive thing about you, Helen, was that you always said what you thought and never let yourself be bullied. I suppose that's why I find it difficult to understand why you worry so much about what Martin's parents think.

HELEN: Is this my bit of advice coming up?

FRANCES: Yes, it is. I know we were poor and they were rich, and I know they think their son married beneath him, and I know they disapprove of the fact that Frank and I aren't married, but for heaven's sake, who cares?

HELEN: I don't.

SOPHIE: You do.

FRANCES: Yesterday when you should have been resting, you cleaned every square inch of the house on the off chance they might arrive.

HELEN: All right. They do put the fear of God into me, but you've never seen them in action. Old Roma prowls through the house hunting dirt and grime like a tax lawyer after a loophole.

SOPHIE: Why do you put up with it? They're monsters.

HELEN: I know, but I've got to live with them.

FRANCES: Of course you have, my dear, but don't let them walk all over you.

SOPHIE: I'll drink to that!

HELEN: Do you really have to go, Mama?

FRANCES: I'm afraid so.

SOPHIE: Are you sure he's sick?

FRANCES: He's full of aches and pains.

HELEN: What's this Sophie tells me about you rowing him around the lake?

FRANCES: Yes, the old boy can be pretty demanding when the fish are biting. He sits up in the stern scanning the lake like Captain Ahab, and all of a sudden he'll shout, 'Head for the broken water near Mosses Point', and no sooner do we get there then he'll yell: 'The buggers are gone. Head for the estuary'. It can be a bit tiring on the arms.

HELEN: The rotten old despot.

FRANCES: Well, it would be a little better if he'd talk to me sometimes, but I'm afraid he just sits there with his jaw slack looking quite imbecilic. Apparently he's thinking.

SOPHIE: You shouldn't feel you have to go up there with him again if you don't want to, Mama.

FRANCES: I'm not really looking forward to it. There are so many things starting to go wrong with him.

HELEN: Like that old Vauxhall we used to have.

SOPHIE: We could never work out how it kept going.

FRANCES: It's a bit the same with Frank.

SCENE NINE

A hospital, Melbourne. FRANK *is in a hospital bed. Tubes drip into him and wires connect him to an oscilloscope.* FRANK *watches the blips on the oscilloscope narrowly.* FRANCES *enters.*

FRANCES: Hello, dear. How are you today?

FRANK: Terrible.

FRANCES: Have they got the results of the tests?

FRANK: Yes. It was a major heart attack. I knew that Melbourne would damn near finish me.

FRANCES: But you're going to be all right now?

FRANK: If I last through the next ten days there's a good chance I'll survive.

FRANCES: You're starting to get a little colour back in your cheeks.

FRANK: They must be putting vegetable dye in the drip, because there's no damn blood flowing. See that weak little blip there? That's my heart.

FRANCES: How long do they think you'll be in here?

FRANK: Three weeks. As soon as I get up we're heading up north.

FRANCES: Will they let you travel?

FRANK: I don't give a bugger whether they will or not. I'm going.

FRANCES: It mightn't be a good idea

FRANK: If you won't take me I'll go by train.

FRANCES: Of course I'll take you, but —

FRANK: I suppose Goneril and Regan have been urging you to stay down here?

FRANCES: Frank —

FRANK: Taking you out to shows and filling you with champagne. It won't last long, you know. As soon as I've gone they'll have you down on your knees scrubbing the floors again.

FRANCES: Frank, how many times do I have to tell you? I love you and I'm staying with you until . . .

FRANK: Until I croak, which mightn't be all that long. My blips are erratic today. Thanks, my dear. I do appreciate your loyalty. I can't offer you champagne every night, but there'll be a magnum when I die.

FRANCES: It's a magnum I'm not really looking forward to.

FRANK: Me neither.

FRANCES: You must be very bored in here.

FRANK: I am. All I can do is sit here watching my own heartbeat on the oscilloscope. It does have the odd exciting moment, though. A circuit blew out the other day and my blip stopped. I thought I'd died.

SCENE TEN

Melbourne. FRANCES, HELEN *and* SOPHIE *discuss* FRANK'*s attack.*

HELEN: There's no question about it, Mama. You're not going up there again now.

SOPHIE: He'll get much better care down here.

FRANCES: He's terrified that if he doesn't go back up north he'll die.

HELEN: Well, he's just being stupid and infantile. I think it's outrageous that he expects you to drive him all the way back up there in that damn camper-van.

FRANCES: I drove it all the way down.

SOPHIE: Mama, the important thing is, do you want to go?

FRANCES: No, of course I don't want to go.

HELEN: Then don't.

FRANCES: Helen, it's not as simple as that. He's really got it fixed in his mind that he won't last more than a few weeks if he stays down here.

HELEN: You're not responsible for the fact that he has totally irrational beliefs.

FRANCES: They're not totally irrational. The cold does thicken the blood.

HELEN: He can sit inside in front of the heater.

FRANCES: It's just not physical, it's psychological. He wants the colours and the light. He really is terrified that if he stays down here much longer he's going to die. I'm the only person that can take him up there and care for him, and if I don't I've got to live with the knowledge that he's sitting down here depressed and miserable and scared.

SOPHIE: Mother, he's not your responsibility.

FRANCES: He is my responsibility. You were both right. I went into this relationship impulsively, I didn't think ahead — and all the things you predicted have come true, so now I've got to live with it.

HELEN: What about your responsibility to us? We do like to see you now and then.

FRANCES: I'll do my best to come down as often as possible.

HELEN: Frank isn't the only one who could use some help. I've been as depressed as hell ever since you left. I'm getting no support or affection from Martin or his parents and I just can't cope and now I've had the baby it's going to be ten times worse.

FRANCES: I know it is, dear. and I wish I could be here to help, but I have to go up north with Frank.

HELEN: I see. Dumped when I was eight and dumped again now.

SOPHIE: Helen, sometimes you don't know when to shut up.

HELEN: Well, that's how I feel.

FRANCES: What exactly do you want me to do. Helen?

HELEN: Come and live in your room again.

FRANCES: What about Frank?

HELEN: Let his daughter look after him. For God's sake, Mama, where do your priorities lie — with someone you've known

two and a half years or with your own daughter?
FRANCES: Helen, you can't use that sort of logic.
SOPHIE: Don't be such a selfish little bitch.
HELEN: Go on. Gang up on me. The both of you. As always.
SOPHIE: No one's ganging up on you.
FRANCES: Ganging up on you!
HELEN: I've never been given a fair go all my life and when I finally ask for a little bit of help I'm called a selfish bitch.
SOPHIE: Well you are.
HELEN: And you're a bloody bully. I haven't forgotten all those ghost stories at night to scare me out of my wits and I remember how you used to put me in the old pram and push me down the hill and roar with laughter every time I fell out.
SOPHIE: You got what you deserved. You were a pain in the arse.
FRANCES: Stop it! You were both pains in the arse. You took after your father.
SOPHIE: Well, she's got no right to say things like that about you.
FRANCES: Yes she has. I should never have left her and I've always known it, and that's exactly why I can't run out on Frank now. I took on this responsibility with my eyes open and I must see it through.

SCENE ELEVEN

The cottage. Light and brightness. Sunshine. A new, bright red phone sits on the coffee table. It rings several times. FRANCES *staggers into the kitchen carrying a carton full of groceries. She puts down her shopping and races to the phone. When she answers it her voice is weary and a little distracted.*

FRANCES: Oh, Saul. Yes. Just a minute till I get a pen. Right. The twenty-second. Right. And that's the eye specialist or the ear specialist? Eye. Ear is on the twenty-fifth. Eye at eleven fifteen, ear at eleven forty-five. Eye at your surgery. Ear at Outpatients. The ambulance will come for ear, but I drive Frank across for eye. Right. And the next visit is on the twenty-seventh at two-thirty. Thanks, Saul.
    [*She hangs up and sighs wearily before going to the groceries*

and starting to unpack them. FRANK *comes in the door of the cottage, leaning on a stick, with a patch over one eye and wearing a hearing-aid. He is frail and moves gingerly; but rather than seeming at death's door, he exudes a certain bright-eyed energy that gives him the air of a geriatric pirate or a Victorian rake. He picks up an egg timer.*]

FRANK: If that was Melbourne you should've been using the egg timer.

FRANCES: It wasn't.

FRANK: Who was it?

FRANCES: Saul. He was checking your specialists' appointments.

FRANK: Did you tell him that my eye is still aching?

FRANCES: No, I'm sorry. I forgot.

FRANK: Blast.

FRANCES: I'm sorry. I forgot.

FRANK: What did that obsequious, red-necked thug who runs the general store charge you for the cashews?

FRANCES: A dollar thirty-eight.

FRANK: That's the third price rise in three months.

FRANCES: He says there's a world-wide shortage.

FRANK: I bet. Some cunning cartel has cornered the world market. I'll warrant that none of the price rise is going into the pockets of the poor peasants picking the things out there in the South American jungles. Did they get in the bran and the brewer's yeast ?

FRANCES: Yes.

FRANK: Did you get the vitamin E tablets?

FRANCES: Yes, they're there.

FRANK: The lentils and leeks?

FRANCES: Yes.

FRANK: The alfalfa and seaweed?

FRANCES: Yes, yes. I got everything.

FRANK: [*looking at his watch*] It's time for my Promite.

FRANCES: I've just put the kettle on.

FRANK: I've been reading this diet book and it appears that it's much better to shred the carrots. You release about seventeen percent more of the vitamins that way. My dear, are you listening?

[FRANCES *is obviously eager to read her letters. She stops opening them and looks up.*]

FRANCES: Yes, dear, I am.

FRANK: Are there any for me?

FRANCES: Not today.

FRANK: I suppose they're from the baby farm down south?

FRANCES: Yes. There's one from Sophie and one from Helen. Sophie's put some photos in. Look at young Tarquin. He'll be five in a week. Can you believe that? Five.

FRANK: Five.

FRANCES: It's incredible isn't it?

FRANK: It's shattering. In the face of a catastrophic South-east Asian war and impending Federal elections, it is nonetheless shattering.

FRANCES: He knows the alphabet.

FRANK: Another two weeks and he'll be reading Shakespeare. Tarquin! Do those idiots down there know who Tarquin was?

FRANCES: He's drawn a picture of a cat at the bottom of the letter.

FRANK: A Roman despot who had the unfortunate habit of raping anything that moved.

FRANCES: Would you prefer me to read the letters outside?

FRANK: Sorry.

> [*Pause.*]

I can't find my spanners.

FRANCES: Spanners?

FRANK: Did you lend them to Freddy?

FRANCES: I don't know.

FRANK: Well, did you or didn't you?

FRANCES: What do they look like?

FRANK: Spanners? The things that tighten nuts! A handle with a bulge at both ends!

FRANCES: I lent them to Freddy.

FRANK: Well, don't lend them to Freddy.

> [FREDDY *knocks at the door and comes in.*]

FREDDY: Did I hear my name being used in vain?

FRANK: Have you got my spanners?

FREDDY: Don't worry. You'll get 'em back.

FRANK: Well, I need them now. I've got hairs in the carburettor again.

FREDDY: [*to* FRANCES] Do you want me to bring it in?

FRANCES: He doesn't deserve it, but you may as well.

> [FREDDY *goes outside and comes in carrying a huge, high-backed reclining chair.*]

FRANK: My God. What's that?

FRANCES: A present.

FRANK: From who?

FRANCES: From me. For your birthday. It's specially designed to give maximum support and relaxation.

FRANK: It looks hideous.

FREDDY: Come on, Frank. Don't look a gift horse in the mouth. Happy seventy-seventh.

FRANK: Where did you get the money?

FRANCES: I saved.

FREDDY: Sit down and I'll show you how it works.

FRANK: What do you mean, 'how it works'? Has it got a four-cylinder engine inside it or something.

FREDDY: Sit down.

   [FRANK *sits down reluctantly.* FREDDY *pulls the back and* FRANK *jerks back into a half-supine position.*]

   Comfortable?

FRANK: Is it real leather?

FRANCES: I'm afraid not, but I can cover it with a nice fabric.

FREDDY: Pull that lever.

   [FRANK *looks at him suspiciously, but pulls the lever at the side of the chair. A foot-support shoots out on an expander mechanism.*]

FRANK: Hmm.

   [*He pulls the lever again and the foot-rest shoots back into the chair.*]

   Hmm. That's quite clever.

   [*He pulls the lever several times, fascinated with it. He reclines and operates the foot-rest again.*]

   Quite comfortable too.

   [FRANCES *moves across with* FRANK's *mug of Promite.*]

FRANCES: Two heaped teaspoons, my dear?

   [FRANK *nods.*]

FRANK: Otherwise it tastes like creek-water downstream from a dead cow.

FREDDY: I've got my own little present wrapped in brown bottles up the hill. I'll be right back.

FRANK: Thanks, Freddy.

   [FREDDY *leaves.* FRANK *operates the chair.* FRANCES *comes across carrying an iced cake with candles on it.*]

   A cake.

FRANCES: Yes, and don't complain. It's wholemeal with no eggs.

[*She opens the other letter and starts reading.*]

FRANK: I'll be able to listen to my concerts in comfort.

FRANCES: [*reading*] Yes, you will.

FRANK: Who's that one from?

FRANCES: Helen.

FRANK: How are things?

FRANCES: Martin is having an affair with another woman.

FRANK: I'm surprised. I would have thought that passion for anything but his sales charts was beyond him.

FRANCES: It's apparently serious. He's shifting out.

FRANK: Who can blame him? Twelve years of that tongue would be enough for anyone.

FRANCES: [*angrily*] She's my daughter and I love her, and from the sound of the letter she's utterly miserable.

　　[*Pause.*]

FRANK: I suppose you'll be going down there.

FRANCES: Yes, I will.

FRANK: How long will you be gone?

FRANCES: Possibly for good.

FRANK: For good? Why?

FRANCES: Why? Because you're a rude, arrogant, despotic old bully and I can't stand living with you a minute longer! And just for your information, Helen has been sending me money for years. It's the only reason we've been able to exist!

　　[FRANCES *storms into a side room in a fury, leaving* FRANK *looking surprised and worried.*]

SCENE TWELVE

The cottage, night. FRANK *is in bed propped up with pillows.* FREDDY *lies on the floor nearby in a sleeping bag.*

FRANK: It's good of you to come down again, Freddy. I appreciate it.

FREDDY: No worries.

FRANK: Normally I wouldn't bother you, but I'm starting to get persistent pains in the back and that is not a very good sign, and if anything did happen it's comforting to think that there's someone here who could get on the phone.

FREDDY: No worries. My wife said I used to snore.

FRANK: She was right. You were in fine voice last night.

FREDDY: Sorry about that.

FRANK: Not at all. In the circumstances it's a very welcome sound indeed.

FREDDY: Still haven't heard from Frances?

FRANK: No.

FREDDY: Why don't you phone her?

FRANK: No.

FREDDY: Or send a letter.

FRANK: I won't beg. I've never done it in my life and I won't start now.

FREDDY: I think you should swallow your pride and admit you were in the wrong.

FRANK: Hmm. Easier said than done.

[*Pause.*]

Who are you going to vote for?

FREDDY: Whitlam.

FRANK: That's quite a turnabout.

FREDDY: Yeah. I still don't like unions, mind you. The one I was a member of made us vote with a show of hands and if we didn't vote the right way we got bashed up later.

FRANK: So why are you changing your vote?

FREDDY: I've changed my mind about Vietnam.

FRANK: Good for you.

FREDDY: I couldn't cop some of those photos of the napalm victims.

FRANK: We're in for a new era, Freddy.

FREDDY: Were you really a Communist once?

FRANK: Yes, for thirty years. There was a wonderful period after the War when Fascism had been defeated and we thought a new order of justice and fraternity was going to sweep the world. It didn't turn out to be that simple.

FREDDY: I think Whitlam's going to toss McMahon.

FRANK: He is. We're in for a new era. Unfortunately, I don't think I'll be around to see very much of it.

FREDDY: Come on, mate. That's no way to talk. Do you want me to get you a mug of Promite?

FRANK: Frankly, I can't think of anything I'd like less.

FREDDY: I could stiffen it up a bit, but I don't suppose Saul would approve.

FRANK: Bugger Saul.
FREDDY: One rum and Promite coming up.
FRANK: Go easy on the Promite.

SCENE THIRTEEN

Melbourne, FRANCES *sits with a tearful* HELEN.

FRANCES: Where are they living?
HELEN: In a flat in South Yarra. I wouldn't mind so much if there was some substance to her but she's a total non-event. She's a mealy-mouthed, washed-out, pouting, simpering, gormless, vapid, stupid little creature without a mind of her own or a thought in her head. For him to run off with someone like that is just an incredible insult.
FRANCES: Does he want to see the children?
HELEN: He may very well want to, but there is no way, no way that he's going to get anywhere near them while he's living with that loathsome woman. He's gone insane, Mama. Apart from everything else she's overweight, asthmatic and has dermatitis. It's just such an insult, Mama. A calculated insult. I've been to my lawyer, and he's going to be very, very sorry.
FRANCES: How have Martin's parents reacted?
HELEN: They've been really wonderful. They've totally disowned him. Roma is round here every day looking after the children and Reg is keeping the garden in shape.
FRANCES: Really?
HELEN: They've been wonderful. They just can't understand how any son of theirs could do that to his children.
FRANCES: Has Sophie been helping out ?
HELEN: Sophie? I've hardly seen her.
FRANCES: Why didn't she take the job she was offered?
HELEN: It wasn't good enough for her. She and Jim are just having one blazing row after another these days and I'm afraid I just don't want to know about it in the circumstances. I'll just go and check the mail. My lawyer says Martin hasn't got a leg to stand on. He's going to lose the house, the car - the lot!
[*She leaves.* FRANCES *sits there looking a little depressed.*]

SCENE FOURTEEN

Evening. FRANCES *sits by the phone in Melbourne.* FRANK *sits by the phone in the cottage. The phone rings beside* FRANCES. *She picks it up.*

OPERATOR: [*voice only*] 233 4509? Mrs Frances Oldfield?
FRANCES: That's right.
OPERATOR: Hold the line, please. Boolindawhy calling.
  [*The phone beside* FRANK *rings. He picks it up.*]
  Boolindawhy. I have your Melbourne number. Go ahead.
FRANK: Hmm. Frances?
FRANCES: Frank?
FRANK: Yes. Hmm. How are you?
FRANCES: I'm well. And you?
FRANK: Could be worse. Hmm. I've been thinking back over my past life, Frances, and I've realised that while I've been in love with mankind in general I've been very thoughtless to some of those I've been involved with in particular . . . Are you there?
FRANCES: Yes. I'm here.
FRANK: So I've rung up to apologise. Hmm. Needless to say I'm missing you very much and if you ever did see fit to return you can rest assured I'd never treat you as badly again. I'd also be willing to contemplate marriage . . . Are you still there?
FRANCES: Yes, I'm here.
FRANK: I'm, er, hmm, sincere about what I say, Frances, so please think it over because I really do, hmm, love you . . . Are you there?
FRANCES: Yes, I'm here.
FRANK: Well, I won't keep you. Saul and Freddy send their love.
  [*Pause.*]
  Well, I won't keep you. Goodbye for now.
FRANCES: Goodbye.
  [*They hang up their respective phones.*]

SCENE FIFTEEN

The cottage interior. Day. FRANK _sits in his chair listening to Bach on the radio. It is the Brandenburg Concerto number five, second movement._ FRANCES _enters._ FREDDY _follows carrying a suitcase. He puts the suitcase down, grins awkwardly at_ FRANK, _and leaves._ FRANK _gets up out of his chair They stare at each other, then embrace._

FRANK: Your description of me as a bully and a despot was hard but fair. I'll be a different man from now on. And I was totally sincere about the marriage.

FRANCES: I didn't come back because of that.

FRANK: Perhaps not, but I meant it. Not in a church. I couldn't go as far as that, but we'll do everything else.

FRANCES: Marriage doesn't mean anything to you Frank.

FRANK: Yes it does. It means you'll think twice before you walk out on me the next time.

    [_They hug._]

Now please, will you marry me?

FRANCES: Yes. If you really want to.

FRANK: Good. We'll do it properly. A honeymoon in Sydney — the lot. Now sit down and I'll make you a cup of tea. [_Putting on the kettle_] I was very lonely without you.

FRANCES: And I was lonely without you.

FRANK: I thought that I'd lost you for good. I know how close you are to your daughters and how close they are to you and I'm touched and a little overwhelmed that you chose to come back.

FRANCES: Frank . . .

FRANK: No, I'm being serious. I've very little to offer anyone and I can't help feeling I don't really deserve you.

FRANCES: Frank. I don't want you to think I don't love you, but the truth of the matter is that I had nowhere else to go.

FRANK: What do you mean? Helen —

FRANCES: Helen and Sophie are working their own lives out. I can't do anything more for them now.

SCENE SIXTEEN

The cottage. Day. SAUL *sits in a chair looking morose.*

SAUL: Frank, you must not go down to Sydney.

FRANK: [*off*] What's that?

SAUL: You must not —

FRANK: [*off*] I'm going.

SAUL: Reason with him, Frances.

FRANCES: [*off*] I've tried.

    [FRANK *enters in his underclothes, black eyepatch and his hearing-aid and proceeds to dress himself in an immaculate white suit.*]

FRANK: We're going to be married and then we're going off to young Brett Whitely's exhibition and nothing is going to stop us.

SAUL: Your heart is going to stop you.

FRANK: Do you want to bet?

SAUL: You know enough to know what those persistent back pains mean.

FRANK: Lumbago.

SAUL: Lumbago. It's your heart protesting. If you don't have a complete rest you'll kill yourself.

FRANK: Fiddle faddle. I'll bet ten dollars that I'll outlive you.

SAUL: Don't joke.

FRANK: I'm serious.

SAUL: I don't make bets about things like that. It's bad luck.

FRANK: Ten dollars.

SAUL: All right. Anything you say. Ten dollars, but will you give up this idea —

FRANK: And when I get back I want something done about this hearing-aid. It amplifies, but there's no clarity.

SAUL: Please, for the last time . . .

    [FRANCES *appears wearing a simple but very pretty dress.*]
Frances, tell him not to go.

FRANCES: I've tried.

FRANK: Look at that. The bridegroom in white and the bride in red. How times have changed.

    [FREDDY *comes in the door carrying a camera and a flashbulb.*]

FREDDY: Frances, you look fantastic. Can I kiss the bride?

FRANK: Not until we're married, and then only briefly.

FREDDY: They look great, don't they, Saul ?

SAUL: Terrific.

FREDDY: Let's have you over here.

[*The camera clicks but the flashbulb does not go off.*]

FRANK: We haven't got time for photographs.

FREDDY: Damn!

FRANK: Come on, man. The train goes in twenty minutes. Can't we take the picture outside?

FREDDY: No, I want one in the cottage. Out of the way, Saul. Let's try again.

FRANK: All right. What do we do? Say cheese? Smile, slouch, lounge or grin?

FREDDY: Just look relaxed.

FRANK: It's hard to when you know you've got nineteen minutes to catch the train.

[*The flash goes off.*]

FREDDY: Right.

FRANK: I hate photos. They never make me look intelligent enough.

FREDDY: [*to* FRANCES] What he lacks in youth he makes up for in modesty.

[FRANK, FRANCES *and* FREDDY *go out the door.* SAUL *shrugs and follows.*]

FRANK: [*off*] Is my toothbrush packed, Frances?

FRANCES: [*off*] Yes, dear. Just get in the van.

SCENE SEVENTEEN

Sydney. FRANK, *dressed in his smart white suit, stands next to* FRANCES *in front of a civil* WEDDING CELEBRANT *whose unctuous, patronising manner indicates that he thinks* FRANK *must be senile.*

CELEBRANT: Can I just say before we begin what a great privilege it is for me to be marrying a couple like yourselves.

FRANK: Why? What's so different about us?

CELEBRANT: I sometimes can't help thinking that the young

    people of today think that happiness is reserved for them and them alone.

FRANK: They're ninety-nine percent right.

CELEBRANT: [*ignoring this*] So I personally find it a wonderful thing when people in the autumn of their lives find love.

FRANK: Then let's get started, shall we, before autumn slips into winter.

CELEBRANT: Can I just say Mr Brown, it is terribly heartening to find someone of your age with so much spirit.

FRANK: The spirit is willing but the flesh is damned weak, so could you stop your patronising chatter and just get on with it.

SCENE EIGHTEEN

A Sydney art gallery. FRANK *and* FRANCES, *still in their wedding attire, approach a desk behind which sits a female* ATTENDANT. *They go to pass but she stops them.*

ATTENDANT: Excuse me, sir, madam. Do you have an invitation?

FRANK: Invitation? Why do we need an invitation?

ATTENDANT: This is a private preview, sir. The gallery is open to the general public tomorrow.

FRANK: This is preposterous. I'm Brett Whitely's father. Go and get my boy immediately and we'll straighten this thing out.

ATTENDANT: Oh. I'm terribly sorry, Mr Whitely. I should have recognised you.

FRANK: Ah, you can't be blamed. I don't often come to his openings. If you want my opinion he's far too obsessed with sex.

ATTENDANT: Well, this show is a little on the erotic side. I hope you're not upset.

FRANK: If we are we'll let him know about it. We didn't bring him up to be like that, did we, Maud?

FRANCES: No. I really don't know where he got it from. Could we have a catalogue, please?

ATTENDANT: Of course. Have two.

    [*The* ATTENDANT *watches them as they go inside.*]

SCENE NINETEEN

The cottage garden. A beautiful sunlit day. SAUL *sits on a bench.* FRANK *comes down to join him. He looks tired and frail, but buoyant.*

FRANK: Frances and I have added our votes to the tide that is going to sweep in a new era. Have you voted?

SAUL: I never vote. Did you enjoy Sydney?

FRANK: Wonderful. And just between you and me, something happened down there that I thought I'd never experience again.

SAUL: If you're talking about what I think you're talking about, it's a miracle you aren't dead.

FRANK: Maybe it was unwise. but we were in a motel room on our honeymoon and we'd just come from that damned Brett Whitely exhibition. The combined impetus was overwhelming.

SAUL: Sit down.

FRANK: I can't. My concert starts in a few minutes. But don't go. Frances will be down in a minute.

[*He goes up the path.* FRANCES *comes down with a mug of Promite.*]

You shouldn't have, my dear. I could've done that.

FRANCES: It's no trouble. I've turned on the radio.

FRANK: Thank you, my dear.

[FRANCES *goes to join* SAUL. FRANK *enters the cottage and settles himself into his reclining chair, operating the foot-rest expander mechanism several times. It still fascinates him. The radio has warmed up and is playing the latter part of Mozart's G Minor Quintet.*]

SAUL: Welcome back. How is he?

FRANCES: He seems a lot better today, but I'm afraid he had a bad night.

SAUL: Was he coughing a lot?

FRANCES: Yes.

SAUL: His heart's too weak to clear the congestion from his lungs.

FRANCES: Saul. be truthful. Is he getting near the end?

SAUL: Yes.

FRANCES: Does he know that?

SAUL: I'm sure he does.

FRANCES: The pain in his back isn't lumbago, is it?

SAUL: No. It's referred pain from the heart. It's a bit like an exhausted runner forcing himself uphill but knowing that he's soon going to have to stop.

[*Up in the cottage the Quintet comes to an end.* FRANK *seizes his paper and pencil.*]

ANNOUNCER: That was the G Minor Quintet, Kochel five-one-six by Mozart —

FRANK: Yes. I know that.

ANNOUNCER: Played by the Amadeus Quartet . . .

FRANK: I thought so.

ANNOUNCER: With Cecil Aronowitz.

FRANK: Who? Speak more clearly, damn you Speak up!

[FRANK *sighs in an irritated manner and puts down his pencil in disgust. He suddenly slumps back into his chair.*]

ANNOUNCER: We will continue this concert with the Vivaldi Concerto in E Minor for Bassoon, played by the Chamber Orchestra of the Saar, conducted by Karl Ristenpart.

[*The music starts.*]

SCENE TWENTY

FRANK *is still in his chair, but has been straightened to an upright position.* FRANCES, *tear-streaked but resolute, reads a letter to* SAUL *and* FREDDY.

FRANCES: No tears, no flowers, no priests, no piety, no headstones, and the first thing you all must do is to drink a full magnum of champagne.

SAUL: I'll go and get one.

FRANCES: No, it's all right.

[FRANCES *goes to the refrigerator and takes out a magnum.*] He always planned ahead.

[FREDDY *opens the bottle as* FRANCES *gets the glasses.*] Oh. He left this envelope for you, Saul.

[SAUL *opens it and takes out a ten dollar note. He reads the message written on the accompanying notepaper.*]

SAUL: Dear Saul. Here is your ten dollars. I'm afraid I can't offer you a rematch, but I think as a gentleman you should have offered me odds, as according to statistics you had a much better prognosis than I did. I'd appreciate it if you and Freddy would help Frances through all the arrangements which are listed separately in envelopes number three, three A and four. Will you thank Frances for the happy years she has given me and apologise to her sincerely for the miserable years I have given her. Tell her she would be well advised to travel south to her family before she gets caught up in the misfortunes of any other old crocks around the district. Regards, Frank.

FRANCES: He used to say that for all his faults he was damn well worth a magnum.

FREDDY: [*solemnly*] And so he was. Let's drink to that.
   [*They drink the champagne. Suddenly the expanding foot-rest on the reclining chair, which has been on full extension, collapses back to its rest position under the weight of* FRANK'S *legs.* FRANCES, SAUL *and* FREDDY *jump with shock.*]

SAUL: My God. I thought for a second that the old boy had come back. Much as I loved him I couldn't have taken another three years.

FRANCES: [*smiling despite herself*] Let's go out into the sunlight.
   [*They take their glasses and move out into the garden.* FRANCES *turns on the radio just as she leaves. It is playing Bach's Brandenburg Concerto number three. The music swells as they walk out into the sunlit garden.*]

SAUL: Do you think you will go back down to your family?

FRANCES: No, I think somehow that I'll go travelling further north.
   [*After a long pause,* FRANK *rises from his chair and comes down to participate in the final bows with the rest of the cast.*]

THE END

BIBLIOGRAPHICAL NOTE

The monograph on David Williamson edited by Ortrun Zuber-Skerritt (1988) contains a large number of bibliographical references which include published and unpublished critical studies, reviews of plays and films, theatre programs.

Peter Fitzpatrick's *Williamson* (1987) is a useful general reference with a select bibliography.

PERFORMANCE PRESS REVIEWS – a select list
The Department
I. Robinson *National Times* 25 August 1975 'Meaning between the lines'.
M. Luke *Australian* 23 September 1977 'The Department'.
E. Perkins *Theatre Australia* October 1990 Review: 'The Department'.
P. McGillick *Financial Review* 28 October 1987 Review: *The Department.*
A Handful of Friends
G. Hutchinson *Australian* 7 September 1976 'With friends like these . . .'.
M. Jones *Sydney Morning Herald* 8 September 1976 'Sophisticated Williamson'.
D. Hewett *Theatre Australia* Christmas 1976 Review: 'A Handful of Friends'.
V. Kelly *Theatre Australia* January 1981 'Refined Tragicomedy'.
P. Goers *Advertiser* 22 September 1992 Review: 'A Handful of Friends'.
The Club
L. Radic *Age* 28 May 1977.
B. Oakley *National Times* 12–17 December 1977 'Survival on the league ladder'.
J. Elsom *Listener* (UK) 24 January 1980 'Dire straits'.
M. Armstrong *Quadrant* XXII.3, 'David Williamson's *The Club*'.
C. Boyd *Times* (Melbourne) 24 October 1990 Review: *The Club.*

The film (1980)

P. Heinrichs *National Times* 7–13 September 1980 'Celluloid grand final'.

Travelling North

M. Rodger *Theatre Australia* October 1979 Review: 'Travelling North'.

J. Peter *Sunday Times* (UK) 11 June 1980 'Lovers on the road to a mirage'.

C. Roberts *Australian* 9 July 1980 'Great but not for the trendies'.

H.G. Kippax *Sydney Morning Herald* 24 June 1980 'Sensitive studies in irony'.

The film (1987)

J. Waites *Cinema Papers* May 1987 Review: 'Travelling North'.

CRITICAL STUDIES – a select list

K. Brisbane 'David Williamson' in *A Companion to Theatre in Australia* Sydney, Currency Press 1994 (forthcoming).

D. Carroll *Australian Contemporary Drama* Sydney, Currency Press 1994 (forthcoming).

R. Fisher 'Clearing the cobwebs' in *The Department* Sydney, Currency Press 1975.

—— 'The play in the theatre' in *The Club* Sydney, Currency Press 1978.

B. Kiernan *David Williamson: A Writer's Career* Sydney Heinemann 1990.

P. Fitzpatrick *Williamson* (Methuen Australian Drama Series M. Williams ed. Sydney, Methuen 1987.

P. Holloway (ed.) *Contemporary Australian Drama* Sydney, Currency Press revised edition 1987.

C.M. Moe 'David Williamson' in *Contemporary Dramatists* (K.A. Berney ed.) London, St James Press 1994 (forthcoming).

P.E. Parsons 'This world and the next' in *Travelling North* Sydney, Currency Press 1980.

T. Sturm 'Drama' in *The Oxford History of Australian Literature* (L. Kramer ed.), Melbourne, Oxford University Press 1981.

I. Turner 'Winners and losers' in *The Club* Sydney, Currency Press 1978.

O. Zuber-Skerritt (ed.) 'David Williamson' in *Australian Playwrights* (Monograph series) Amsterdam, Rodopi 1988.

Also in this Series

PATRICK WHITE Collected Plays Volume I
The Ham Funeral
The Season at Sarsaparilla
A Cheery Soul
Night on a Bald Mountain

PATRICK WHITE Collected Plays Volume II
Big Toys
Netherwood
Signal Driver
Shepherd on the Rocks

DAVID WILLIAMSON Collected Plays Volume I
The Coming of Stork
The Removalists
Don's Party
Jugglers Three
What If You Died Tomorrow

JIM McNEIL Collected Plays
The Chocolate Frog
The Old Familiar Juice
How Does Your Garden Grow
Jack

DOROTHY HEWETT Collected Plays Volume I
This Old Man Comes Rolling Home
Mrs Porter and the Angel
The Chapel Perilous
The Tatty Hollow Story